Inhabiting Displacement

Shahd Seethaler-Wari, Somayeh Chitchian, Maja Momić (eds.)

Inhabiting Displacement

Architecture and Authorship

Birkhäuser
Basel

Acknowledgments

This book is the result of the collective contributions of many people over several years. Each of those contributions was essential to this book in its own unique way, and without which the book would not have been possible. We would like to use this space to express our deepest gratitude to all contributors.

Foremost, we acknowledge the *inhabitants*, meaning the lives and conditions of those that the contributors of this volume have engaged with on a deep level, those who made this publication and our thinking possible. Those whose names are not mentioned, but who opened up their lives to us, and allowed us to enter. Our aim and aspiration are to write with them, not for or about them, and we hope we have risen to the occasion. We acknowledge that we only act as intermediaries, struggling to find new meanings of what research and writing could fundamentally contribute. This book is not dedicated to them, it has arisen from them.

This work would not have been possible without the support of Prof. Steven Vertovec, the director of the Max Planck Institute for the Study of Religious and Ethnic Diversity in Göttingen, which launched the research project "Between Accommodation and Integration: Comparing Institutional Arrangements for Asylum-Seekers" in February 2017, and concluded it, in January 2019, with the architectural workshop "Inside Out – Outside In: Shifting Architectures of Refugee (In)habitation." From the beginning of the project, Prof. Vertovec believed in the importance of architecture and space in the context of migration and refugee studies, at a time when the surrounding academic environment was mostly focused on social and political sciences. It is due to his belief, encouragement, and support that the research project gained spatial and architectural perspectives, which inspired this volume. In this spirit, we express our deepest gratitude to the entire staff of the institute; to the administration, the maintenance team, the IT team, the library team, the student assistants, and the scientific staff for their support both throughout the project and in the organization, moderation, and success of its closing workshop.

Our thanks and gratitude equally go to the Volkswagen Foundation for their generous support of the above-mentioned research project, its concluding workshop, and this resulting volume.

We thank the participants of our workshop for their contributions in creating a platform for all of us to engage in a lively, interdisciplinary, multiscalar, cross-regional discussion which, subsequently, inspired this book. A particular thank you to the authors of this volume for their patience, support, and hard work. Their papers were written and edited amid a pandemic, in challenging conditions, while juggling family life and work from home. Their commitment to the project was exemplary!

Last but not least is the unconditional support and care that our families, friends, and loved ones provided throughout the process, giving us the opportunity to sacrifice time with them to make this publication possible. Those family members who left us, came into our lives, became inaccessible due to the pandemic, and those we returned to for mutual care, all are an important part of this process, and for whom we cannot be more grateful.

Introduction

Shahd Seethaler-Wari, Somayeh Chitchian, and Maja Momić

This co-edited volume builds upon the workshop "Inside Out – Outside In: Shifting Architectures of Refugee Inhabitation," held in January 2019 at the Max Planck Institute for the Study of Religious and Ethnic Diversity in Göttingen, Germany.[1] The workshop brought together a group of scholars, architects, urbanists, planners, designers, and sociologists, from both academia and practice, working at the intersection of architectural spatial research and migration/refugee studies. This workshop focused on the reciprocal relationship between design, displacement, and practices of inhabitation, seen through the lens of the shifting and changing architectures of shelter(ing). Contrary to the architectural disciplinary orthodoxies of permanence and durability, these architectures are in a constant state of flux, ephemeral, and blatantly showcasing the impermanences and fragilities of our contemporary conditions. Furthermore, the workshop aimed at challenging the humanitarian, interventionist, and technocratic understandings of architectural spatial production and its subsequent dualisms between the figure of the "architect" and that of the "refugee" – putting one at the giving end and the other at the receiving end of technical expertise and, by extension, knowledge (Chitchian, Momic, and Seethaler-Wari 2020). This volume builds upon these ideas and expands them further.

"Crisis" of migration or crisis of the nation-state?

The abovementioned workshop, and this subsequent publication, have undeniably grown in the European post-2015 context; a context that has been riddled with notions such as "crisis," "influx," "flood," and "threat" of migrants/refugees. The inherent Eurocentrism of these discourses is not only evident through the language of crisis – a crisis not *in* Europe but *of* Europe (Tazzioli and De Genova 2016) – it distinctly reproduces Europe's concomitant fortified geographies through the constant ideological construction of the Other (that imagined lesser form of humanity, in an oppositional relation to an Us/the Self) and that outside place of otherness, of fear, and threat (Fanon 1963; Said 1978; Anderson 1983; Duncan 1993).

The contemporary questions of migration and refuge are foundational to and intertwined with the project of modernity and its particular conceptions of time and space. According to Arturo Escobar, "the contemporary migrant [and migration] constitutes a historical problematic that embodies in a particularly acute manner the pasts, presents, and futures of the world known as Western modernity" (2019, 96). In other words, immigration and citizenship controls are crucial technologies and strategies for the project of nation-making (and nation-maintaining), particularly, as Nandita Sharma puts it, in the Postcolonial New World Order and the territorialized and, thus racialized, global hegemony of Europe and the United States since the end of World War II (2020, 3). As Sharma poignantly argues, the separation between, what she calls, Natives (autochthons) and Migrants (allochthons) is a legacy of imperialism in both the colonies as in the metropoles and, thus, co-constitutive of the hegemony of nation-state power (Sharma 2020, 13). This world order fundamentally contains and excludes possibilities for decolonized formations through its superstructure, as argued by Sharma. The frame of national governmentality and biopolitical form of state power, based on the territorial divide of the "people of place" and the "people out of place," will always be a colonial one.

From the perspective of imperial metropoles, the geographies of former colonies, where the majority of displaced populations are both ousted and sheltered, are often not only marginalized but made invisible. They are marked outside of frames of "crisis" and "state of exception," which are in particular reserved for imperial metropoles. This is what Escobar alludes to as normalized and dominant worldwide ways of being, doing, and knowing, or what he refers to as "onto-epistemic historicity" that has come to "colonize other historical ways of world-making" (2019, 96). Hence, a critique of contemporary migration should also "*begin with the foundations that gave rise* to a particular conception of nature, liberalism, secularism, secular humanism, anthropocentrism, capitalism, and the modern state and much else that modernity developed as central to its project," as argued by Hallaq in his critique of Orientalism (2018, 4, original emphasis).

Thus, the discourse of crisis is not confined to the post-2015 moment alone, nor the particular condition that made this work and research possible. Rather, the crisis in question is that of modernity and the modern nation-state altogether; it is the crisis when a certain order of things (Foucault 1994) starts falling apart, blatant in its manifestation, and crudely visible as we write these pages during a global pandemic. In this framework, it is undeniable to claim the Euro-American centrism of much of modern frames of knowledge and thought, and its compartmentalization into "disciplines" in the past two centuries. As Syed Farid Alatas, along with others, has said, the formation of much of the modern social science disciplines in the context of colonial expansion, and its institutionalization in the imperial metropoles and colonies, have left social sciences marked with fundamental, limited characteristics.[2] Alatas summarizes these characteristics as: (a) the inability and/or the lack of creativity to look outside of the Euro-American cultural arena for the generation of knowledge and methods of analysis; (b) the uncritical adoption of imitation of Western theories and models, which Alatas refers to as *mimesis*, and their imposition on non-Euro-American contexts; (c) textualism, or rather the assumption of correspondence between a normative textual reading and reality; (d) stereotyping, or the essentialization and racialization of modernity's Other; and finally (e) absence of subaltern voices that lie outside of the dominated elitist perspective in social science, all contributing, according to Alatas, to *academic imperialism* (2000). Hence, the call for "alternative discourses" for decolonization, indigenization, de-Orientalization, sacralization, feminist alternatives, and multiplication of social sciences, or what Alatas refers to as counter-Eurocentric sociology (2006), is the more recent manifestation of a longer trajectory of diverse groups of scholars and thinkers, from a wide range of disciplines, who have been reading, seeing, and thinking from/with an *elsewhere* – outside of the geotemporal frame of Western modernity alone. This book aims to implement this call for alternative discourses within the modern, institutionalized, and technocentric discipline of Architecture.[3]

Spatial authorship

Since 2015, a plethora of events, funding opportunities, conferences, workshops, open discussions, research groups, task forces, and debates have taken place, in Europe and beyond, focusing on questions of migration and refuge. Dominated mainly by the fields of social sciences, these debates oftentimes neglect questions of space, architecture, and the overall built environment. Meanwhile, in the institutionalized and professionalized modern field of Architecture – and the design discipline more broadly (Fry and Nocek 2021; Abdulla et al. 2019) – the focus is primarily on the architect/designer as the problem-solver and the innovator of "better shelters." Institutionalized architectural thinking is often framed as an object-based discipline, using the container as its archetypal problem solution, thus, pairing linearly the "boxed space" of the container with the solution of shelter and containment. The container, as such, stands as *the* spatial typology of sheltering displacement. It is replicable, universal, transportable, a unit made to be out-of-time and out-of-place, containing and transporting both goods and life, hiding them, pausing them in the hidden universalized time-space of mobilized immobilities. It is precisely the containers' modularity that has permitted the phenomenal increase of its quantity and scale, "its staid metal walls" bringing about "the radical opacity of its contents," as Charmaine Chua puts it (2016, 43). It is precisely this universalized, modern architectural space and architectural form, through its totalizing language of spatial authorship, that has entirely disregarded its inherent complicity in violent forms of domination, dispossession, and displacement (Sorkin and Sharp 2021; Weizman 2007, 2019; Herscher and Siddiqi 2017; Rael 2017; Kenzari 2011).

As such, the evident gap we have found between the fields of design, architecture, urban planning, and spatial disciplines more broadly, and those of the social sciences in the past years with regard to questions of migration and refuge motivated us to organize the above-mentioned workshop, and this successive edited volume. We hope these platforms will contribute to debates among both academics and practitioners working at the intersection of spatial and social disciplines on the alternating nature of spaces and architectures of both displacement and refuge. Both these disciplines, with all their problematic structural limitations and Eurocentric colonial legacies, would benefit dramatically from participating in each other's debates.[4] On a methodological level, for example, the use of architectural drawing, as included in this volume, not as a mere technique of representation, but, rather, as a prime analytical tool for sociological and ethnographic research, allows the authors/inhabitants of space to be the authors/teachers of (academic) research as well. In addition, these disciplines could engage in a critical dialogue for alternative merging grounds of knowledge formation – knowledge that is foundationally grounded in seeing, thinking, and being, from a non-modern, non-colonial elsewhere and elsewhen. Considering this broader frame, we ask the following question: What are the possibilities, but also the limits, of Architecture to unlearn and rethink the boundaries and parameters of its canonization and predefined authorship, and to fundamentally recast a different disciplinary approach altogether? The first step towards this architecture would be to recast a new (or rather, recenter its perennial) spatial author: *the inhabitant* (Chitchian, Momic, and Seethaler-Wari 2020).

Displacement has a long history and different forms of manifestation, both spatially as well as on a temporal level, and is associated with various subject positions of displacement: from socio-politico-environmental conflicts and crisis situations to uneven forms of economic and spatial development; global war-making apparatuses and military occupations; refugee migrant movements and (im)mobilites; class struggles; ethno-racial and religious "otherings"; global land grabs and water grabs; gentrification and various practices of segregation; changing institutional terrains of governance from the local to the supranational etc., resulting in various subject forms of *displacement*, including but not limited to the migrant/refugee displaced populations. These apparently arbitrary categories (Dadusc, Grazioli, and Martínez 2019) are produced and reproduced by modern bordering regimes – in their various forms and scales of manifestation – as a method of division as well as of multiplication of differences powered by the nation-state (Mezzadra and Neilson 2013). In addition, this multidimensional and multiscalar discussion poses the question of how various dimensions of displacement are fundamentally interrelated with other subaltern positionalities – urban poverty; the dwindling, saturation, and commodification of (social) housing; detention and incarceration of urban inhabitants; precarious labor regimes, etc. – requiring a broader cross-connection and linkage between these various levels of analyses (Sanyal 2012, 2015; Roy 2011).

Colonial capitalism has consequently triggered, and fundamentally benefited from, these various modalities of displacement and uprootedness, and, as Escobar puts it, is "an integral element of Eurocentric modernity and its post-World War II manifestation in Asia, Africa, and Latin America" through the language of "development" (2004, 157). As Escobar further explains, while the logic of the simultaneous creation *and* prevention of displacement (that is, uprooting *and* re-placing) is central to the operation of colonial capitalism, it is precisely the widening of this gap – the breaking down of mechanisms of re-placing, or what Mezzadra and Neilson have framed as *differential inclusion* (2013) in relation to the logic of displacement – that lies at the heart of our contemporary neoliberal "crisis" condition (163). In addition, by understanding the displacement of both space *and* time to be foundational to the project of modernity, we can further argue that displacement is not a geographical/spatial condition alone in which a subject is displaced from one point to another (for example, from the subnational to the supranational scale). Rather, without any spatial movement, one could be *displaced* in time (located outside of the imagined timeframe of modernity). By doing so, the project of modernity not only displaces space in/through time, making its colonization possible, it displaces itself in return. Thus, the modern subject is a displaced subject.

Looking at the question of displacement through an architectural lens, Andrew Herscher, in his book *Displacements: Architecture and Refugee* (2017), shows how modern histories of architecture have usually reproduced the nation-state's exclusion of displaced people as those who are "out of place." He, thus, argues that mass subjects created by violent displacement were usually marginalized or normalized in histories of modernity – from proletarianization, through colonization, to expulsion and other forms of coerced exile – and through these populations architecture came to define its modernity. As such, he locates architecture at the two historical points, mentioned by Escobar earlier: namely, the mass population displacements (caused by rural enclosure, colonial conquest, total war, and other forms of modern and contemporary political violence) and the arts and technologies of mass population placement (that is, re-placing) imagined and enacted by modern and contemporary architecture.

Within this framework, we revisit the notion of re-placing from a different perspective, and ask: How can a critical understanding of the notion of displacement help us unpack the complex, and often marginalized and invisibilized, spatial productions by displaced populations as modes of architectural re-placing? In other words, can the frame of displacement offer us a different understanding of architecture? By using the concept/condition/spatial process of inhabitation, we aim to deconstruct the techno-material foundations of architectural (knowledge) production by positing it instead as a mode of subject position in/of space. Thus, inhabitation acts as a mediation between conditions of displacement and re-placing of the state, and place-making and re-placing from below – that is, an architectural vocabulary of authorship of the many, beyond the state, and beyond its technocrats.

Inhabitation as architecture

This volume centralizes the concept of inhabitation as an epistemic shift of both the *site* and the *subject* of architectural (knowledge) production. It uses the concept of inhabitation as an expansive understanding of architecture through the central subject figure of spatial production, namely, the inhabitant. The modern professionalization and institutionalization of the discipline of Architecture has gone hand-in-hand with the elimination, or decentralization, of the notion of inhabitation as its a priori (Boano and Astolfo 2020, 562–63). In other words, the architect, the legitimized builder became detached from the inhabitant, the daily user, and maker of space; and, as a result, inhabitation (the simultaneous act of living and altering space) became detached from the process of design itself (Boano and Astolfo 2020, 562–63).

We enter the vast concept of inhabitation through the particular spatialities of migrant displacements. By doing so, the sheer nakedness and violence of these conditions visibilize inhabitation practices that might otherwise be invisible or unseen by the broader discipline of Architecture. By formulating inhabitation in relation to displacement, defined here as the *inhabitation-displacement nexus*, we aim to conceptualize a broader understanding of architecture as a merging ground, a field of negotiation, a domain of encounter, of all the various voices, subjects, and agents involved. In this frame, architecture is seen as a domain of both violence *and* care, both construction *and* destruction, sheltering *and* uprooting, repair *and* abandonment with various levels and hierarchies of authorship, in relation to, but also beyond the figure of the modern "architect." In other words, it is a domain of both displacement *and* inhabitation, of dis-placing *and* re-placing. Architectural inhabitation, therefore, can be conceptualized beyond its association with the design and the materiality of the built environment alone. Rather, it can be seen as a domain, a zone, or a plane of arrangements – material and otherwise – through which alternative subjectivities and understandings of politics and power can be imagined, one that is inherently communal.

Framing displacement and inhabitation as co-constitutive of each other allows for the possibility of understanding and analyzing a different stitching together of space, a different modality of socio-spatial arrangements – architecture or otherwise. It is this porous ground of merging and emergence that we are looking at, the potential of becoming, that which is displaced and emplaces itself anew, albeit invisible to the modern eye, to the modern spatial lexicon, in a time outside of the linearity of progress or in a space outside of the universalized global. Inhabitation is local, it adjusts itself to its encountered conditions, it is not on the individual scale, it is communal, relational, dependent on its circumstances, it pulls in what it can, it improvises based on its ascribed condition. It is written through a different process of spatial authorship, that of inhabitation by/for the inhabitants. Furthermore, it problematizes various binarisms and dualisms of modern spatial thinking due to how it weaves through them and positions itself at an interstitial position of in-between; the dualisms of architecture/urbanism, the camp/the city, the architect/the refugee, the formal/the informal, the material/the nonmaterial (or beyond-the-material). It argues for interdependencies and co-constitutive nature of each of these categories of analysis and offers an empirical and theoretical framework for bridging the dualities mentioned.

What we are alluding to here, however, is not the individual agency of spatial alteration, or the individual subject and its "overrepresentation" being at the center of our thought (Wynter 2003). Rather, inspired by notions such as the vernacular, processes of auto-construction etc.,[5] we refer to a communal understanding of what constitutes space-making and space-building altogether. It is one which is not bound by the regulatory frames of the modern architectural sovereign and which, while in a constant state of negotiation and struggle with it, perhaps even defies it; one that sees the architect not as an individualized act, but rather as a communal entity.

Book structure

Based on the discussed conceptual frame, this volume includes academic articles, one autobiographical essay, and one interview. The featured contributions present a range of themes, methodologies, disciplinary backgrounds, foci, geographies, and modes of representation and analysis. While there are multiple ways that this volume could be structured and read, we have centralized the various inhabitation practices of displacement around two main perspectives: (1) *Inhabiting the "Camp"* and (2) *Inhabiting the "City."*

Each of the two parts opens up with a testimonial voice of a "refugee" and an "architect." In their respective contributions (an autobiographical essay and an interview), each reflects on their specific roles and experiences in different modalities and processes of architectural spatial production. In doing so, while acknowledging their different hierarchies and positionalities within the field, they both, in their own particular way, portray the limits of the normative frames oftentimes assigned to their positions and experiences. While Samah Al Jundi-Pfaff argues that "in camps, people are the architects who create anew that which has been destroyed" as illustrative of their spatial agency and authorship, the interview with Gregor Brune discloses restrictive conditions (hyperbolically speaking, even lack of agency) that practicing architects face in planning and design processes of refugee shelters. These examples, as particular as they may be, challenge, in a way, the normativity of Architecture (as a discipline) and the Architect as an agent of spatial change/intervention, and by extension the supposed architect-inhabitant binarism and dichotomy. The established structures of displacement, institutionalized and state-run (together with nonstate and supra-state actors), repeatedly foster a humanitarian, interventionist, and authored understanding of architectural shelter, particularly in conditions of mass displacement, and thus create a dualism between the figure of the architect and that of the refugee (or the migrant), putting one at the giving end and the other at the receiving end of technical expertise, as mentioned before. As such, we see these testimonials giving voice to the oftentimes voiceless in academic research and debates surrounding these themes.

While grouping the contributions around these two foci, our goal, as we elaborate on further in the epilogue, is to argue that the division between the camp and the city is actually a porous one. The city, as various critical urban studies scholars have argued, is a partial representation of the extended urban geography. In addition, camps in their various spatial formations, are also one instance of a larger geography of displacement, as our contributors also show.

Part I: Inhabiting the "Camp"

The first part of the volume, *Inhabiting the "Camp,"* looks at spatial inhabitation practices from below in the condition of the (refugee) "camp." The featured camp spaces are located both in Southern geographies and in makeshift modalities thereof in European territories – representing a geographical "outside" scope of supposed peripherality and marginality, both within the fortified geographies of Europe together with its outside Third World regions.[6] These contributions represent various instances of inhabitation practices; spaces that are constantly made and remade, altered, changed, updated, negotiated as an act of accommodating needs and supporting survival. These spatial alterations bring various traditions and temporalities together, in which the extension of a past, prolongation of the present, together with the anticipation of a possible future are all brought together in complex and precarious ways; a time-space continuum in which distances and durations are in a constant state of negotiation and change – permanently temporary or only temporarily framed as permanent;[7] a time-space continuum in which various subjects, positioned in different relational hierarchies, also produce spaces that are in different relation to each other. These various spaces are, in essence, coproduced and co-constitutive of each other, albeit labeled differently. Examples of these spatial practices in camps in Syria, Jordan, Kenya, Lebanon, Germany, and France are included here.

This section opens with an autobiographical essay by **Samah Al Jundi-Pfaff**, titled *In, Out, and Beyond the Camp,* a personal, scenic, and poetic account on the experience of displacement and refuge. Al Jundi-Pfaff fluidly depicts different memories and spaces, thus blurring the boundaries of the *here* and the *now* and that of the *there* and the *then,* seamlessly connecting, both spatially as well as temporally, Germany to the Middle East, Friedland Transit Camp to Al Yarmouk Camp, Lattakia to Dheisheh and to St. Norbert Church. Moving beyond that which is called an ethnographic account or qualitative methodology, Al Jundi-Pfaff lives her own observations. By so doing, she lives and witnesses inhabitation as a modality of everyday life in the camp and beyond, comparing the time in the camp to the experience of being in a storm – surreal, out-of-place and out-of time. By showcasing practices of survival, getting by, appropriation, and inhabitation, she argues that the people in the camp are the authors of space, in reality *they* are the architects.

The following paper – *Reversals: The University and the Camp,* by **Anooradha Iyer Siddiqi** – complements the previous paper by inviting the reader to take the concerns and the problematics of decolonizing the mind seriously by imagining an architecture in which the humanitarian becomes the student, the refugee the professor, and the space of the camp that of the university. She, thus, asks: "What if camps did not serve empiricist ends of knowledge, but instead, theoretical ones?" "What if the inhabitation of the camp generated theory, practices, and ritual knowledge of its own?" Through the example of the Chairlady of Ifo camp, Dadaab, along with a registered refugee who partook in the shelter initiative program, something, according to Siddiqi, originated in the refugee camps *as an architecture*, affecting a political subjectivity, different from the usual understanding of the political sphere producing built form. This is the architecture she asks us to imagine, outside of the conventionally understood epistemic frameworks, and outside of the agency of any interpreter's translation thereof.

Another rigorous theoretical piece – *Architecture on the Move: (Re)Creating a Place in a Displaced World* by **Irit Katz** – follows in this part. Based on the work of Hannah Arendt on refuge and the human condition, Katz focuses on practices of homemaking in the makeshift Jungle camp in Calais and examines the meaning of the "moving architecture" of "moving people," as they attempt to create a place for themselves in their unstable world of displacement and human mobility. These spaces, as Katz shows, are inhabited and move both externally in their geographical location following the workings of regional and local powers, and internally through the creation and change of their architectural forms. These temporary environments are an active realization of a "place in the world" that answers the human needs of their inhabitants, destabilizes who architects are, and redefines what architecture is and what it could be.

The following paper, *Madafah: Who is Hosting Whom? The Everyday of Za'atri Refugee Camp and the Architectural Encounter* by **Aya Musmar**, adds a complementary layer by interrogating the often-cited notion of the refugee camp as a place where refugees are "hosted." Rather, Musmar's article, grounded in a decolonialist feminist methodology, offers a critical reading of the *Madafah* as a place whereby refugees in the camp become the hosts, enacting, thus, the ethic code of hospitality and performing a sense of ownership over the extraterritoriality of the camp. Central is the understanding of hospitality as an ethical and moral relationship rather than a juridical one. Through the shifting terrain of the host and the hosted, Musmar interrogates how the gendered, classed, and raced power positions are played out between refugees and NGO representatives and community mobilizers in Za'atri camp through the space of the *Madafah*.[8] She, thereby, exhibits the *Madafah* as an architectural space of encounter, producing an assemblage of positionalities and temporalities through the encounter.

This section concludes with the article *Between Securitization, Appropriation, and the Right to Dwell: A Multiscalar Analysis of Azraq Camp*, an architectural ethnography by **Ayham Dalal**, **Petra Heber**, and **Leticia Palomino** that focuses on the multiscalar tension and fundamental interlinkages between securitization and technologies of discipline and control, on the one hand, and the refugee appropriation and inhabitation of space from below, on the other. By focusing on the Azraq Camp in Jordan, Dalal, Heber, and Palomino situate dwelling as their prime cursor for exploring these spatial practices and tensions. Despite all the attempts to restrict refugees and "fixate" them in space, the authors show how refugees manage to find ways in which they humanize the space of the camp, from the scale of the shelter, to the plot, and finally to the larger camp setting through incremental and tactical acts of transformation. These practices of appropriation and inhabitation defy the contours of disciplinary powers, enabling refugees to both occupy the camp *and* to dwell.

Part II: Inhabiting the "City"

The second part, *Inhabiting the "City,"* takes the scale of the city as its starting point of analysis, and asks: What do inhabitation practices look like in conditions of displacement within the larger scale of the city and the urban? How do these practices differ from, or relate to, modes of inhabitation discussed in the prior section within the "camp"? What makes them particularly urban spatial interventions? In a complex interplay between the architectural scale and the interiority of the institutionalized spaces of shelter (for example, reception camps, accommodation centers, long-term and short-term housing solutions) and that of the larger urban scale, articles in this part show, each in their unique way, how inhabitation practices are manifested on different scales through different geographies and temporalities of operation, while offering (and resulting from) different capacities of mobility/immobility of their inhabitants. Each successive paper adds another layer of analysis and differentiation to inhabitation practices, thus helping us blur, and complexify, our presumed boundaries of thought.

This part opens with an interview carried out by Shahd Seethaler-Wari with the architect **Gregor Brune**, addressing the response of German cities to the so-called refugee crisis and the readiness of urban planners and designers in general, to react effectively in emergency situations. The interview aims to understand the challenges that practitioners face on the ground in designing and building refugee accommodations in a rapidly changing geopolitical context. Brune shares his experience in designing and transforming a hospital building complex in Lower Saxony, Germany, into refugee accommodation, and explains the twists and turns that complicated the implementation of his project. In the discussion, the interview addresses the chances and opportunities that emerged in the otherwise rigid planning and building system in Germany, precisely due to the "crisis" situation.

In the following architectural ethnography, *Inhabiting Refugee Accommodations: A Comparison of Two Temporarily Transformed Buildings*, **Shahd Seethaler-Wari** centralizes the voice of refugees and their inhabitation practices in two refugee accommodations in the city of Göttingen, showing how these practices are in a complex interplay between institutional frameworks, their restrictions, and their constant update of those spaces. The author combines architectural drawings with qualitative research methods to present the similarities and differences between the spatial layouts, the daily lives, and their respective inhabitation practices. In the context of blurred definitions and boundaries of private and public, she illustrates how the inhabitants use the resulting margin to redefine those boundaries and appropriate spaces to better meet their diverse needs. Finally, the paper shows how different actors, through their different roles and practices, are makers and authors of architectural space.

Maja Momić's paper, *Between Inhabitation and Dwelling: (Im)mobilities in Everyday Life*, centralizes an urban analysis through the tracing of different trajectories and practices of inhabitation in the city of Hamburg. By doing so, she showcases the many spheres of life – the legal, the material, the lived – that intertwine with these trajectories, from interrelations with policies and regulations to factors such as unequal mobilities and distribution of rights, thus sharing the *de jure* possibilities, restrictions, and experiences of various inhabitation practices. Furthermore, Momić illustrates how inhabitation operates as a ground for both resisting oppressive mechanisms and shaping the urban sphere. She conceptualizes inhabitation as a mode of relationality with others *and* the city through practices of mutual care and repair, and by imagining – and performing – that which could be. Finally, the paper explores the ambivalent relation between mobility and immobility based on the example of different dwelling patterns, thus demonstrating how movement and change can be examined only in relation to immobility and relative settledness.

Subsequently, in her paper *Architecture and Beyond: In/formal Spaces of Urban Refuge – Berlin*, **Nassim Mehran** further expands on the limits of thinking through the formal architectural paradigms of refugee accommodations and, instead, connects them to their broader urban context. In other words, she argues that the abstract architectures of refugee accommodations, as she frames them, operate beyond their initial, bureaucratic physical layout and, depending on their local particularities and circumstances, develop a distinct relation to their urban vicinity. Consequently, spaces of "urban refuge" constitute a wide and complex merging ground of in/formal networks of urban relationalities that form a decisive part of refugees' multiscalar trajectories of resettlement. Moving beyond the frame of temporality, impermanence, or exceptionality characterizing refugee accommodations, Mehran showcases how refugees reclaim their spatial agency and autonomy through an alternate definition of what it means to settle and to inhabit, thus blurring the boundaries between the formal and the informal, the individual and the communal, the architectural and the urban.

Lina Sánchez Steiner's paper, *Displacement, Arrival, and Housing: The Case of Leipzig (Germany) and Mocoa (Colombia)*, starts from an urban lens and zooms out to the interregional scale by contrasting and comparing two cities, Leipzig and Mocoa. The author analyzes long-term housing solutions of displaced populations in both cities showing similarities and differences between both contexts in the Global North and the Global South. She illustrates the complex interplay between the spatial interventions done by refugees and by other institutional and humanitarian actors. For each case, the author describes the arrival processes of displaced populations and their phases of settlement and addresses the roles of governments and other local actors in the provision of long-term housing in these very different institutional contexts. Sánchez Steiner shows how displaced persons assume an active role to solve their long-term housing problems by fulfilling the roles of urban planners and architects in Mocoa, and by appropriating and adapting their apartment layouts to their cultural needs and household sizes in Leipzig.

Finally, in her paper *Architectures of Displacement: On the Aesthetics and Politics of Humanitarian Shelter*, **Romola Sanyal** critically interrogates the iconography of refuge. Contrasting the dominant iconography – that of the camp – she examines the ways in which camps have come to take their current form and how they are aestheticized through different technologies, asking what they do for different stakeholders. The author argues that this aestheticization of displacement is not merely a convenient technology to deliver aid and support, but also serves to elicit sympathy and support for specific forms of suffering while ignoring other spaces and populations who are equally marginalized. Analyzing the challenges that the urban shelters face in imagining refuge, Sanyal draws these distinct spaces together to critically interrogate what it means to talk about architectures of displacement, urging us to rethink what architectures of refuge can be and how we can be part of a progressive conversation that pays attention to a wider range of spaces that refugees inhabit in the city.

Epilogue

This volume finishes with an epilogue by **Somayeh Chitchian**, *Inhabitation: A Story of Return*. In this final contribution to the volume, she asks: How does displacement differ from, or relate to, categories such as exclusion, dispossession, classed conditions, etc.? How can a new critical understanding of the spatialities of displacement help us unpack the complex subjectivities that are emerging under contemporary conditions of exclusion and dispossession more broadly? Chitchian argues for a relational understanding of allegedly opposite spaces (camp/city) and subjects (refugee/non-refugee) of displacement. Furthermore, she illustrates how state subjects of displacement, that is, "refugees" and/or the internally displaced, are fundamentally connected to other subaltern positionalities within the "imperialist, white supremacist, capitalist, patriarchal" interlocking systems of domination (i.a. hooks 1984). Hence, she emphasizes the vital importance of an intersectional understanding of displacement within modernity's broader systems of domination. In sum, the paper moves beyond both the binarism of the camp and the city towards subjects and spaces of architectural inhabitation, along the either/or frames of camp/city (space) and architect/refugee (subject).

1 Event page link: http://events.mmg.mpg.de/inside-out-outside-in/ **2** This project is indebted to, and positions itself in alliance with, the intersectional work of many decolonial, feminist, abolitionist, anticapitalist, and antiracist pieces of scholarship that have given us fundamental frames of critical thought and analysis for understanding how modernity's liberal secularism, humanism, and anthropocentrism are structurally intertwined with violence, and are incapable of sympathizing, let alone fundamentally engaging, with the nonliberal, nonmaterial, nonsecular, and nonhumanist modes of ethical thinking. **3** Here we would like to make a distinction between architecture and Architecture with capital 'A,' a distinction between the average, everyday building in our cities versus the high-art design by the master architect. Robert Bruegmann, in his 1986 essay "Architecture Without the Capital 'A'," quotes Nikolaus Pevsner's opening line of his book *Outline of European Architecture*, telling us that "[a] bicycle shed is a building; Lincoln Cathedral is a piece of Architecture" (capitalization our own). While on the surface this may seem, as Bruegmann argues, merely a distinction between high-art and low-art design, in essence, this type of distinctive binary thinking has allowed for much of the illnesses and complicity of modern architecture in its violent dominations and dispossessions, while negating much of the everyday, the vernacular, the non-professional, and in sum, the non-modern architecture and design. Henceforth, in this introduction, when Architecture is used with capital 'A,' it is referring to this distinctive frame. **4** While acknowledging academic movements known as turns – whether in social sciences and its "spatial turn," or a subsequent plea for a "social turn" in spatial studies – our understanding of an ultimate merging ground of these disciplines would be an onto-epistemic shift altogether, i.e., the fundamental recasting of the modern/colonial imaginary of time (linearity, development, and progress) materialized in/through space (universality and segmentation, e.g., developed vs. developing). **5** As Marion von Osten states (*e-flux Architecture* 2009): "The didactic model of vernacular and self-built architecture [...] has to be critically examined in the context of colonial and global modernity." The "learning from premodern architectural form" by, for example, Bernard Rudofsky and his *Architecture without Architects* exhibition, according to von Osten "needs to be contextualized against its ambiguous and asymmetrical postcolonial histories [...] it becomes important to acknowledge the impossibility of projecting any new utopias from the aesthetic regimes of planned worlds, the universal abilities of the human subject, or the 'creativity of the poor,' studied by the modern sciences only to improve Western design practices." **6** This framework falls within the understanding of "internal colonialism," conceptualized by Leo Marquard (1957) with respect to South Africa, and later on expanded and popularized by González Casanova (1965) with his work on Mexico. Other scholars have further used and elaborated on this concept and related it to others such as "uneven development." See: Marquard, L., *South Africa's Colonial Policy,* Johannesburg, Institute of Race Relations, 1957; Casanova, G. P., "Internal Colonialism and National Development," *Studies in Comparative International Development* 1, no. 4, 1965, 27–37, https://doi.org/10.1007/BF02800542; Hechter, M., *Internal Colonialism: The Celtic Fringe in British National Development,* Berkeley, University of California Press, 1975; Wolpe, H., "The Theory of Internal Colonialism: The South African Case," in *Beyond the Sociology of Development*, edited by I. Oxaal, T. Barnett, and D. Booth, London, Routledge & Kegan Paul, 1975. **7** For a fundamental elaboration and expansion on the notion of "permanent temporariness," see the work of Sandi Hilal and Alessandro Petti, entitled *Permanent Temporariness*, edited by Nick Axel and Maria Nadotti, Art and Theory Publishing, 2018. **8** This refugee camp in Jordan is mentioned in a few articles in this volume. Each author has chosen a different spelling of the Arabic name (مخيم الزعتري). It will appear as Za'atari, Zaatari, Za'atri, or Alzaatari in the volume.

References

Abdulla, D., A. Ansari, E. Canlı, M. Keshavarz, M. Kiem, P. Oliveira, L. Prado, and T. Schultz. 2019. "A Manifesto for Decolonising Design." *Journal of Futures Studies* 23, no. 3: 129–32.

Alatas, S. F. 2000. "An Introduction to the Idea of Alternative Discourses." *Southeast Asian Journal of Social Science* 28, no. 1: 1–12.

Alatas, S. F. 2006. *Alternative Discourses in Asian Social Science: Responses to Eurocentrism*. New Delhi: Sage Publications.

Anderson, B. 1983. *Imagined Communities: Reflections on the Origin and Spread of Nationalism*. New York: Verso.

Boano, C., and G. Astolfo. 2020. "Inhabitation as More-Than-Dwelling: Notes for a Renewed Grammar." *International Journal of Housing Policy* 20, no. 4: 555–77.

Bruegmann, R. 1986. "Architecture Without the Capital 'A': Documentation in a Post-Modern Age." *Art Documentation* 5, no. 3: 103–05.

Chitchian, S., M. Momic, and S. Seethaler-Wari. 2020. "Architectures of an 'Otherwise': Inhabiting Displacement." *Contingency, Ardeth. A Magazine on the Power of the Project*, no. 6, edited by D. Cuff and W. Davis: 249–55.

Chua, C. 2016. "The Container: Stacking, Packing, and Moving the World." *The Funambulist: Object Politics*, no. 6: 40–45.

Dadusc, D., M. Grazioli, and M. Martınez. 2019. "Introduction: Citizenship as Inhabitance? Migrant Housing Squats Versus Institutional Accommodation." *Citizenship Studies* 23, no. 6: 521–39.

Duncan, J. 1993. "Sites of Representation: Place, Time, and the Discourse of the Other." In *Place/Culture/Representation*, edited by J. Duncan and D. Ley, 39–56. London: Routledge.

Escobar, A. 2004. "Displacement, Development, and Modernity in the Colombian Pacific." *International Social Science Journal* 55, no. 175: 157–67.

Escobar, A. 2019. "De/coloniality and Displacement: Ontological Occupations and the Aporias of Neoliberal Mobility." *Socioscapes. International Journal of Societies, Politics and Cultures* 1, no. 12: 95–109.

Fanon, F. 1963. *Black Skin, White Masks*. Harmondsworth, UK: Penguin.

Foucault, M. 1994. *The Order of Things: An Archaeology of the Human Sciences*. New York: Vintage Books.

Fry, T., and A. Nocek, eds. 2021. *Design in Crisis: New Worlds, Philosophies and Practices*. London: Routledge.

Hallaq, W. B. 2018. *Restating Orientalism: A Critique of Modern Knowledge*. New York: Columbia University Press.

Herscher, A. 2017. *Displacements: Architecture and Refugee*, edited by N. Hirsch and M. Miessen. Critical Spatial Practice 9 series. London: Sternberg Press.

Herscher, A. and A. I. Siddiqi, eds. 2017. *Spatial Violence*. New York: Routledge.

Hilal, S. and A. Petti. 2018. "Returns." In *Permanent Temporariness*, edited by M. Nadotti and N. Axel, 29. Stockholm: Art and Theory Publishing.

hooks, b. 1984. *Feminist Theory from Margin to Center.* Boston, MA: South End Press.

Kenzari, B., ed. 2011. *Architecture and Violence*. Barcelona and New York: Actar Publishers.

Mezzadra, S., and B. Neilson. 2013. *Border as Method, Or, the Multiplication of Labor*. Durham, NC: Duke University Press.

Osten, M. von. 2009. "Architecture Without Architects: Another Anarchist Approach." *e-flux Architecture: Journal*, no. 06, edited by J. Aranda, B. Kuan Wood, and A. Vidokle. https://www.e-flux.com/journal/06/61401/architecture-without-architects-another-anarchist-approach/.

Rael, R. 2017. *Borderwall as Architecture: A Manifesto for the U.S.-Mexico Boundary.* Oakland, CA: University of California Press.

Roy, A. 2011. "Slumdog Cities: Rethinking Subaltern Urbanism." *International Journal of Urban and Regional Research* 35, no. 2: 223–38.

Said, E. 1978. *Orientalism*. London: Routledge & Kegan Paul.

Sanyal, R. 2012. "Refugees and the City: An Urban Discussion." *Geography Compass* 6, no. 11: 633–44.

Sanyal, R. 2015. "Refugees and Urban Poverty: A Historical View from Calcutta." In *The City in Urban Poverty*, edited by C. Lemanski and C. Marx, 137–57. Basingstoke, UK: Palgrave Macmillan.

Sharma, N. 2020. *Home Rule: National Sovereignty and the Separation of Natives and Migrants*. Durham, NC: Duke University Press.

Sorkin, M., and D. Sharp, eds. 2021. *Open Gaza: Architectures of Hope*. Cairo: The American University in Cairo Press and Terreform.

Tazzioli. M., and N. De Genova, eds. 2016. *Europe/Crisis: New Keywords of "the Crisis" in and of "Europe."* New Keywords Collective: A Collaborative Project of Collective Writing. Brooklyn, NY: Zone Books. https://research.gold.ac.uk/27156/1/New-Keywords-Collective_11.pdf.

Weizman, E. 2007. *Hollow Land: Israel's Architecture of Occupation*. London: Verso.

Weizman, E. 2017. *Forensic Architecture: Violence at the Threshold of Detectability*. Brooklyn, NY: Zone Books.

Wynter, S. 2003. "Unsettling the Coloniality of Being/Power/Truth/Freedom: Towards the Human, After Man, Its Overrepresentation – An Argument." *CR: The New Centennial Review* 3, no. 3: 257–337.

PART I
INHABITING THE "CAMP"

In, Out, and Beyond the Camp

Samah Al Jundi-Pfaff

> *"In camps, people are the architects who create anew that which has been destroyed"*

While shifting between doing and being, I stepped into a world where individuals, institutions, and organizations have come together to reshape history and overcome global challenges. Since 2015, the place-making of Friedland Transit Camp has led me to question what I thought was universal and to recognize my biases; these discoveries are chronicled in incomplete notes in my journals. The collection of Museum Friedland, which mirrors the history of the camp, has touched my soul and grounded me in front of the discourse of World War II and its paradoxes. At the museum, there are no ancient ornaments, no funerary tombs and statues, to make you travel in time and space; instead, the memories and the voice of the *dead objects* are reborn with every tour I make. My task is to bridge the gap between the camp and its museum so the residents can reflect and shape their new life. Therefore, this paper questions the "normal" of the camp and reveals the personal emotional engagement and the contextual understanding towards historical empathy in the era of refugee crises.

After many "touch-and-go" games with different camps, I am stuck in transit in the Friedland Transit Camp where pulling the covers over my head will not lead to sweet dreams, and the euphoria of having arrived and being able to start again vanishes the moment I stand in the queue. Seeking to sort out the untested stories and to know what is around the corner grants me a life that is beyond Scheherazade's imagination. To keep my head up, I gave myself permission to start writing a journal, although, very often, it is hard to conceptualize my ideas. The reward of working on the operational level at the Museum Friedland's *Let's Make It* project is the chance to get close to the people's side of things and to walk around Friedland. The project is an assortment of educational activities built on the teach-a-person-to-fish approach. Founded in August 2016, the project aims to build a bridge between the Friedland Transit Camp and the seventy years of history of camp management represented in the new museum. Building this bridge makes my task as multilayered as the refugee crisis itself.

I am not collecting data over a period of time; I live my own observations. The notes I put down are controversial and not complete due to the accelerated pace of events and the ever-changing social and cultural fabric of the camp. It is hard to keep track of the significant changes and miscellaneous incidents that take place in that spot of Germany. Very often, the hours of the day allow no space or stamina to fill in the dots or to clarify the exclamation marks. In fact, some observations are indescribable.

Words cannot reflect my ears' pain while listening to the complaints that there is no water faucet and no hose at the camp toilets. Luckily, my mouth creates a funny story: "Perhaps the Syrian architects follow the French system in building their toilets! The German architects cannot match your standards. Use toilet paper and wash your hands!" Words cannot describe the blink of my upset eyes, shifting from the respectfully lined-up shoes on the wet towel inside the room to the random piles in the corridors of the camp's residential complexes. A funny story does not work when it is about the residents' private space, so my sense of humor could not move the wet towel to the shared corridor to collect the dust there, too. No words can delve satisfactorily into that moment when Karim, a teen from Romania, painted his hand over the painted hand of Alice, a pretty teen from Iran, to express his love. The paintings they left behind tell their stories. In this article, there is no hypothesis to test. I am sharing my lived experience as a refugee at the camp and a member of the Museum Friedland team. Academia calls it ethnography or qualitative methodology but, for me, it is a chance to dive deep into what, why, and how.

> *The camps I know are not like* Grenzdurchgangslager – *Friedland Transit Camp!*

Historically, on September 20, 1945, the cattle sheds of the Friedland experimental estate of the University of Göttingen were converted into a camp to provide immediate aid and relief for refugees along the common border of the British, American, and Russian zones of occupation. Within a short time, the barracks and the so-called Nissen huts, and most of the features of the camp that we see at present were built on the current site. The facility has witnessed the humanitarian crisis facing Germany after World War II and played a crucial role in the lives of four million individuals.

The camp was designed to be the first way station for refugees, evacuees, and returning soldiers of the war that I have lived through in movies and books but did not firsthand smell their blood mixed with gunpowder and dust. It made me touch the

Figure 1. A photograph taken in the 1950s showing the central square with the *Kantine* (House 15) in the Museum Friedland. Source: Museum Friedland/Fritz Paul

lives of refugees from Chile, the boat people from Vietnam, the Tamils from Sri Lanka, the refugees from Albania, the Iraqi Christian minority, and the people of the 2015 Refugee Crisis. Whenever I recite the story of their transit time in the camp, a new life chapter is added to mine. Wandering among the camp barracks, passing by the Homecoming Bell, and whispering my prayers at St. Norbert Church – each experience suggests the possibility of a silver lining in that in-between space where the ghosts of history and the confusion of the arrivals overlap and intertwine.

The history of camps I have been in before 2015 is no longer visible except as shops and street names such as Haret Alfedaeen (fedayeen quarter), and Jafra Youth Center in Al Yarmouk Camp, Damascus. Al Yarmouk Camp was built from scratch and designed by its dwellers, who used their common sense to create what was apt for the moment. I used to play cards there with my friends and listen to the stories of the adults, the Tamim family. The cards competition ended after buying some *kunafa nabelsia*, a sweet cheese pastry, and *za'atar* from Share'a Falastin street and when the adults' story time started. The Palestinians, who were refugees, started building their camps in 1957, then, over time, improved their housing and used new materials; there was no space or money for (conventional) architecture. The camp was located far away from the district of the city of Damascus where the ancient Roman canals used to be the swimming place. Their stories were full of images of the place that was turned from green countryside where they used to collect the sweet *sabara* (cactus figs) to a concrete forest. Those night-time talks amplified the tall tale of the arrival and new beginning of every refugee. The nostalgic stories of Al Yarmouk Camp have no clear names or dates but the dried out hands and the scars on the shoulders of the storytellers bear witness to their wanderings from temporary stays in mosques, schools, and abandoned houses before starting to build clay homes on the rented ground.

In front of the old train station, which is redesigned into a vivid museum, the old man who fled Al Yarmouk Camp mentioned that there was an official order to backfill the historical Roman ruins to dedicate a cemetery for the camp; he also chatted about how he could move the fig tree into his yard, the one he had left behind. A little vigilance and hope thrived when the talk turned to how to build *halawa* and *kunafa* factories, and Palestinian embroidery shops in Germany.

Mokhayam Alraml – as the people of Lattakia call the camp – is the place of family meetings and wedding parties, where the friends of my grandmother sing, and the guava trees listen and dance. It is the reward for being "a good girl" and the place of freedom where I can feel the fine cold sand under my bare feet. It is the beach where I learned to swim and to fly kites. Walking along the small paths of the camp, I read the short poems and slogans in graffiti that taught me the names of Palestinian cities and the poetry of Mahmoud Darwish. Like *normal people,* the residents of the camp go to school, go to work, get married, hold their children's hands, and bury their loved ones in the dedicated camp cemetery. Many underprivileged Syrian families lived on the outskirts of the camp until their homes merged into the fixed boundaries of the municipality. The 2015 war in – and on – Syria, doubled the population of the camp and tripled the residents of Palestinian homes in this camp with the displaced relatives from Al Yarmouk and Nairab camps. Displaced Syrian families also found shelter here. Cooperating with the Youth Program (UNRWA), I conducted a three-day-workshop called "Make a Difference" in 2014, where the participants filmed a profound message addressing both local and global audiences to promote the idea of learning with the displaced Palestinians and Syrians, not just learning about them. During the workshop, the youths talked about the lack of the basic infrastructure services like roads, sewage, clean water, electricity, telecommunication, to name a few, although the camp was recognized officially as property number 1140, act number 2316, in 1968. The three days of listening to the youths' concerns and challenges taught me that the long-term housing plan is at the will of the policy makers, no matter how active or passive the locals are. Many self-organized events, which were held by the residents of the camp and their supporters, failed simply because they could not figure out which governmental entity was in charge of the service delivery. In essence, the good memories of Mokhayam Alraml had already vanished when the pungent smell blew in from the seashore, and the participants informed me that the municipality had removed the waste containers for security reasons, which had meant the truck drivers had not dared to collect the garbage from the camp.[1]

I must build my tent, then cry!

The best years of my life were the ones in which I learned that my problems are my own and I must build my tent, then cry. At Scout camps in Slinfeh, in the countryside of Lattakia, I touched the stars and walked among the fir trees. At that time, camps were where and when making the fire and singing until dawn enriched the memory with the smell of the cedar and pine trees. Dismantling the Scout camp, by its very nature, started at the sunset with the song "The Fire Guard – Hares Alnar," while we baked potatoes and corn, and finished when we were sitting on the luggage tired and overwhelmed. Just remembering the special, improvised uniform that Yousef put on to sing ignites memories of the last Scout camp in Hatay, Turkey. In every camp I was in, the rituals of demolishing the tents, swapping the Scout neckerchief, and exchanging the handmade souvenirs were the time of profound hugs, happy tears, and a hope to meet next year. In fact, camps were established to be demolished at the end; that is, until I experienced seeking asylum at *Grenzdurchgangslager* Friedland Transit Camp and working for Museum Friedland.

Have you ever played with the white crystal aromatic ball of naphthalene when folding a tent and sleeping bags? Have you ever backfilled the trench you dug around your tent and put out the big fire pit with soil and tears? Have you folded the flags and gathered the masts for next year's camp? To be in a camp means to live on the minimum, and to accept what you have in that moment, because your possessions are safe and waiting for you at home.

Packing for a camp takes a long time. It is not easy to make the transition all at once and to choose what you need with limited space and time. Just a wild imagination could arrange the puzzles of everyday routine to pack strong shoes, waterproof jacket, sleeping bag, camping knife, and a dish and a cup made of stainless steel. The children, the documents, the family photos, and the most valued possessions have no space in your backpack, but they are safe at home. I have not ever packed a mirror or hand cream because my campmate tells me how I look, and olive oil is the balm and the medicine. The life you know and live far from the camp is guaranteed and your address is fixed. The sleepless nights and the hard days in the camp pass away and lead towards the demolishment of the campsite and the farewell ceremony. At home, a long bath and a big bowl of hot chicken soup prompts the to-do list and the start of normal life.

In Friedland, the camp was transformed into a place with history, present, and future. I am face-to-face with the history of the place, the uncertain present I am trying hard to accept and celebrate, and the unknown future in which paper is more valued than I am. Being a Friedlander puts me on my cross and changes me dramatically. My cross is not empty, and I am still here, collecting the stories of those who have experienced the darkest betrayal, torture, deception, and abandonment. I wander around the corners of the camp and my eyes kiss all the buildings. The narration says that the residents – my campmates – started life from scratch, but it does not tell how long they needed. Harmonizing the heart-wrenching tales of pain of everyday people is my first life motto; I conduct activities that encourage Friedlanders to find resilience and hope – resilience and hope that erase the double-blind bias that we bring to the camp. The second one is to create chances of behavioral architecture where Friedlanders open their eyes to discover that *nothing is intrinsically wrong with me and everything is figure-outable.* "Let's figure it out" and "let's make it" are what I have in my tool kit. Admittedly, no one received the owner's manual at birth. Under the conditions of camps, acting precedes thinking and the language of the manual is far removed from the known alphabet. Forming the manual is like giving birth from the loins!

> *"Wherever you stand, be the soul of the place."* (Rumi)

"Names are neutral. We place our personal bias on them!" These words ended the conversation with my German colleague, who advised me not to use the word *"Lager"* due to its connotations in German history. She generously explained that a German associates the word with the concentration camps. Later that same day, I consulted the report in the chronicle *Grenzdurchgangslager Friedland*, but the two huge albums, where the timeline of the events and the development of the camp is seen throughout newspaper extracts, photos, graphs, and handwritten notes, added more unanswered questions. That semantics incident and the images of the staff members collecting the content of the report made me stand with reverence in front of the illuminated box where the albums are kept. In its turn, the report is witness to how the people of the camp turn their misery into a road map towards results. At present, I walk around the *"Lager"* trying to relate the places that hold my body and soul with the reality behind those places. The steps towards the camp become my daily pilgrimage and the details of the *Let's Make It* project are my prayers.

Figure 2. *I Feel* exhibition at the Nissen hut. Source: Museum Friedland/Stephan Beuermann

Very often, different assumptions between my reality and the historical background of the monuments create a kind of humor and a new story. While the Nissen hut, for example, is simultaneously the green hut, the meeting point, the visual educational tool to help with understanding the notion of integration, the children's green maze, and my personal new beginning; for the museum team, on the other hand, it is just the ethnic German history. The hut, with its interactive educational built-in time, is just a grocery store (*Dokan*) for some refugees.

Figure 3. People paint to reshape their arrival. Source: Author

Stepping into the Nissen hut is the beginning of the long process of psychological rehabilitation as the guests touch the old furniture that goes back to the time of World War II and talk to the imagined soldier who slept on that iron bed. Some children and adolescents jump onto the bed to act like that soldier, no matter how I try to prevent this performance.

Holding the wooden door to open the hut and listening to its squeaking sound reminds me of the first World Refugee Day 2016. During the event, people were invited to sign their names on a white-flag mural. Alan's name was added only three years later, when his parents and his sister Elin also joined to celebrate the museum's International Day 2019. Perhaps we are not folding the pages of the past, but rather rereading them regularly and consciously.

The uncolored part of the hut inflames the artist in me to fancy the mural of faces I would like to paint. *I am afraid that I would be sent to court to be charged with stealing the history of the place*! The Nissen hut is the eyewitness of adding Hi/Story.[2] It would tell the story of Mohamad's first exhibition that led him to study architecture at Kassel University. It would smile empathetically at the children as they touched the old fire siren from way back. It would thank the other Mohamad for turning it into a barbershop and giving free hairstyles to the refugees and to the Service Civil International Study Camp group 2016. I miss touching the old hanging socks and the old, green box of Persil that used to be exhibited there.

By mere coincidence, once, I had to improvise a tour for some frightened children around the camp fountain that is located opposite the hut to prove that there was no hidden surveillance camera in the hut. If the Nissen hut could speak, it would give voice to the children's chalk paintings and teach us to watch our words and to choose what promotes togetherness and feelings of trust and integrity.

Losing this green hut as a meeting point for *Let's Make It* activities and the documentation of Dheisheh Refugee Camp – the Palestinian refugee camp in Ramallah – added more questions to my list. I wonder what would happen if an ethnic German demanded a "return to the Nissen hut!" How would Herr Shahinian react if a refugee visited the *Kapela* one day and asked to celebrate an achievement simply because he had visited the *Kapela* when seeking asylum? Could I plan a reunion party at the Nissen hut for the 3,500 people who were there in August 2015? Would it be possible to ring Friedland Bell to celebrate the end of the war in Iraq? Am I the only one who repeats the call for prayers when listening to the bell of St. Norbert Church? Looking at the photos of Dheisheh taken by Luca Capuano, the famous Italian photographer who was commissioned by UNESCO to document the 44 sites of the Italian

World Heritage, changes my definition of camps. They are communities of people, not places, where "the term 'compact' is coined for new deals for countries hosting refugees to boost their economies and give direct support to the communities where refugees are living" (CRRFs – Comprehensive Refugee Response Frameworks).[3]

Do places affect the lives we lead and create opportunities for us?

I do not pretend to have all the answers and there is no scientific evidence to confirm the stories I share, but this question indicates its answer. When we arrive, we are confused, confounded, and perplexed, but by spreading the *culture of trying-it-before-denying*, a feeling of control thrives. Ibrahim, for example, spent the waiting time at the camp making special rosaries and accessories using the seeds of dates. Alaa was not only the hairdresser but she learned new skills from the African lady who only speaks her own local language. In the transit camp, when the language barrier is too high, the residents build on what they have to communicate and to live life, especially when they get an inspiring push.

Acting like a storyteller to motivate people will not bring back what has already been lost, but it made Saeed redesign the bunk bed into a sofa. His red woolen carpet turned the room into a Bedouin tent in Palmyra. He set up his private museum to honor the silver tray, the colored glassware, the rosary, and some small items he managed to fold safely among his clothes. Creatively, the bunk bed has a third floor so he can lie down and recite the Quran with less noise from the children. The heating pipe became the bookshelf, too.

"Your time at the camp is a short, unforgettable honeymoon!" Can you imagine the vastly different responses I get to this statement? Some faces turn red and others glow, then a flood of memories runs mixed with their notions about certain places in the camp. In fact, there is no evidence that this statement led to the spontaneous engagement party that took place at House 41 in the camp. Moreover, I have no permission to share the names or the photos of the sweets offered by the families to celebrate the arranged marriage between two teen brothers and two sisters planned by the middle-aged parents who met at the resettlement orientation week in Egypt. Surprisingly, three weeks were enough to make a decision, which would have taken three months and more if they were not in a transit camp. Taking into consideration that the two families used to live in different cities in Syria makes such marriages unlikely to take place otherwise.

The myth of the honeymoon encouraged Mariam to whisper into my ears the story of her arranged marriage. I will leave out the painful pictures and contradictory details, to celebrate her as an interior designer. She managed to spread her wedding coverlet on the beds. The children were on another bunk bed behind an improvised curtain to allow some kind of intimacy. The next day, her husband baked pies on the back of the frying pan. The pies tasted special, but not the same as when using Syrian ingredients. We spent some time talking about his future catering project. The clever, serious questions made me listen attentively and wish them both good luck while I enjoyed my first cardamom tea.

Stories are born every day and, luckily, these stories always find their way to the *Let's Talk* activity where I meet those who speak English and Arabic during the mealtime. At the cafeteria, I join people to chat and build a rapport while they stand in line waiting to stamp a color-coded card to get their meal. The picture is almost the same no matter what nationality they are. A few are talking to each other and many are just looking silently through the windows waiting their turn. Some cross the line, especially children. I can almost hear the monologue in their heads wondering what food is on the tray. Very often after mealtime, men smoke outside while women are busy with the children. It is not the same with the ethnic German or the non-smoking males.

The complaints about food form another myth to tell to ease the dissatisfaction. When the complaint is about spicy food, the myth includes nutrition facts about ginger and red pepper, and when it is about the lentil soup, there are more dietary tips to offer. When it is about the plain fish, I am speechless. After two or three days, they learn how to bring their favorite tastes to the meal; onion, garlic, cumin, and curry are in their pockets.

Figure 4. A photograph taken on Samah Al Jundi-Pfaff's cell phone on January 29, 2020, showing how Saeed turned his camp room into a private museum using what he collected on his trip to Germany. Source: Author

Talking about camps is in vogue, but not for me. I hold many camp images dear due to my grandmother's stories about her life after leaving Yafa in 1948. Her stories about the vaccination when they reached Beirut Port pounced strong and vivid when the nurse was tapping the needle to inject me with the flu vaccination. At the camp clinic, the nice nurse felt embarrassed and confused for not being able to stop the crying episode of an adult woman. The next visit to complete the obligatory vaccination was a real drama that I could not control or explain. The same nice, embarrassed nurse asked me to take off my top not knowing that this would lead to another story of my grandmother and to another panic attack.

My camp stories are summed up in Luca Capuano's photos. They capture the moment professionally. The light coming through the windows and the shadow of a tree on what looks like a curtain dangling from the roof of the home evoke memory and awaken all butterflies in the stomach. As a matter of fact, only those who live in a camp know that the water on the street smells fishy and will make shoes dirty in the morning. The camp's dwellers know that the sky has no stars and that the sister of Mahasen Malek Shahin – the graffiti shows her name – is shedding hot tears on the other side of the closed door.

Speaking about the closed door, in February 2016, I pushed the heavy solid door of St. Norbert Church, looking for the entrance to plan my work that day, and was taken by surprise by the rainbow colors of the stained-glass windows on the brown wooden benches. That surprise granted me a peaceful tour till the sound of the bell brought me back from the Omayyad Mosque windows and grounded my feet in Friedland. Later, I created a story to justify the three bells hanging in the church tower and use it to break the "wall" between East and West Germany again and again! The fabricated story I tell in the friendly playful Syrian dialect of Homs says that "they brought one bell from the east and the other from the west and the one in the middle was sent from Homs." This myth helps to clear some misinformation from the media that the Syrian refugees bring with them.

Figure 5. In camps, closed doors hide the tears and the bewilderment; and the street water is fishy. Source: Project DAAR/photographic dossier Luca Capuano

The prevalence of hate speech and rumors on social media inspired me to add the theme of religion to my project, hence, visiting St. Norbert Church is often included. The churches in my Syrian memories have one bell but the same colored glass windows. They have icons, crosses, candles, and a bowl made of stone, full of olive oil to dip our fingers in and then rub our foreheads to be blessed. Often we smile at each other and show compassion to the people who dip a small piece of cloth in the oil to take it home. Normally, it is a sign that there is a sick person waiting for the blessed oil to be healed. Sharing these stories encourages the camp residents to step in and to remember the voice of the local churches.

St. Norbert Church is my shelter to hide my tears or to cool down in the hot German summer. The cold water in the metal bowl tempers me. I could swear that the water smells of jasmine and the colored windows recite the story of Younes, the Prophet! Looking at the sun's rays on the floor transports me to Al-Hamidiyah Souq, too. The big open space in front of St. Norbert Church initiates dramatic talk about monuments and turns the participants into architects sharing their own descriptions of certain memorials they used to visit before fleeing. I cannot explain why the people who speak Arabic link the light that comes from the memorial for the victims of World War II on Hagenberg with the Holocaust. They even link the old chimney of the nearby factory to "the gas chamber." To send the children to bed without fear and nightmares, I sometimes do not wait till adults open their mouths to ask. The story of Hagenberg monument is a topic of every tour and every small conversation near the fountain of the camp. After enjoying the Aha! moment with them, I ask who implanted this idea in their heads, but I get no reply. Once, two ladies visited the area of Hagenberg monument alone and shared the chamomile they collected with me. Very often, the visit to the memorial makes me miss the train back home, but I enjoy the picnic and smoking shisha. Of course, I do not count the time as working time!

Which is first, the camp or the refugees?

This question formed itself after I listened to the stories of the people who passed the Syrian-Turkish borders in 2012. The narrative says that the camp was ready for them as if it had already been built. They swear they took the mattresses and pillows out of their plastic bags. Searching for an answer diverted my attention away from the large amount of misinformation based on conspiracy theories. Besides, the wide variety of terminologies that describe a person living in the camp makes my search and my question drift. What camps? Summer camps, study camps, concentration camps, prison camps, and so forth? What refugees? The displaced, the forced displaced, the asylum seeker, the outsider, the stateless, and so forth?

To help me shape an answer, Mais told me, "a camp is somewhere far away from home." Then she proceeded, "Friedland Transit Camp is the camp that lives in me although I haven't lived in it." I read on one of the Museum Friedland postcards, "A camp is a camp," so simple, so deep! In my notebook:

> Each camp is born to solve a demographic local problem and to create a new global reality. The world we know today shares its history with the personal history of the refugees. Human first, then refugees, then UN agencies and NGOs. Human first, then all the classifications and speeches. Refugees first, then the chessboard is created to classify human names. Ironically, the name changes according to the speaker and the listener, not to the holder of that name!

Was it a moment of nostalgia, or a sense of history, or an impulse of my constant partying life? No answer and the attempt to find answers makes me agree with Professor Hein de Haas that human migration is a hotly debated but poorly understood issue. Migration raises high hopes and deep fears and perceptions which need to be investigated taking into consideration the fact that no one gets up in the early morning aiming to willingly cross international borders. No one chooses to deny their own citizenship in order to become a mere number in migration statistics, or a suspect, or an illegal, or an *ungrateful* refugee.

It is never a decision with a free will or a free made family strategy. To go to a camp is the result of dirty wars where unimaginable terror and fear take place and accelerate like cancer. Consequently, after the first night at the camp, the state of destitution challenges our souls before our bodies. Soon, the self-settled behavior is activated, and the empty tuna can is the ashtray, the broken suitcase is the shoe cabinet, and the leftover bread is the bird food. To make a football out of old stockings is an old trick but to make it out of headscarves – the hijab – is the Friedlander's brand. Some dolls and rugs are born, but the best is the baby swing-cradle made out of broken suitcases. The very best is the wooden glasses frame that Mohamad had to carve so the old lenses fit to satisfy his father.

Luckily, unanswered questions can be ice-breakers to reach out to Friedland adults, particularly the reserved ones; they can evoke stories and some details about the jobs and the skills they have. The talk with the history teacher taught me this trick when he recited memories of Jordan and the cup of tea which led him to eat *Mansaf* at Irbid Camp. Talking like an anthropologist, he said:

> To leave Alzaatari Camp, I need a permit, but to talk to the old peddler, I need a glass of tea. The peddler was born in a tent in Irbid Camp. When he started going to school, his father started to replace the tent with a mud shelter. Later, he replaced the mud with concrete to redesign the home so his first son could get married. Later, the kind man and his son managed to get me permission to visit their home. After the delicious meal, he showed me the documents he was able to collect from Safad, Palestine, and told the story of the Altal family who owned the land of Alzaatari Camp. The surprise is that his son is the soldier who helped me and my family to cross the Syrian-Jordanian border.

The many details led to a Syrian cup of coffee and the story of the big building known as Nidal Bashabsheh – which was the history teacher's transit camp for almost a week. Getting to know that they have been transferred to a mobile caravan justifies his question: "Where are we going after the Friedland honeymoon?"

The history talk puts me on the stage to give him a tour around Friedland Transit Camp, specifically, to 1911 when Friedland's experimental farm was set up as an agricultural station; then to 1924, when it was incorporated into Göttingen University's Institute of Animal Nutrition. In the fall of 1945, the buildings and the stables served as transit accommodation for the refugees of that era. Consequently, we walked towards Museum Friedland to read the extract that was taken from the British military government's war diary and documented by the National Archives: "Refugee Transit Camp, capacity 2000, opened at Friedland. 10–20 September 1945."

On that day, another storyteller took us to 1922 and to the Agriculture School located in the rural area of Lattakia where he planted vegetables, medical herbs, and guava trees. With a hazy memory, he described the photos he saw in the school archive and in the collection of a Palestinian bookshop owner in the heart of the village. He shocked his listeners, and the conversation grew loud, when he said that the bookshop owner took care of the four guava trees and bought all the fruit. Luckily, the weather was nice, so to stop their speculation we visited the Friedland Garden. There, thyme, peppermint, parsley, and cilantro are on their lips and in their future gardens and balconies. They rejected my dream to plant flowers but not jasmine and roses, and agreed to plant olive, lemon, guava, pistachio, and walnut trees. Ali, the passionate farmer, sent me the photo of the olive tree he wants to plant after a few months, but I have not been able to convince the staff of the garden to plant it yet.

"Did You Know," the website of the Museum Friedland declares, "Friedland would now be larger than Berlin, Germany's capital city, if everyone registered in the camp had stayed here." What a sustainable idea we missed! Transforming the temporary into permanent. Could camps be built with the intent of creating places, which are meaningful, functional, and economical so the camp residents can produce the needed products and have better access to services? Could camps offer places that connect people with the world outside the walls, windows, and doors so its residents can live normal lives and the locals in the host country move on building on what they have? Could camps be designed with the intent to remove barriers, reduce stress, and lower heart rates? *Refugees as city-makers is my first wish to the Genie so I should search for the magic lantern.* I would ask for a monumental building without overly designed architecture that adapts to activities when people bake their bread, sew their handbags, plant their herbs and vegetables, make their teas, clean their rooms, and recycle their waste. The third wish would be to help IKEA perform a miracle and give my project a shelter and a chance to prove that building and managing a camp by "experts" who do not leave their air-conditioned rooms is like giving a paracetamol to the patient.

In camps, people are the architects of destruction; while they are waiting for a miracle, their time in a camp will always be like being in a storm, and when the storm is over, I, like my people, cannot remember how I escaped it, and very often will not really know whether it ended or not. There is only one certainty after living in a camp: I am not the same person who entered it.

1 The municipality considered the camp's dwellers to be a security threat and claimed they might place bombs in the garbage. Thus, it took the waste containers away and stopped collecting the waste as a punishment. The garbage polluted the area and made it smell dreadful.

2 I coined "Hi/Story" to draw attention to the intrinsic connection and tension that exists between personal stories, particularly oral stories, and the broader narrative of history.

3 https://www.unhcr.org/uk/comprehensive-refugee-response-framework-crrf.html

Reversals: The University and the Camp

Anooradha Iyer Siddiqi

If we take seriously the concerns and problematics of decolonizing the mind, we might begin by looking for sources of knowledge in the refugee camp. Camps have long been sites of empirical research: in their darkest form, as sites of detention and concentration; and in a putatively lighter form, as liberatory vehicles for the rescued and their saviors. What if camps did not serve empiricist ends of knowledge, but instead, theoretical ones? If so, then the humanitarian would become the student, the refugee the professor, and the architecture of the camp that of the university. This article imagines this architecture. This text draws from the keynote address given on January 25, 2019, at the "Inside-Out/Outside-In: Shifting Architectures of Refugee Inhabitation" workshop, convened by Somayeh Chitchian, Maja Momić, and Shahd Seethaler-Wari at the Max Planck Institute for the Study of Religious and Ethnic Diversity.

In this article, I would like to raise several ideas, without necessarily attempting to cohere them. My hope is that this will be generative, rather than didactic. My thoughts relate to a course I teach, "Colonial Practices," that attempts to disentangle architectural historical traditions from colonial practices. For example, my students and I work through the contingent relationships between colonialism and humanitarianism. One of the premises of the course has been that, if we take seriously the concerns and problematics of decolonizing the mind, we might begin by looking for sources of knowledge in the refugee camp.[1] This thinking comes from Ngũgĩ wa Thiong'o and Frantz Fanon, by way of Isnina Ali Rage, Chairlady of Ifo camp, Dadaab (Thiong'o 1986, 2009; Fanon 1967, 1968).

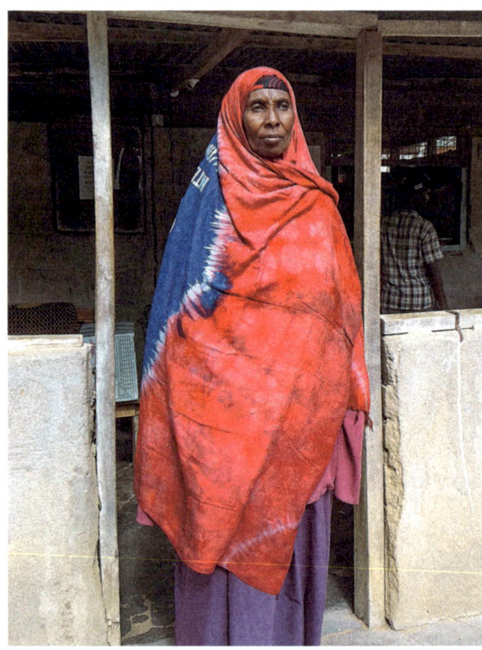

Figure 1. Isnina Ali Rage, Ifo camp, Dadaab, Kenya, 2011. Source: Author

Isnina Ali Rage is a Somali woman who lived in a refugee camp in Kenya and represented that camp to foreign governments. I hope my photographic portrait conveys her strength. She didn't require any country's "emergency relief," nor any aid agency's "gender mainstreaming," nor any "humanitarian care" – she was a refugee and also a sovereign person. She was a giver of refuge, in my opinion. I met with her while working in Dadaab for the Women's Refugee Commission, a research and advocacy unit whose parent organization is the International Rescue Committee. I interviewed her for a report on relationships between livelihoods and gender-based violence on the day that I took this photograph.

Putting her into dialogue with Ngũgĩ wa Thiong'o and Frantz Fanon requires an epistemic shift. I argue that as an elected political leader and recognized thinker, her work is akin to that of theorists. Without wishing to make false parallels across a variety of material, social, political, and epistemic asymmetries, my hope is that we might work to recognize the shift I propose, in order to better understand ways in which the camp and university relate to one another, and ways that the former might perform the liberatory aspects of the latter. Such a shift must be performed by the camp, through its own affect, not through the agency of any interpreter's translation of it – for example, any scholar's empirical analysis of it. Camps have long been sites for empiricism: in their darkest forms, sites of detention and concentration, and, in lighter forms, as missions or liberatory vehicles, for the rescued as well as the saviors. But what if camps didn't serve empiricist ends for knowledge production? What if they didn't provide the conceptual or material object for instrumental study? Instead, what if the inhabitation of the camp – to use our organizers' words – generated theory, practices, and ritual knowledge of its own? This epistemic shift is a decolonial method.

Decolonial theory and practice grew out of anti-colonial struggles, such as the Negritude, Pan-Africanism, and Black Consciousness movements. Decoloniality is a response to an ongoing condition of coloniality. Nelson Maldonado-Torres explains:

> Coloniality is different from colonialism. Colonialism denotes a political and economic relation in which the sovereignty of a nation or a people rests on the power of another nation, which makes such a nation an empire. Coloniality, instead, refers to long-standing patterns of power that emerged as a result of colonialism, but that define culture, labour, intersubjectivity relations, and knowledge production well beyond the strict limits of colonial administrations. Thus, coloniality survives colonialism. It is maintained alive in books, in the criteria for academic performance, in cultural patterns, in common sense, in the self-image of peoples, in aspirations of self, and so many other aspects of our modern experience. In a way, as modern subjects we breathe coloniality all the time and every day (Maldonado-Torres, 2007, 243; Ndlovu-Gatsheni 2015, 487).

Thinking on decoloniality begins with thinking on "the dark side of modernity" – that is, understanding modernity as intrinsically linked to the colonial (Mignolo 2011). Decoloniality is not an approach to eliminate colonialism. It is to understand colonialism as a force that rationalizes, erases, and denigrates people – but as only one of many historical forces, no more important than non-colonial, non-violent histories and practices.

Decolonial theory is subversive. It is intended to be reparative, restorative, and liberatory. It seeks to reverse larger forms of colonial violence, which are ongoing. It aspires to acknowledge, validate, and elevate the life and work of formerly and presently colonized people, people of color, Indigenous people. As Sabelo Ndlovu-Gatsheni writes, decoloniality pushes to shift the "geography of reason from the West as the epistemic locale from which the 'world is described, conceptualized and ranked' to the ex-colonized epistemic sites as legitimate points of departure in describing the construction of the modern world order" (Ndlovu-Gatsheni 2015, 485–96). To return to Ngũgĩ wa Thiong'o, to decolonize the mind means to think outside the strictures of coloniality, to think outside of colonialism as an all-encompassing force.

If we follow this, a decolonial approach to architectural history might be to recognize its structural entanglements with the colonial, but not see these as systemic. One way to reverse the colonial, in turn, might be to think through the camp by thinking through the university. Some concrete histories may be of use here, particularly of the Decolonize the Curriculum movement, which grew out of and was linked to the Rhodes Must Fall and Fees Must Fall movements. It began with an action on March 9, 2015 (Fairbanks 2015).

Chumani Maxwele, a student of political science on a scholarship at the University of Cape Town, traveled by *matatu* (minibus) to attend courses. People traveled for hours on these buses, often relieving themselves at roadside stops. At a stop on the way, Maxwele picked up a bucket of excrement by the roadside. Later that day, he hurled it at a bronze statue of the nineteenth-century British colonialist Cecil John Rhodes on the university campus. This action became known as the "poo protest." Three days later, more than one thousand students gathered and demanded that the statue be removed from campus. Within five weeks, there were hundreds of students amassing, tagging the statue with graffiti, covering it in black garbage bags, and singing anti-apartheid songs. They shut down the campus. The vice chancellor sent the staff home, and the statue was removed. It led to other protests. At Rhodes University, students demanded an institutional name change. At Stellenbosch, students protested the use of the Afrikaans language. Some campuses shut down for weeks.

Maxwele was part of a generation of students known as the "born frees." This generation is the first in South African history raised with almost no direct memory of apartheid.[2] He came of age in a time of a falling South African currency, with tuition fees being raised by 20 percent. Amit Chaudhuri writes that the ambition of the Rhodes Must Fall movement lay beyond the removal of statues; it aimed "to bring out into the open institutional racism in university life in South Africa and Britain and to decolonise education" (Chaudhuri 2016). The movement named unequal access to opportunity and mobility as a structural norm and called for structural transformation. At issue was an ethos that gave space and pre-eminence to such a figure but hesitated to interrogate Rhodes' legacy. That legacy did not merely include Rhodes' financial bequests and their educational offshoots, such as the Rhodes Scholarship, but the vision embodied in his will, which calls for:

> the establishment, promotion and development of a Secret Society, the true aim and object whereof shall be for the extension of British rule throughout the world, the perfecting of a system of emigration from the United Kingdom, and of colonisation by British subjects of all lands where the means of livelihood are attainable by energy, labour and enterprise and especially the occupation by British settlers. Then he names several lands.[3]

Surely, these incendiary words must have meant something different to Rhodes in his context than they do now? Moreover, would not a historical contextualization of these words have value and counter their capacity to injure? For the movement, this was beside the point. The movement demanded precisely that these words *should* be interrogated *in the present* because they undergirded an ideology that produced profound structural inequality through ongoing colonial practices; not colonialism in the abstract or in the past, but very specific colonialisms, at specific times, in specific places in the present.

There was a great deal of controversy over the attacks on the statues, on the physical property, on the icons. These statues came to represent authority so powerfully that they became ready, meaningful targets. They became the iconographic locus for protests. Their vandalism produced a forum. This forum is not meant in the sense raised in the *Forensis* project, which in important ways holds scientific rationality as a basis for analysis (Keenan 2014; Weizman 2014). This forum, instead, lies in the tradition of iconoclasm: a kind of aesthetic disruption, sometimes literally by vandalism.

This iconoclastic generation of a forum did not occur only through a material intervention, but also through conceptual ones. It is important to note that the Rhodes Must Fall, Fees Must Fall, and Decolonise the Curriculum movements were connected to very particular power centers – Cape Town and Oxford – and circulation between these centers returned focus to certain thinkers. These thinkers had never lost their immediacy, but they suddenly became quite urgent again. Several programs started to take the exercise of curriculum revision quite seriously: for example, at Oxford and Cambridge, and perhaps particularly the School of Oriental and African Studies (SOAS). SOAS played a special part in the colonial history of European higher education institutions, as it specializes in the study of Africa, Asia, and the Middle East. The students' union articulated a new set of educational priorities: expansion of the curriculum, greater diversity and inclusion in enrollment and hiring, and the cessation of economic exploitation of campus workers. Ironically, these demands stood – *in theory* – in opposition to an aim of the school's establishment: to produce the figure of Asia, Africa, the Middle East, as bounded epistemological categories, and within that practice, to perform multiple forms of subjugation.

The Decolonise the Curriculum movement recalls protests on campuses worldwide in 1968, when many similar calls were made to change the purpose and tenor of the university. I started researching this when I began teaching students at Barnard College, Columbia University, where I often worked in the library of Avery Hall. Avery Hall is the home of the architecture school and came to play a significant role in the aftermath of the 1968 student occupation of the campus. Though the events of this campus occupation come from a different historical context, they suggest alternate intellectual traditions for the Decolonise the Curriculum movement.

In February 1967, members of a group called Students for a Democratic Society (SDS) staged sit-ins to protest the US Central Intelligence Agency's workforce recruitment on campus, as well as the university's involvement in the Institute for Defense Analyses, a think tank of the US Department of Defense. As the year progressed, vocal opposition to US imperialism in the Vietnam War increased. In 1967, University President Grayson Kirk issued a ban against any picketing or demonstrations inside all campus buildings. By March 1968, the SDS defied this policy. They staged a demonstration inside Low Library, an iconic library at the top of the steps on Columbia's main campus.

A few years earlier, in 1959, plans had been initiated to build a gymnasium for Columbia College, the core liberal arts undergraduate unit at Columbia University. The gym was intended to sit on two acres of public land inside Morningside Park, just adjacent to Columbia University, in Harlem. The New York legislature approved the plans, which included community access, albeit limited. However, opponents of the gym were critical of its design. Columbia is in Morningside Heights and sits on a steep cliff separating it from Morningside Park, down below, in Harlem. The cross section of the gym was intended to bridge that steep divide. The Harlem community was eventually allotted only the basement space. The state-of-the-art gym was at the top level, reserved for the Columbia students alone. The Society of Afro-American Students (founded in the mid 1960s) vocalized opposition to Columbia University's land use practices, real estate negotiations, and treatment of its neighbors, which crystallized in the spatial planning of this gym.

This tension reached a crisis in April of 1968. A rally held on campus led to a violent march on the gymnasium site. Students started ripping down the construction fences. They staged a sit-in inside one of the major halls on campus. They formulated demands that the administration stop construction on the gym, sever all ties with the Institute for Defense Analyses, and that President Kirk and the trustees resign their positions. They made serious demands of the university leadership, six in total, and staged sit-ins in some of the major halls on the campus. At first, the black students and white students protested together. After some time, the Hamilton Hall protest segregated. There are many stories about why this happened. The white students were evicted from Hamilton Hall, and the different elements of the student body began to take up different but equally radical causes. Some of the students focused on Columbia's relations with and impacts on its neighboring community. Some focused on what kind of knowledge the university produced and for whom. The students eventually occupied Low Library and the president's office. The administration summoned the New York City police, and 712 students were arrested. The students had formed a Strike Coordinating Committee to call for a student-faculty strike, in an attempt to mobilize the full population on campus. The ensuing strike lasted through the end of the school term, shutting down the campus. The strikers also disrupted graduation. They marched out of the formal commencement proceedings and held a counter-commencement outdoors. They formed what they called a Liberation School. Its counter-classes suggested that university instruction should be about real things. In other words, they called for a decolonized curriculum.

Please note how architecture, spatial history, and broader sorts of engagements with the built environment have come into play in this reformulation of the university. The architecture school itself went on strike after these events.[4] The school then radically experimented with a form of reparations. It admitted and provided free education to a cohort of African-American students. Sharon Sutton has recently documented this in a book that compiles a set of oral histories with that cohort (2017). I raise all this together by way of pointing to moments of imagination in the university. Not only is a different university being imagined, but the entire premise of the university is being questioned.

Another reason I focus on Columbia University is that its spatial history is tied to its colonial history. The embedded links between traditions and architectures of higher education, colonialism, and humanitarianism suggest relationships between the epistemic order of the university and that of the camp. Columbia University embodies a contradictory entanglement of liberal and oppressive traditions, particular to the history of the United States. It was founded by Royal Charter in 1754 as King's College and is the oldest institution of higher learning in New York, the fifth oldest in the United

States. Its classes were suspended during another revolutionary period – the American Revolution – in 1776. The college reopened in 1784, eliminating the name King's College, and opting for the new name Columbia, an expression of New World patriotism, but one which normalized the contradictory colonial hegemonies embedded in US history.

Along these lines, it is important to note other contradictions. In 1784, the first professor of Oriental languages was appointed at Columbia University. That was the same year that the Asiatic Society was founded in Calcutta, the Indian headquarters for British East India Company and later the capital of the British Raj. While the direct relationship between architecture's epistemic traditions and the colonial Orientalist tradition has been well documented (Borden and Rendell 2000; Çelik 1996; Crinson 1996, on James Ferguson), it is also important to note connections between the liberal university and humanitarian discourses and architectures, which tie together colonial and liberal thought and action. Thinking from New York about this contradictory alignment, we might look to the founding students and trustees of King's College and later Columbia University. One of these people was John Jay, who became the first Chief Justice of the United States. His grandson, also named John Jay, was a lawyer and a diplomat, who, in 1834, was manager of the New York Young Men's Anti-Slavery Society, and, in 1847, the secretary of the Irish Relief Commission during what became known as the Potato Famine. He authored abolitionist papers. He was also the president of the American Historical Society and helped found the Metropolitan Museum of Art, institutions with an inclusive reform mission toward the people of New York. He remained an active member of the Metropolitan Museum of Art and the National Academy of Design. Within three generations of this family, a thread appeared between colonial practice and philanthropic humanitarian practice.

With such an articulation of contradiction in liberal thought and action, how can a historical tradition linked so intimately to the colonial be understood? These problems were raised at Columbia during the events of 1968 and, later, as part of the recent Decolonise the Curriculum movement. Through those histories, in spite of the foreclosure of radical thought that followed, we can follow the imagination in experiments that attempted to reverse the university politically and epistemically. The structures, people, values, currents, all which generated knowledge and expertise, were replaced with others – even if only momentarily. Can we imagine the same for the camp? This is the question I want to raise. To return to its concerns, and to Isnina Ali Rage and the questions raised by her subject position, I would put forward that the camp has a role to play in an epistemic shift. It does so in three major ways.

Firstly, the camp provides aesthetically and historically precise forms for analysis, architectures of real and lived places. This architecture has not been constructed as a symbol and is not an abstraction. The camp offers a view into the social life of an architecture that is an aggregation of modern materials and designed space. This architecture offers the empirical texture for a process of very close looking and, through this process, the exposure of unexpected histories.

Secondly, the camp helps us refine methods of studying architectural histories through its normalization of a variety of documentary archives. The archive of visual material on Dadaab includes many artifacts of militaristic surveillance of refugees, both the rational universal perspective of overview maps and satellite photographs and the ground views of ethnographers. But there are also many other perspectives and kinds of images. For example, an architect hand-sketched a plan and took a photograph when he visited Dadaab in 1992, just after Ifo camp was established in 1991, and these images remain among the first visual representations of any of the settlements. The analytical work of abstraction rendered in this plan suggests something architectural can generate a different kind of knowledge of the past, a response to the affective. The hand sketch based upon sensitivities and experiential learning on the ground expands the sensibilities to be probed within the official archive.

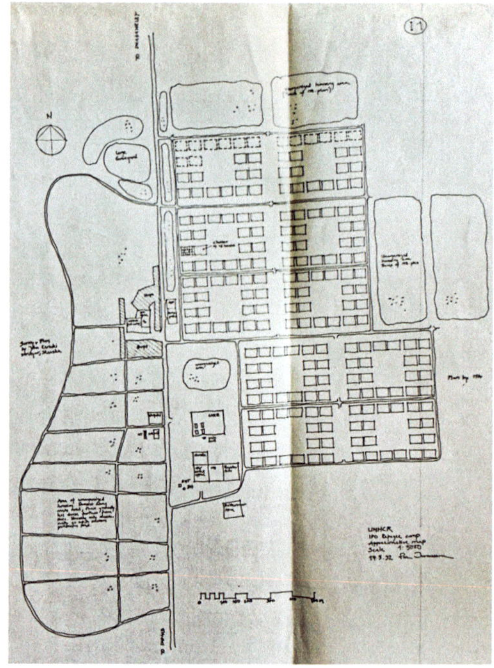

Figure 2. Plan of Ifo camp, Dadaab, Kenya, 1992. Source: Per Iwansson

Thirdly, the materials and media of the camp inform the construction of fields of theory, databases of institutional knowledge, and new knowledge institutions. For example, there is the institutionalization of humanitarian knowledge. Nongovernmental organizations establish a radically different archive than that of colonial or state authorities. For another example, there is artistic or aesthetic knowledge. Curation and exhibition are important archiving practices. A further example is that of knowledge institutions related to political-economic development, whether private or state-based. The advocacy-oriented field of refugee studies grew in part out of a response to the Dadaab refugee camps in Kenya.

From these examples, we might induce that the construction of such knowledge might have been the work of experts and thinkers outside conventionally understood epistemic frameworks outside of the modern intellectual and geographical centers of knowledge. As such, all these forms of knowledge production reverse power positions and the position of the historical protagonist. The example of Shamso Abdullahi Farah illustrates this epistemic shift.[5] Farah was a registered refugee from Bula Hawo, Somalia, who arrived at Ifo camp in 2003, 12 years after it was established. The emergency situation in Ifo camp was such that within the first three years of Farah's arrival, shelter aid had gained equal importance to the distribution of water and food. Shelters provided by CARE, the organization that had previously managed the settlements, proved unsafe, as heavy winds blew off their roofs.

Figure 3. One of the first photographs taken of Ifo camp, Dadaab, Kenya, 1992. Source: Per Iwansson

In response, the Norwegian Refugee Council was contracted to work in Ifo, building upon its core competence in shelter aid while hiring project managers trained in architec-

Figure 4. Shamso Abdullahi Farah inside shop, Ifo camp, Dadaab, Kenya, 2011. Source: Author

ture or construction, many from European architecture schools. The organization valued architectural expertise, attention to design details, and a rational building process. Through the largesse of the Norwegian government, it produced an architecturally detailed and well-made object, of squared, wire-cut, kiln-fired, cement-stabilized soil blocks together with a mud plaster protective exterior, supported by foundations set 10 bricks deep into the ground, for durability and longevity. The building process was, therefore, central to humanitarian operations. For establishing a sense of ownership and empowerment in the refugee communities, the Norwegian Refugee Council instituted skill-building activities that centralized the communities' craft and labor as part of their shelter aid package.

By 2011, when I interviewed Farah and other refugees and aid workers who worked with the Norwegian Refugee Council, the international humanitarian system had thoroughly transmitted "participatory" building practices inspired by the 1960s and 1970s self-help models. However, in this camp condition, "participation" was handled asymmetrically, as residents were not citizens, land users were not empowered to own property, and refugees were denied the right to labor for wages.

This shelter initiative was fiercely opposed by most refugees in Ifo camp, who saw it as unjust and over-demanding. Farah, however, positioned herself differently on these matters and, instead, utilized the Norwegian Refugee Council's shelter aid package to her and her family's advantage. She requested additional building materials to construct a storefront in order to trade goods and supplement her family's ration. She worked from specifications provided by the organization, and, accordingly, supervised workers, including her husband and children. It could be argued that she achieved economic, social – and by extension political – realization in the camp through this work. Political actualization may seem a wild claim in this ambiguous situation; however, it highlights the question of "how subjecthood and subjectivity are formed when the urgent domesticities of forced migration and emergency inscribe practices not necessarily coterminous with the nation-state" (Siddiqi 2018) or other normative political economies and frameworks. One perspective could be that Farah's engagements presented a form of petty capitalism, or that her experiences offered a vivid example of the humanitarian apparatus's oppressive development practices. From a different perspective, however, this example illustrates that architecture is capable of producing authority, even legitimacy. Her intersection with a transnational system, negotiated through the space of the camp, materialized and made visible her situated expertise – a modality of power, subjectivity, and mobility.

Figure 5. Shop designed and built by Shamso Abdullahi Farah and Norwegian Refugee Council, Ifo camp, Dadaab, Kenya. Source: Author

The architectural construction of the Dadaab settlements was a joint effort by formally certified architects as well as refugees. However, in this setting, Farah's spatial practice renders visible the banality of various matters, architectural and professional licensing included. Her integral work destabilizes the understanding of the figure of the modern "architect" as legitimized solely by the state, representing its authority from a distance. Rather, Farah enacted a local form of architectural authority, forcing a re-narration of architectural production and its spatial authorship.

Shamso Abdullahi Farah was among many refugees who engaged deeply with humanitarians, with institutions, and the state, regardless of any asymmetries in power that may have stemmed from the circumstances of physical or political displacement (Siddiqi 2018, 2020a, 2020b, forthcoming 2021). If the same circumstances describe Isnina Ali Rage's position above, she might be understood further as a theorist and intellectual, an organizer of the community's will and ideas, due to her status as an elected leader. In considering their cases, I argue that something originating in the refugee camps *as an architecture* effected a political subjectivity. This is different from the usual understanding of the political sphere producing built form.

Thinking this way returns us to the decolonial. Decolonial thinking means that producing knowledge and living it are not separate. Thus, decolonial thought applies itself to the past as well as the present and makes visible both a history and its connection to the telling of a history. It illuminates the links between knowledge, social practices, and social action – between architecture, architectural history, and spatial practice.

In this article, I have tried to complicate and churn things rather than neatly resolve them. As we work on reversing the university, on the one hand, and the camp, on the other, I leave you with a question. Can we imagine this architecture?

I would like to thank the Max Planck Institute, the organizers of the "Inside Out – Outside In: Shifting Architectures of Refugee Inhabitation" workshop, and Romola Sanyal, the keynote respondent at the workshop, especially for her work on citizenship (Desai and Sanyal 2012). I would also like to acknowledge recent collaborations relevant to the workshop and this article (Bilsel and Maxim forthcoming 2021; Chee, et al. forthcoming; Chowdhury and Karim 2018; Siddiqi and Lee 2019, forthcoming 2021–22, forthcoming 2022), as well as insights gained from refugees and aid workers – on "decoloniality," on "inside and outside," on architecture, and on history.

A shorter version of this paper is published in Contingency (Ardeth 6, 2020), guest-edited by Dana Cuff and Will Davis. Parts of this article reference "Writing With: Togethering, Difference, and Feminist Architectural Histories of Migration," published in Structural Instability (e-flux Architecture and PennDesign, 2018), edited by Daniel Barber, Eduardo Rega, and e-flux Architecture.

1 The terms "refugee camp" or "the camp" here refer to historical places captured in the slides that accompanied this keynote address rather than abstract concepts. This specificity attempts to value people's histories and lived experiences and name the violence that may be enacted by abstractions of these terms. **2** The apartheid system was put to an end in approximately 1994. **3** "of the entire Continent of Africa, the Holy Land, the Valley of the Euphrates, the Islands of Cyprus and Candia, the whole of South America, the Islands of the Pacific not heretofore possessed by Great Britain, the whole of the Malay Archipelago, the seaboard of China and Japan" (Chaudhuri 2016). **4** In my Colonial Practices course at Barnard College and Columbia University (most recently taught in fall 2020), I show a slide of Avery Hall picketers during the strike following arrests of students on campus, with a large banner hung across the building's entrance, reading "Avery Is On Strike." See photo in *Columbia College Today*, Spring 1968 (Columbia University 1968, 1998; Wilk 2008). **5** This section references "Writing With: Togethering, Difference, and Feminist Architectural Histories of Migration," in *Structural Instability*, guest-edited by Daniel Barber, Eduardo Rega, and *e-flux Architecture* (2018).

References

Bilsel, C., and J. Maxim, eds. Forthcoming. *Architecture and the Housing Question*. London: Routledge.

Borden, I., and J. Rendell. 2000. *Intersections: Architectural Histories and Critical Theories*. London: Routledge.

Çelik, Z. 1996. "Colonialism, Orientalism, and the Canon." *The Art Bulletin* 78, no. 2: 202–05.

Chaudhuri, A. 2016. "The Real Meaning of Rhodes Must Fall." *The Guardian*, March 16, 2016. https://www.theguardian.com/uk-news/2016/mar/16/the-real-meaning-of-rhodes-must-fall.

Chowdhury, Z. and F. Karim. 2018. "The Art and Architecture of Partition and Confederation." Getty Research Institute symposium.

Columbia University. 1998. *Columbia University 1968*. http://www.columbia.edu/cu/computinghistory/1968/.

Crinson, M. 1996. *Empire Building: Orientalism and Victorian Architecture*. London: Routledge.

Desai, R., and R. Sanyal, eds. 2012. *Urbanizing Citizenship: Contested Spaces in Indian Cities*. New Delhi: SAGE.

Fairbanks, E. 2015. "Why South African Students Have Turned on Their Parents' Generation." *The Guardian*, November 18, 2015. https://www.theguardian.com/news/2015/nov/18/why-south-african-students-have-turned-on-their-parents-generation.

Fanon, F. 1967. *Black Skin, White Masks*. New York: Grove Press.

Fanon, F. 1968. *The Wretched of the Earth*. New York: Grove Press.

Keenan, T. 2014. "Getting the Dead to Tell Me What Happened." In *Forensis: The Architecture of Public Truth*, edited by Forensic Architecture, A. Franke, and E. Weizman, 35–55. Berlin: Sternberg Press.

Maldonado-Torres, N. 2007. "On the Coloniality of Being: Contributions to the Development of a Concept." *Cultural Studies* 21, no. 2–3: 240–70.

Mignolo, W. D. 2011. *The Darker Side of Western Modernity: Global Futures, Decolonial Options*. Durham, NC: Duke University Press.

Ndlovu-Gatsheni, S. 2015. "Decoloniality as the Future of Africa." *History Compass* 13, no. 10: 485–96.

Siddiqi, A. I. 2020a. "Ephemerality." *Comparative Studies of South Asia, Africa, and the Middle East* 40, no. 1: 24–34.

Siddiqi, A. I. 2020b. "The University and the Camp." *Contingency, Ardeth. A Magazine on the Power of the Project*, no. 6, edited by D. Cuff and W. Davis, 137–51.

Siddiqi, A. I. 2018. "Writing With: Togethering, Difference, and Feminist Architectural Histories of Migration." In *Structural Instabilities*, edited by D. Barber, E. Rega, and *e-flux Architecture*. Special issue, *e-flux Architecture* (July 28). https://www.e-flux.com/architecture/structural-instability/208707/writing-with/.

Siddiqi, A. I., et al. *Insurgent Domesticities*. https://www.socialdifference.columbia.edu/projects-/insurgent-domesticities.

Siddiqi, A. I. Forthcoming 2021. "Humanitarian Home-maker / Emergency Subject." In *Architecture and the Housing Question*, edited by C. Bilsel and J. Maxim.

Siddiqi, A. I., and R. Lee, eds. 2019. "On Margins: Feminist Architectural Histories of Migration." *Architecture Beyond Europe*, no. 16.

Siddiqi, A. I., and R. Lee, eds. Forthcoming 2021–2022. "Of Migration," *Canadian Centre for Architecture*; with the introductory essay "On Diffractions: Feminist Architectural Histories of Migration."

Siddiqi, A. I., and R. Lee, eds. Forthcoming 2022. "On Collaborations: Feminist Architectural Histories of Migration." *Aggregate*.

Sutton, S. E. 2017. *When Ivory Towers Were Black: A Story about Race in America's Cities and Universities*. New York: Fordham University Press.

Thiong'o, N. 1986. *Decolonising the Mind: The Politics of Language in African Literature*. Nairobi: Heinemann.

Thiong'o, N. 2009. *Re-membering Africa.* Nairobi: East African Educational Publishers Ltd.

Weizman, E. 2014. "Introduction: Forensis." In *Forensis: The Architecture of Public Truth*, edited by Forensic Architecture, A. Franke, and E. Weizman, 9–32. Berlin: Sternberg Press.

Wilk, J. K., and Columbia University Libraries. 2008. "*1968: Columbia in Crisis.*" Online exhibition. https://exhibitions.library.columbia.edu/exhibits/show/1968.

Architecture on the Move: (Re)Creating a Place in a Displaced World

Irit Katz

Refugees, irregular migrants, and other people on the move often plan to remain in their spaces of refuge only temporarily, yet they invest time and efforts in these ephemeral environments. Based on the work of Hannah Arendt on refuge and the human condition, and by focusing on actions of homemaking in the makeshift Jungle camp in Calais, this paper examines the meaning of the "moving architecture" of "moving people," as they attempt to create a place for themselves in their unstable world of displacement and human mobility. By analyzing the spatial transformations of emergency shelters and camp environments conducted by their inhabitant-fabricants, the article argues that actions of place-making and homemaking materialize a political call of the displaced of their need for an elaborate human place in the world, even if this place makes part of a temporary environment of displacement and refuge.

At the end of November 2015, the makeshift Jungle camp in Calais was a bustling clutter of tents and shacks laid out on the wet ground of the derelict industrial site from which refugees and irregular migrants were attempting to cross the English Channel to the United Kingdom. The Jungle's main street, curving between the camp's Afghan, Syrian, Somali, and other neighborhoods, was busy with a constant stream of people walking and cycling up and down the road or chatting next to the grocery stores, barbershops, bakeries, and restaurants that served the camp's residents and volunteers. At the camp's several schools and libraries, residents took language lessons while others visited one of the churches or mosques or were busy building new huts in cleared areas between existing shelters. Some of the huts that had been built for quite a while had front porches or flowerbeds near their entrances, while others were decorated with flags and graffiti, sometimes with political messages on the right to free movement and open borders. At the same time, as the camp revealed itself as an elaborated vivid human environment, it was clear that this was also a violent site of deep neglect and precariousness. The large black puddles and piles of garbage that dotted the camp and the rows of portable toilets and communal taps where people washed and filled buckets with water, indicated that this was a place where men, women, and children were abandoned with no basic

Figure 1. Calais Jungle main street, November 2015. Source: Author

Figure 2. Restaurant in the Jungle camp, November 2015. Source: Author

infrastructure, services, or amenities. The long queues of people waiting for donated food and clothes were also a reminder of the precarious provision on which those living in the camp were dependent.

This was my first visit to Calais Jungle, on which I was accompanied by two fellow architects following an invitation from activists who asked for assistance in designing and building robust shelters in the rapidly growing camp before the European winter set in. We came to the camp, as many others, to act in solidarity with people "on the move" who tried to confront the UK and the EU exclusionary border regime. As three architects, we were to cast the role of "the professionals" who came to counteract the structured institutional violence and support those who were considered as "people in need" who lived in the camp. Yet the camp's residents, it was already clear during that visit, did not really need architects to assist them. Similar to other refugee and migrant camps worldwide, despite scarce resources, the Jungle had evolved into an elaborate self-built environment grounded in the residents' needs and skills, a makeshift camp that developed rapidly by and around them (Katz 2017).

Migrants planned to remain in the Jungle only briefly until they could successfully depart and complete their journeys, and it was clear that the site itself would not last, yet many of them had nevertheless put time and effort in building and improving their ephemeral shelters, businesses, and institutions in the temporary camp. But why invest so much in a place one is aiming to leave? Why build and improve a site that will eventually be demolished? The Jungle, it was clear, was a place that was about more than emergency shelters and basic protection and provision. As such, this article reflects, primarily through an Arendtian perspective, on the meaning of the Jungle as both a temporary site of irregular human movement and an environment developed as an elaborate place that exceeded its functional role in sustaining the life of those "on the move." By focusing on the spatial movement of shelters and camps generated by their builders-inhabitants, the article examines how actions of homemaking and place-making materialize a political call of the need of displaced people for a human place in the world, even in the ephemeral environments in which they settle for only a short time.

Figure 3. Alpha House shelter and art school in Calais Jungle, November 2015. Source: Author

No place in the world

Migration, including forced migration and seeking refuge elsewhere, is as old as the history of human existence, yet since the early days of modernity, people have lived in an increasingly mobile world. They move, flee, cross borders, and this constant human movement, especially of forced migrants, creates continuous spatial movement in different realms and scales. Refugee camps and makeshift encampments such as the Jungle are continuously built and then demolished often only to be created again in a different form elsewhere (Katz 2019), generating an *external spatial movement* across geographical regions. At the same time, these spaces also move internally by the constant changes of their inhabitation. While their residents have left their homes, hometowns, and home countries behind, they also carried these places with them through their memories, experiences, social ties, and cultural traditions, which form the ways they inhabit their new environments. The homemaking and place-making processes create an *internal spatial movement* that continuously morphs and reshapes these environments.

These external and internal spatial movements, when camps, emergency shelters, and other spaces of displacement change location and form, make part of what Zygmunt Bauman (2000) calls "liquid modernity," the condition of constant shifts that exist not only in the actual and often imposed movement of people, but also in the relationships, identities, and global economics of constantly re-created contemporary society and its spaces. Hannah Arendt, prior to Bauman, was one of the most significant scholars to consider displacement and refuge, describing the "uprootedness and superfluousness which have been the curse of modern masses since the beginning of the industrial revolution," while reflecting on how displacement and undesired people in excess "have become acute with the rise of imperialism [and] the break-down of political institutions and social traditions" (Arendt 1962, 475). Arendt describes this uprootedness and displacement, following her own experience as a refugee escaping Nazi Germany and then Europe, as world-shattering: "We lost our home, which means the familiarity of daily life," she wrote in her 1943 essay "We Refugees" (Arendt 1994, 110), gesturing with her interpretation of "home" to the Latin notion of *habitus* as an intimate condition of inhabitation from which those uprooted are ruptured. The only solution "the world had to offer the stateless," identifies Arendt, was the camp, which makes the displaced "deportable again" (1962, 284). For those forced into such temporary sites, it was not only impossible to return to their lost homes but also to create a new one in conditions of uncertainty and exclusion.

The meaning of displacement for Arendt is indeed not only the world that was lost but also the world that is being denied to those displaced: "to be uprooted," she writes, "means to have no place in the world, recognized and guaranteed by others"; "to be superfluous means not to belong to the world at all" (Arendt 1962, 475). By "world," Arendt means the human world created by people over time through social, political, and cultural structures and institutions. This is the "man-made world of things" that creates "a home for mortal man," which is distinct from nature (Arendt 1998, 173), a world assembled by what people have created and is therefore distinctively and familiarly human. In order to understand what kind of world is lost and being denied in displacement, and what people in sites and camps such as the Jungle sometimes reconstitute, it is first important to identify the meaning of the human world and its conditions.

In *The Human Condition* (1958), Arendt reflects on three human activities – labor, work, and action – which are fundamental to *vita activa,* the active human life. Labor, whose human condition is life, "corresponds to the biological process of the human body," with the vital necessities of "growth, metabolism, and eventual decay" (Arendt 1958, 7) provided by repetitive and cyclical activities such as preparing food or cleaning. Differently, the human condition of work is worldliness, which "corresponds to the unnaturalness of human existence" and "provides an 'artificial' world of things [...] within its borders each individual life is housed, while this world itself is meant to outlast and transcend them all" (Arendt 1958, 7). Lastly, action, which for Arendt means political action, corresponds to the condition of plurality, "to the fact that men, not Man, live on the earth and inhabit the world" (Arendt 1958, 7). These different human activities and their conditions are interrelated yet have different temporalities. Labor is about our temporary and cyclical biological existence; work is about our ability to create a more permanent world that outlasts our temporary lives; and action is about our ability to gather at the same time in order to act together politically and change our world.

In the modern age, for Arendt, having a place in the human world is inherently connected to the political modern systems of citizenship and rights. In the age of modernity, the earth has been frantically divided into nation-states through which people are subjected to material, social, legal, and political systems that protect their freedom and rights, and as such have become fundamental to our human existence. In this tightly knit modern global arrangement of nation-states, those ejected as displaced people from "the trinity of state-people-territory" are not only deprived of their intimate homes and familiar life, but also lose their "place in the world which makes opinions significant and actions effective," a world acknowledged by a political community that guarantees their humanity and, ultimately, their basic "right to have rights" (Arendt 1962, 281–82). Those who are denied citizenship might also be placed, as either humanitarian objects or undesired people on the move, in temporary in-between spaces, such as the Jungle, where they are denied a recognized and legitimate place. The Jungle, however, as an in-between bottleneck site of waiting, has become much more than what the municipality of Calais intended when it instructed a set of separate individuals to concentrate their makeshift shelters on the specific derelict industrial site where the camp was formed (Reinisch 2015, Katz 2017). Such makeshift environments of refuge are designed to be unworldly and often violent spaces of "the undesirables" (Agier 2011), yet they could also become places of "world-building" (Singh 2020) which are actively transformed by the spatial agency and spatio-political actions of their inhabitants into an elaborate home in the world.

Unworldliness by design

The designated space for refugees, stateless people, asylum seekers, and undocumented migrants left outside the state-people-territory trinity is often, as highlighted by Arendt and many others since, the temporary space of the camp, whether refugee camps, migrant camps, detention camps, or camps of other forms and titles (hotspots, reception facilities, hospitality centers). These sites are marked by their technologies of control and minimal provision (Martin et al. 2020) and function as spatial instruments of containment of those displaced. Camps create what Agamben calls "spaces of exception" (1998), which exist within the state territory yet outside the normal juridical and social order. Those suspended in these spaces are given ephemeral shelters rather than houses or homes in order to control them as temporary undesired guests (Agier 2011) rather than permanent inhabitants.

Such prefabricated emergency shelters tend to be primarily designed with standardized features for anonymous universal users and are the product of rationalization, industrialization, and standardization. Their design prioritizes budget and logistics so they can be easily transported as flat-pack kits to be rapidly erected in different parts of the world. The impersonal spaces and environments they create go together with the objectives of the states and aid agencies who purchase and deploy them for only temporary use. These shelters are primarily designed for the *external* spatial movement of camps which are created in emergency situations across different geographical regions only to be liquidated as soon as possible. They embrace a strictly technocratic approach generated by elementary biological needs and technical measures based on the standardized human body that both assembles and inhabits them (Katz 2017, 2020). The institutional camp, often composed of these prefab temporary shelters laid out in a rigid grid for a better-controlled environment, creates a biopolitical space in itself that answers only the basic necessities of its inhabitants with food and hygiene facilities provided outside the minimal shelters. As such, institutional camps and emergency shelters work in tandem to create a system which keeps displaced people as temporarily warehoused living bodies while ignoring their more meaningful human needs. Informal emergency camps, where basic forms of informal shelters and minimal provision are used, are also often erected and function to answer only the essential needs for the mere survival of their dwellers.

These shelters and camps correspond to no more than the basic condition of life and to its related activity of labor, conducted to maintain not more than basic biological existence. They also correspond to Arendt's analysis of modern mass society that tends "to 'normalise' its members" (Arendt 1958, 40) with interest in maintaining "life process itself," and aims only for the "survival of the animal species man" (Arendt 1958, 321). As the structures provided for the displaced are only the most basic, with only the minimal needs of food and hygiene met, in order to be erected and liquidated as quickly

Figure 4. The Calais container camp within the Jungle camp, April 2016. Source: Author

Figure 5. Prefabricated shelter with added extension in the camp near Dunkirk, April 2016.
Source: Author

as possible, such shelters and camps create detached, unhomely, and alienating environments. Their purpose is no more than sustaining the life of those who are deprived of control over their own destiny and the spaces they inhabit. Displaced people often name such shelters after spaces for animals – the prefabricated shelters in a camp near Dunkirk, for example, were nicknamed "chicken houses" – and describe their feeling in such shelters as being "like animals" (Woensel Kooy 2016, Katz 2017, 2020), manifesting their purpose of merely sustaining life. Camp dwellers such as those in the Jungle and the abovementioned camp near Dunkirk, however, sometimes use their capacities to reshape their environments, creating *internal* spatial movement through which their basic spaces are transformed to become a temporary home in the world.

Worlding a displaced world

The displaced people living in the emergency shelters and camps often refuse to comply with the restrictions of these minimal spaces and actively reshape them as articulated places of refuge. The prefabricated timber shelters erected in the camp near Dunkirk were significantly expanded from the first day they were occupied, and in other camps around the world the refugees have turned their minimal shelters into elaborate homes built according to their cultural traditions, forming memoryscapes of the environments left behind (Peteet 2005). In the Jungle, while prefab emergency shelters were transformed and reformed in both shape and function, informal shelters and temporary institutions were carefully designed according to the cultural and social traditions, preferences, skills, and the limited resources of their builders. Traditional Darfurian semicircular compounds, Afghan restaurants with elevated hookah lounges, wide mosques with specific entrance features, and an Ethiopian Orthodox church with raised roof sections and turquoise-colored entrance gates, were all sophisticated interpretations of places left behind and of places needed for a particular form of life that is distinctly human. The builders' available skills and resources have created specific architectural qualities of well-articulated spaces, which, through processes of "precarious placemaking" (Hinkson 2017), confronted the perilous environments within which they were formed.

Migrants and refugees, as Brun and Fábos (2015, 14) argue, re-create places as particular articulations of their past and current realities, as environments that exist "in a range of different places across space and time" and "within circumscribed geographic, historical, and political contexts." The Jungle's residents created spaces that exceeded the basic provision of shelter, seeking to sustain the fundamental aspects that establish who they are as people with specific backgrounds, identities, and particular modes of living (Katz 2017, 2020). In addition, these environments evolved from a collection of isolated and isolating shelters and camp spaces to a collective enterprise of complex social and cultural practices that go beyond the survival of their residents as an arbitrary gathering of isolated outcasts. The creation of such articulated environments, it is important to note, was not limited to the Jungle but happened, and still is happening, in informal and institutional refugee camps around the world (Peteet 2005, Doraï and Piraud-Fournet 2018, Refugee Republic, n.d.).

These spatial actions that transform the minimal shelters and camps could be linked to Arendt's discussion on work (Singh 2020) and its related human condition of worldliness, which has three key attributes. First, worldliness, or the human world, is constituted by producing things that are durable, "works and deeds and words" that transcend the lives of those who create them and "at least to a degree, are at home in everlastingness" (Arendt 1958, 18–19). These durable things have the function of "stabilizing human life" (Arendt 1958, 137), creating a world that was there before us and will continue after us and therefore confronts our uncontrolled biological movement in time and space. In addition, the ideal parts of this man-made world, for Arendt, are not instrumental but are created for their own sake. Such work, differently from labor, is not "a matter of utility but of meaning" (Arendt 1958, 154); it is not created "in order to" but "for the sake of," and can appear as an end in itself and not as a means to an end, transcending "both the sheer functionalism of things produced for consumption and the sheer utility of projects produced for use" (Arendt 1958, 173). It is therefore not surprising why it is the work of art, including architecture, which for Arendt is "the most intensely worldly of all tangible things" (Arendt 1958, 167). Lastly, our human world must also be acknowledged by others, going beyond the realm of the private creation while existing in, and creating, the public sphere. "In order to be what the world is always meant to be, a home for men during their life on earth," writes Arendt, "the human artifice must be a place fit for action and speech" (Arendt 1958, 173), and unless it creates the "web of human affairs and relationships and the stories engendered by them," this world "lacks its ultimate raison d'être" (Arendt 1958, 204).

Inhabiting a place, and particularly emergency shelters and camps, it could be argued, is a substantial part of world-making. If, as examined earlier, these initially instrumental spaces could be identified as aimed at the mere biological lives of their residents and to the labor of sustaining them, including the labor of assembling these shelters, then the reappropriated shelters and camp environments could be identified through their relation to work and its condition of worldliness. These transformed spaces were not only created for the bare necessities of life but were also formed as carefully crafted spaces intended for particular human uses and sometimes for the sake of their very creation.

As one of the Jungle's Sudanese residents stated, "I do not want to stay, I want to go to England, but when I am here, I want my Calais home to be nice so it reminds me of my home in Sudan" (Ma 2016), reflecting on how his beautified home in the camp did not answer only his basic needs of physical protection, but was also decorated for the sake of aesthetic preference and the feeling of a homely connection to the home left behind. This form of homemaking in the camp should not be dismissed as an insignificant act of a person on the move who is bound to eventually abandon his temporary informal home. Rather, it should be linked to a variety of studies showing how everyday inhabitation practices of beautification and modification of precarious spaces allow people to "establish a sense of home, as well as constructing a clear sense of self and agency" (Handel 2019, 14; see also Parsell 2012, Hinkson 2017). This active form of homemaking in the camp means a form of control over a space which is otherwise uncontrollable for its inhabitants. As Parsell (2012, 160) explains in relation to people sleeping rough, this form of homemaking and "control over a space also means the ability to exercise a degree of autonomy over their lives." The active process of making a shelter a home therefore also means the remaking of human agency in the dehumanizing space of the camp.

Yet it was not only their own homes that the refugees in the Jungle were creating; they were also transforming the camp itself into a worldly human environment. The Ethiopian church, for example, with its elaborate roof structure that incorporated windows of transparent plastic sheets that allowed the sunlight to enter the space from above, was created for elevating religious purposes. The space of the camp itself was also carefully organized, with shelters and institutions not scattered arbitrarily but relating to one another to form a meaningful space, whether it was a neighborhood or a main street, turning the camp into a human environment formed by logic and intention. This *internal* spatial movement of shelters and other camp spaces by their reappropriation and careful creation was transforming the camp from a mere functional space into a space created for human life as a whole with purposes beyond providing for the body's basic needs.

This is related to the important attribute of the endurance of these camp spaces. Although these camps are considered temporary, and the Jungle indeed no longer exists, this environment could nevertheless be considered as a space of endurance. This is in part because the representations of the camp still endure in the human world through media reports, academic analysis, West End theatre shows, and architectural exhibitions and discussions, all preserving the Jungle beyond its physical existence. But the human endurance of the Jungle and similar camps was and still is formed through their very materialization as spaces that encapsulate and maintain the particular cultures, spatial traditions, social ties, practices, and memories of their inhabitants-builders, and therefore allow their human world to endure within and through them. This works despite and often against their builders' uprootedness and rupture, temporariness and uncertainty, which are often enhanced by unstable and alienating environments of the informal and institutional camps. Instead, such transformed spaces allow for identities and the very humanity of their inhabitants-creators to be represented and endure during and beyond the precarious situation of uncertain realities and unknown futures.

While these spatial transformations often happen in radical conditions in the camp, they are not dissimilar to other ongoing actions of homemaking and place-making in "ordinary" environments, which are also seen as part of an ongoing and never-ending process of change (Massey 2005). Such continuous processes of constant transformation, which are an inseparable part of modern environments, question the idealized, stabilized conditions of home and inhabitation and their related permanent, fixed, sedentary, or not-in-motion modalities. As Nowicki (2014, 788) argues, places are constantly being "made, unmade, and remade" as part of continuous "temporal, material and geographic fluidity of the homespace," and processes of homemaking in the camp could also be seen as being part of this broader spatial fluidity. While these rapid homemaking and place-making actions in the camp could be seen as hyper processes of inhabitation, they are not dissimilar to mundane processes of inhabitation which are always in-motion, never static, and entangled to various scales, geographies, and temporalities of spatial production and operation, as identified by Bauman's liquid modernity. As people in the camp who are rendered out of place and those who inhabit prosaic places worldwide constantly transform them in a variety of forms and rhythms of home- and place-making, they together challenge rigid place-related notions such as being "at home" or an "outsider," a "refugee" or a "citizen," which are violently tied to the "Postcolonial New World Order" (Sharma 2020).

Arendt's third aspect of worldliness, the recognition by others, becomes an inseparable part of worlding the camp in terms of both internal and external recognition. The Jungle and other camps such as Za'atari in Jordan and Dadaab in Kenya, have become iconic spaces of refuge manifesting the human resourcefulness and creativity of their residents and were broadly recognized by scholars, journalists, artists, and the general public external to the camp. Yet, as importantly, the articulated spaces in the Jungle, as in other camps, allowed their residents to recognize one another as human beings with different backgrounds and life trajectories in their self-created camp environments. By together establishing new relations and realities in their spaces of refuge, as a plurality of people with unique identities, rather than the unifying identity imposed

Figure 6. Calais Jungle church, November 2015. Source: Author

on them as excluded and contained refugees and irregular migrants, the space of the camp itself became not only the object of speech but created in itself the scene "fit for action and speech" (Arendt 1958, 173) between its inhabitants. This was done not only through actions of homemaking in the camp's private realms of the shelters but importantly also through the actions of place-making that reshaped the camp's public realm and exposed the unique humanity of its dwellers to one another.

The Jungle, therefore, similar to other rearticulated camp spaces, is revealed as a worldly place, whose creation beyond mere functionality and with endurance and recognition by others, have together made it a home in the world for its inhabitants. Such a space should be looked at not only as an environment fit for speech and action, but also as a political action in itself conducted by its residents, reconnecting them to one another and to the world outside the camp, an action that works against the form and intention of the camp's original function.

Acting through architecture

In a reflection on Arendt's thought, architectural theorist Kenneth Frampton (2002) shows how architecture relates to both labor and work. Architecture, argues Frampton, combines the never-ending processual labor of building and dwelling necessary for our purely instrumental needs. At the same time, the fact that a work of architecture is usually enduring and intentionally created for our particular human use, and occasionally as a work of art, for its own sake, that is widely recognized, makes it a worldly creation. While the spaces of the emergency shelters and camps, with their instrumental functionality, could be related to the labor around the mere biological necessity of shelter and minimal provision, the reappropriated shelters and camps could be linked to the work of their inhabitants, which transformed them into spaces that are distinctively human.

Architecture is defined as the "formation or construction resulting from or as if from a conscious act" (Merriam-Webster 2020). The internal movement which transformed camp spaces from being purely for functional provision into worldly human spaces through the intentional and conscious acts of their residents could therefore be recognized as an architectural creation, turning the instrumental spaces into carefully designed dwellings and institutions that were constructed and related to one another in a meaningful manner. Contemporary architecture is often considered as being designed only by professional architects, while being an architect today requires the qualification and accreditation of authorized educational and professional state-related institutions. Yet those who redesigned their minimal shelters or makeshift institutions in the camp could also be defined as architects. These refugee-architects, who are not only unauthorized by the state to design buildings but are also deemed unqualified as citizens, have nevertheless transformed their designated minimal environments into articulated places of human life. But these spaces are not only articulated everyday spaces or an architectural work of art. More profoundly, they form performative spatial actions creating worldly environments by those denied a place in the world, creating places formed by those deemed out of place. By that, they are not only environments of labor and work, as reflected Frampton, but they are also spaces of political action through which the displaced resist the isolating naked biopolitical environments in which they are contained.

For Arendt, political action constitutes the highest realization of the human condition. It is based on the human condition of plurality, which "is the condition of human action because we are all the same, that is, human, in such a way that nobody is ever the same as anyone else who ever lived, lives or will live" (1998, 8). In our human world, the arrival of every one of us creates a new beginning, and as our realities change, we can generate further beginnings through political actions that aim to create together a better world for ourselves. It is therefore natality, for Arendt, which is the ontological condition of political actors as beginners who realize their human freedom to begin something new through action; "[b]ecause they are initium, newcomers and beginners by virtue of birth, men take initiative, are prompted into action" (Arendt 1998, 177). It is the political action and its condition of plurality that discloses the identity of the agents as unique individuals who are also political actors capable of new beginnings by interrupting the routine and the expected and creating the unanticipated while realizing their freedom.

The internal movement of camp spaces through reappropriation and change is how the inhabitants are recognized by one another as unique human beings and how their plurality is spatially articulated and expressed. Within a confining environment that was designed to treat people en masse according to their biological similarities rather than their human differences, this spatial action is in itself a political action that enacts the human plurality and freedom that were deliberately denied. These rearticulated spaces could be considered as the materialization of the power of people living together as unique individuals who can further act politically together after recognizing one another as such. This further political action happened in the Jungle through protests and demonstrations, similarly as in other camps, until the camp was violently destroyed by the French authorities. By these actions of spatial creation and protest, the self-created architecture in these camps is submerged in multiple layers of political meaning of a dehumanizing space that becomes worldly by its residents. The unique human significance of the Jungle's improvised spaces was not only meaningful to its inhabitants but was also acknowledged by French legal and political authorities. The French court repeatedly halted attempts to demolish businesses and public institutions in the camp, recognizing that the Jungle is characterized by "collective spaces whose purpose is to provide services of a social, cultural, medical or legal nature," and that "these places have been carefully arranged, and that they correspond, by their nature and their functioning to a real need of the exiled living spaces," and therefore should not be destroyed (Calaismag 2016).

For architecture to represent a collective value, argues Frampton, its "representative role would have to be contingent on the establishment of public realm in the political sense" (2002, 42). This political power, argues Frampton, is dependent "on its social and physical constitution, that is to say, on its derivation from the living proximity of men and from the physical manifestation of their public being in built form" (2002, 42). The creation of articulated places by encamped people with compromised freedom, rights, and provisions formed a specific political relation between the status of these people and their buildings, which enables their plurality to, literally, take place. Such a collective value of people living together as humans in the camp, which is undoubtedly represented by the camp's architecture and facilitated by it, makes the camp a public realm in the political sense derived from the living together of those who were denied such a space altogether yet created it, nevertheless.

In this respect, the Jungle could be identified as Arendt's definition of the *polis* as a political public space. The polis "is not the city-state in its physical location," writes Arendt; "it is the organization of the people as it arises out of acting and speaking together, and its true space lies between people living together for this purpose, no matter where they happen to be" (1998, 198). For Arendt, such polis stands for the "space of appearance," the space "where I appear to others as others appear to me, where men exist not merely like other living things" but as explicitly human. Such public space of appearance can be always re-created anew where individuals gather together politically, that is, "wherever men are together in the manner of speech and action." The Jungle's insurgent place-making, or rather polis-making process, re-created the camp as an elaborate "home in the world," where voices and acts of residents were articulated, seen and heard and where architecture was formed as distinctly political.

Conclusion

The space of Calais Jungle was on the move from the day it was formed in January 2015 until it was demolished in October 2016. The camp was created, grew, changed shape, and was eventually demolished according to the various forces of irregular movement and the attempts to control it that worked within and upon it, forming, together with many other formal and informal migrant and refugee camps around the world, a mobile space that constantly moved geographically and spatially. These spaces moved *externally* in their geographical location following the workings of regional and local powers, but they also moved *internally* by the creation and change of their architectural forms. Their initial spaces, which were created as instrumental environments aimed to answer only the biological necessities of their residents, were then reappropriated by them and transformed into human worldly environments based on plural particular needs, preferences, and skills.

While the first external movement is related to the will, need, and active demand for free global mobility and the right to move from one place to the other and the attempt to block it, the second internal movement is related to the need for a meaningful environment and an active realization of a "place in the world" that answers the human needs of its inhabitants. Such a place is connected to the multiple aspects of being human in intertwined social, cultural, and political ways, as opposed to what these spaces were originally planned to do – to sort and store people on the move outside and away from the human world. As such, these shelters and camps have turned from dehumanizing spaces into worldly places created by architectural and political action of homemaking, place-making, and polis-making of their inhabitants-architects.

Yet, while considering the resourcefulness and endurance of the camps' fabricants in their precarious situation, these environments should not be idealized and sentimentalized, and their broader context should not be forgotten. While their dwellers were and still are making remarkable efforts to live as human beings, many of these spaces have been and still are violently disconnected from the environments around them, blocking the physical, social, and human mobility and mobilization of their inhabitants to become an equal part of the human world. While they create a place in the world for their inhabitants, they are also the materialization of their forced exclusion from everyday environments to which they must have the freedom to belong. These reappropriated camp environments should therefore not be read as an answer or as a solution but rather as a demand. And this demand is expressed by their humanized re-creation, which articulates a clear political call to provide their inhabitants with a place in the world.

When, back in November 2015, we went to the Jungle as architects who wanted to support those living in the camp with a minimal shelter for winter, we realized that, while such shelters were indeed necessary, the more elaborate environment that the camp inhabitants created was equally important. In the visits since, we not only witnessed how camp inhabitants were acting as architects and through architecture, but we also realized how our own role as architects has changed into being activists that work for and demand political change. It is therefore not only spaces and their meaning that are continuously shifting in the camp, redefining what architecture is and what it could be, but also subjectivities and identities of those connected to these environments, including the destabilization of who architects are and in what ways they can act.

References

Agamben, G. 1998. *Homo Sacer: Sovereign Power and Bare Life*. Palo Alto, CA: Stanford University Press.

Agier, M. 2011. *Managing the Undesirables*. Cambridge: Polity.

Arendt, H. 1962. *The Origins of Totalitarianism*. Cleveland, OH: Meridian Books.

Arendt, H. (1943) 1994. "We Refugees." In *Altogether Elsewhere: Writers on Exile*, edited by M. Robinson, 110–19. Boston, MA: Faber and Faber.

Arendt, H. (1958) 1998. *The Human Condition*. Chicago, IL: The University of Chicago Press.

Bauman, Z. 2000. *Liquid Modernity*. Cambridge: Polity.

Brun, C., and A. Fábos. 2015. "Making Homes in Limbo? A Conceptual Framework." *Refuge: Canada's Journal on Refugees* 31, no. 1: 5–17.

Calaismag [online magazine]. 2016. http://www.per-ou-paris.org/pdf/Actions/CALAIS_16_mag_anglais_ON-LINE.pdf.

Doraï, K., and P. Piraud-Fournet. 2018. "From Tent to Makeshift Housing: A Case Study of a Syrian Refugee in Zaatari Camp (Jordan)." In *Refugees as City-Makers*, edited by M. Fawaz, A. Gharbieh, M. Harb, and D. Salamé, 136–39. Beirut: American University of Beirut.

Frampton, K. 2002. *Labour, Work and Architecture*. London: Phaidon.

Hinkson, M. 2017. "Precarious Placemaking." *Annual Review of Anthropology* 46: 49–64.

Katz, I. 2017. "Between Bare Life and Everyday Life: Spatialising the New Migrant Camps in Europe." *Amps: Architecture_Media_Politics_Society* 12, no.2: 1–21.

Katz, I. 2019. "En Route: The Mobile Border Migrant Camps of Northern France." In *Architecture on the Borderline: Boundary Politics and Built Space*, edited by A. Pieris, 119–38. London: Routledge.

Katz, I. 2020. "Adhocism, Agency and Emergency Shelter: On Architectural Nuclei of Life in Displacement." In *Structures of Protection?* edited by T. Scott-Smith and M. E. Breeze, 235–46. New York: Berghahn Books.

Massey, D. 2005. *For Space*. London: Sage.

Ma, A. 2016. "Homes in Calais' Refugee Camp Reveal Stories, Hopes, and Dreams." *HuffPost*, February 29, 2016. https://www.huffingtonpost.co.uk/entry/calais-jungle-refugee-camp-homes_n_56d45a9be4b0bf0dab32b77f?ri18n=true.

Martin, D., C. Minca, and I. Katz. 2020. "Rethinking the Camp: On Spatial Technologies of Power and Resistance." *Progress in Human Geography* 44, no. 4: 743–68.

Nowicki, M. 2014. "Rethinking Domicide: Towards an Expanded Critical Geography of Home." *Geography Compass* 8, no. 11: 785–95.

Parsell, C. 2012. "Home is Where the House Is: The Meaning of Home for People Sleeping Rough." *Housing Studies* 27, no. 2: 159–73.

Peteet, J. 2005. *Landscape of Hope and Despair: Palestinian Refugee Camps*. Philadelphia, PA: University of Pennsylvania Press.

Refugee Republic [website]. n.d. Accessed December 30, 2020. https://refugeerepublic.submarinechannel.com.

Reinisch, J. 2015. "'Forever Temporary': Migrants in Calais, Then and Now." *The Political Quarterly* 86, no. 4: 515–22.

Singh, A. L. 2020. "Arendt in the Refugee Camp: The Political Agency of World-Building." *Political Geography*: 102–49.

Sharma, N. 2020. *Home Rule: National Sovereignty and the Separation of Natives and Migrants*. Durham, NC: Duke University Press.

Woensel Kooy, E. 2016. "Living In Between: How Refugees and Volunteers in Negotiation (re)Construct Citizenship and Humanitarian Care in the Camps of Grande-Synthe, France." Master's dissertation. Utrecht University.

Madafah: Who is Hosting Whom? The Everyday of Za'atri Refugee Camp and the Architectural Encounter

Aya Musmar

The refugee camp is often cited as a place where refugees are hosted, yet I suggest that through the everyday life of Za'atri refugee camp, *Madafah* emerges as a place whereby refugees host NGO community mobilizers. Who is Hosting Whom? aims to interrogate how the dynamics associated with the power positions of the host and guest are played out between refugees and community mobilizers, respectively. The contrast between the host (refugee) and the guest (community mobilizer) works to challenge the image of the refugee present in conventional humanitarian discourses, that of people whose relationship with humanitarian NGO consists of debt.[1] I cite the *Madafah* by dwelling on one of the autobiographical notes that I wrote during my fieldwork.[2] While grounded in a decolonialist feminist methodology, I engage with the note to unpack the gendered, classed, and raced power relations implied in the *Madafah* as an architectural encounter. I exhibit the architectural encounter of the *Madafah* as an assemblage of positionalities and temporalities produced through the encounter.

Early in the morning, my colleagues seemed certain about their destination when I asked, "Where are we going?" "To Abu Saleem's." "Aha," I nodded. "Aya, do you not remember him?! We used to visit his place when you were here with us as a community mobilizer two years ago?!" one of my colleagues asked as he tried to remind me of the place.[3] *By the time I returned to Za'atri as a researcher, I felt that I had a vague memory of what the place looked like two years ago. It was not different in character, yet it felt unusual. The arid air, wide cul-de-sacs, deserted earth, and the white geometrical surfaces of the caravans and water tanks – all of which are numbered and signed by blue, orange, red, and green NGOs logos and colorful flags – have not changed. I looked to my friend and shook my head with*

Figure 1. (*Madafah*-مضافة): a noun in Arabic that designates "the place of guests." Derived from the verb, (Daf-ضاف) which translates to "hosted." Source: Author, Spring 2016

uncertainty. Jordanians that work here know that one year in the camp sets otherwise in the flesh of our time outside the camp. My colleague seemed to also recall that fact when he tried to ease the intensity of his previous exclamation by excusing my memory: "How would you remember?! We used to work with the communal kitchens. You may have mentally marked the place with a reference to District Three's blue-painted kitchens. There are no kitchens here anymore as you have probably noticed."

Walking from the base camp to meet the District Three main representatives was never a direct route.[4] *No matter how short the shortcut was that we would attempt to take, there were many detours and turns that we would end up taking. As my colleagues and I walked, our path was composed in accordance with the calls, shouts, and shout-outs exchanged between my colleagues (community mobilizers) and the inhabitants of District Three. "Come and join us at Abu Saleem's, we will discuss further details there," my colleague referenced Abu Saleem's Madafah to the people he encountered on his way. We arrived, having reached the corner that takes us to Abu Saleem's Madafah. A red bike was parked there. "Whose bike is that?" I asked. "It is the bike of his son-in-law," my colleague responded.*

As we became visible to Abu Saleem, he smiled at us from a distance. Leaning against the floor with the heels of his hands, Abu Saleem supported himself when rising from his floor-seated position. He stood up, waved with his right hand and gestured to invite us in. "Hawlouw/حولوا" he shouted. This is a term that would have sounded strange to Jordanians before they encountered Syrian refugees from Dara'a. It means "change the direction of your path and come here"; it cites hospitality and generosity. We waved back. Following the steps of my colleagues, at the entrance of the Madafah, I took off my shoes and greeted Abu Saleem and his guests. Close to where my colleagues and Abu Saleem were seated, I sat on the cushion that lay near the exit. My colleague introduced me as a previous community mobilizer and a now-researcher. Despite his efforts to hide his grimace and welcome my presence with a smile, Abu Saleem seemed uncomfortable with my current occupation. He followed my colleague's introduction of me as a "researcher" with a story about Al-Assad's investigatory apparatuses and how that cost his village the disappearance of many young men. On the same day, he told us that he writes poetry in a notebook that he keeps with him. I asked him if I could have a look at his lines out of a personal interest in poetry, but he did not approve it.

During my first few visits to Abu Saleem, I had the chance to be perceived differently; I spoke more about architecture than I did about research. I spoke to Abu Saleem about my interest in the Madafah that he had established, furnished, and sheltered. He explained his process to me: "First, I planned the boundaries that I needed for the Madafah, mixed the concrete material with the assistance of a skilled neighbor from the same district, poured the concrete and leveled its surface so it looks even like how it looks now. I also replaced many of the caravan wooden floors inside my place with concrete to seek some stability."[5] *Silence. I thought about how to ask a question that would draw out a comparison between the two sides of refugees' lives: their life now in the camp and their life before in Syria. This line of questioning had become tedious for some refugees to answer, and as a result I shied away from asking. Abu Saleem interrupted my stillness by catching my*

Figure 2. Abu Saleem speaks to my colleague. He smiles to the camera, but he pretends to not pay attention to it. Source: Author, Spring 2016

shying eyes and saying: "The Madafah's importance as a place originates from our rural culture. Back in Dara'a my family was one of the families that opened its Madafah to guests all the time. Our Sheikhs listened to people's problems and tried to mediate and solve them."[6]

Seated at the center of the side that marks the entrance to his Madafah (replicating his family Sheikhs back in Dara'a), Abu Saleem welcomed guests all throughout the day. He was an official leader and never aspired to be one.[7] *Abu Saleem's good reputation was not only known to community mobilizers and other NGO representatives, but people in the district where he lived also trusted him and looked to him as a leader. During the time I spent in the camp, many of the formal and the informal meetings between refugees and NGO representatives took place in his Madafah. During the times that I was hosted at Abu Saleem's Madafah, many of his neighbors came in to discuss their daily issues. Abu Saleem listened to people attentively and when he spoke it was always with confidence. With his euphonic assertive voice, whenever he spoke everyone listened. Only when he mentioned NGOs did his tone become tense. Despite the pattern of the UNHCR blue logo that adorned the plain surface of the shelter-sheet that dangled from behind Abu Saleem, he did not conform to the power that everybody else thought the UNHCR had over refugees' lives in the camp. When I asked him about how happy he was with NGO services inside the camp, he said, "I have never needed an NGO to provide me with aid and I will not ask for it. They owe me, I do not owe them. I know how to sustain myself and keep my extended family sustained too." As he went on to explain, it was hard for Abu Saleem to perceive the UN humanitarian agenda in isolation from its "implicit interventions that bred the war in Syria."*

Hospitality

Derrida describes hospitality as an "aporia" (2000), defined in the dictionary as "an irresolvable internal contradiction or logical disjunction in a text, argument, or theory" (EOD, 2018). Ultimately, the singular law of unconditional/absolute/inclusive hospitality and the plural laws of conditional/exclusive hospitality are in conflict. For example, if conditional hospitality means asking the guest about their name and family origins in order to allow them into a pact of hospitality, the law of

Figure 3. Abu Saleem's six necessary gadgets: a cell phone, a pack of cigarettes, a lighter, an ashtray, his notebook (not the poetry one), and a pen. Source: Author, Spring 2016

Figure 4. Taken during our walk, one minute before we reach Abu Saleem's *Madafah*. One Arabayeh (mobile seller) is parked in front of Abu Saleem's. The seller was being hosted in the *Madafah*. Source: Author, Spring 2016

absolute hospitality conceives hospitality as a duty, and it therefore demands a break from the law. Derrida writes:

> [A]bsolute hospitality requires that I open up my home and that I give not only to the foreigner (provided with a family name, with the social status of being a foreigner, etc.), but to the absolute, unknown, anonymous other, and that I *give place* to them, that I let them come, that I let them arrive, and take place in the place I offer them, without asking of them either reciprocity (entering into a *pact*) or even their names (2000, 25).

As he structures unconditional/absolute hospitality as "inconvincible and incomprehensible" (Derrida 2002, 362), he argues that this paradoxical relation between unconditional hospitality (the "singular law" of hospitality) and conditional hospitality (the "plural laws" of hospitality) is a complementary relationship. Westmoreland explains this paradoxical relationship between the singular law and plural laws of hospitality by stating that "they are not symmetrical, equally opposing one another. Rather, a hierarchy exists in which the law is above the laws, outside the laws. However, the two complement each other in that the law of hospitality requires the laws so not to be abstract" (2008, p. 8).

Although Derrida's deliberation of hospitality (as exchanged through the host-guest relationship) stays loyal to the boundaries of the unit of the house (as constructed by the host), territory and politics are two key structures that feature within Derrida's critique of conditional hospitality. The domestic setting, through which the host-guest relationship is articulated in Derrida's writings, cites geopolitical relationality to a broader territorial and political landscape of nation-state regimes (Rosello 2001).[8] For

Figure 5. That day, we walked together with the team of social workers from the Case Management unit. We were all heading to Abu Saleem's *Madafah*. Source: Author, Spring 2016

example, if the boundaries of the house represent the territory of the state, the host then becomes a representative of the state by being the head or the master of the house, and the guest represents the "foreigner," or those in transition who have come from "abroad" (Derrida and Dufourmantelle 2000, ix). The latter are also those who have been left out of what Emma Haddad refers to as the "trinity" of state-nation-territory (2008). Thus, Derrida's critique of the host-guest relationship in conditional hospitality comprises an analysis whereby political concepts like power, sovereignty, and violence are essential in order to comprehend the laws that rule the exchange of hospitality (Derrida and Dufourmantelle 2000).

To understand how the laws of hospitality (singular and plural) are enacted through the *Madafah*, it is important to ask: how does hospitality translate spatially (Dikeç, Clark, and Barnett 2009)? In spatial terms, the hyphen in host-guest conveys a contrasting spatial relationship as well as a merging of the inside (host) with the outside (the guest). To expand, the inside is the host's house where he occupies a powerful position as the master of his place, while the outside or "abroad" is where the "foreigner" guest comes from (Derrida and Dufourmantelle 2000, 3). Visualizing the space where hospitality laws are enacted as situated at the edge between the private and the public, Derrida invites us to understand hospitality as an "interruption" (Westmoreland 2008, 1). Through this thinking, the *Madafah* can also be understood as a space where the interruption of hospitality takes place (Westmoreland 2008, 1). In this interruption, where the outside trespasses the inside by moving towards/meeting/crossing/clashing/transgressing the inside, the *Madafah* performs the *threshold* that provides rules as to how the inside is encountered by the outside.

In the following text, I start my critical reflection with the same question that I asked earlier on my walk with the community mobilizers: "Where are we going?" Thinking of community mobilizers as wanderers, travelers, and maybe foreigners themselves, I approach this question as one of the foreigner. For Derrida, the foreigner is "the one who puts the first question or the one to whom you address the first question" (2000, 3). Following my colleague's answer about our destination: "to Abu Saleem's" (citing his *Madafah*), I reflect on trespassing the threshold of the *Madafah*. Keeping in mind the intimate entanglement between the two, the infrastructure of humanitarian governance and the infrastructure of social relations that community mobilizers embody, I argue that the laws that dictate the pact of hospitality in the *Madafah* have been already constructed and agreed on through the chronological evolution of the two structures (Graham and McFarlane 2014). Thus, for the community mobilizers, trespassing the *Madafah* was rather a performative act that paid respect to the *Madafah* as a pact whereby an exchange of hospitality took place according to certain terms. Moving on to describe my own crossing of the *Madafah*, which Abu Saleem perceived as intrusive due to his unfamiliarity with my presence, I reflect on my position as a foreigner and how substituting "researcher" with "architect" shifted how I was perceived by Abu Saleem. To elaborate, while the power that I generated through the title "researcher" was perceived by Abu Saleem as threatening, that which I amassed due to the title "architect" was rather generously and respectfully welcomed by Abu Saleem. By the end of the text, I argue that despite the decline of the *Madafah* as a space where community mobilizers could dwell, the laws of hospitality that had been enacted through the space of the *Madafah* were still otherwise performed.[9]

"Where?": the question
"Where are we going?"

> The question "where" is ageless, transitive, it gives as essential the relation to place, to dwelling, to placelessness, and in its very function refuses thought in its comprehending relation to the object (Derrida and Dufourmantelle 2000, 52–54).

Caught by their occupational duty to mobilize the community through their everyday five-hour walk, a place where they can quickly stop or where they can rest hinders their transitive quest.[10] For community mobilizers, to mobilize the community is to help people, or to help people help themselves. It is to work to build relations, to maintain them, and most importantly to belong to them. Belonging to these social relations is not to be understood as a plain-sighted imitation whereby community mobilizers assimilate into refugees' communal relations; rather, belonging is choosing to be vulnerable, to be cracked so to allow these social relations in. As Butler, Gambetti, and Sabsay argue in the introduction to *Vulnerability in Resistance*, "vulnerability emerges as part of social relations, even as a feature of social relations" (2016, 4). Choosing to be vulnerable to social relations cannot be better explained than the explanation offered by one of my interviewees: "People in the camp feel more comfortable around those who can feel their pain more than others trying to technically solve their problems. At least when you are unable to solve the problem, the refugee will know you honestly tried to and they will be satisfied by that!" For community mobilizers, a place ("where") that satisfies their quest is a place in which they can dwell (Mommersteeg 2014), or in Ahmed's terms, a place that they can "inhabit" (2006). The same interviewee continued by saying, "Our management often criticizes the time that we spend 'sitting with' refugees as time wasting. Management complains of our capacities in formal reporting, saying that reporting is the 'real work.' But I genuinely think that 'sitting with' refugees is the real work." Consequently, a place of dwelling for community mobilizers is a

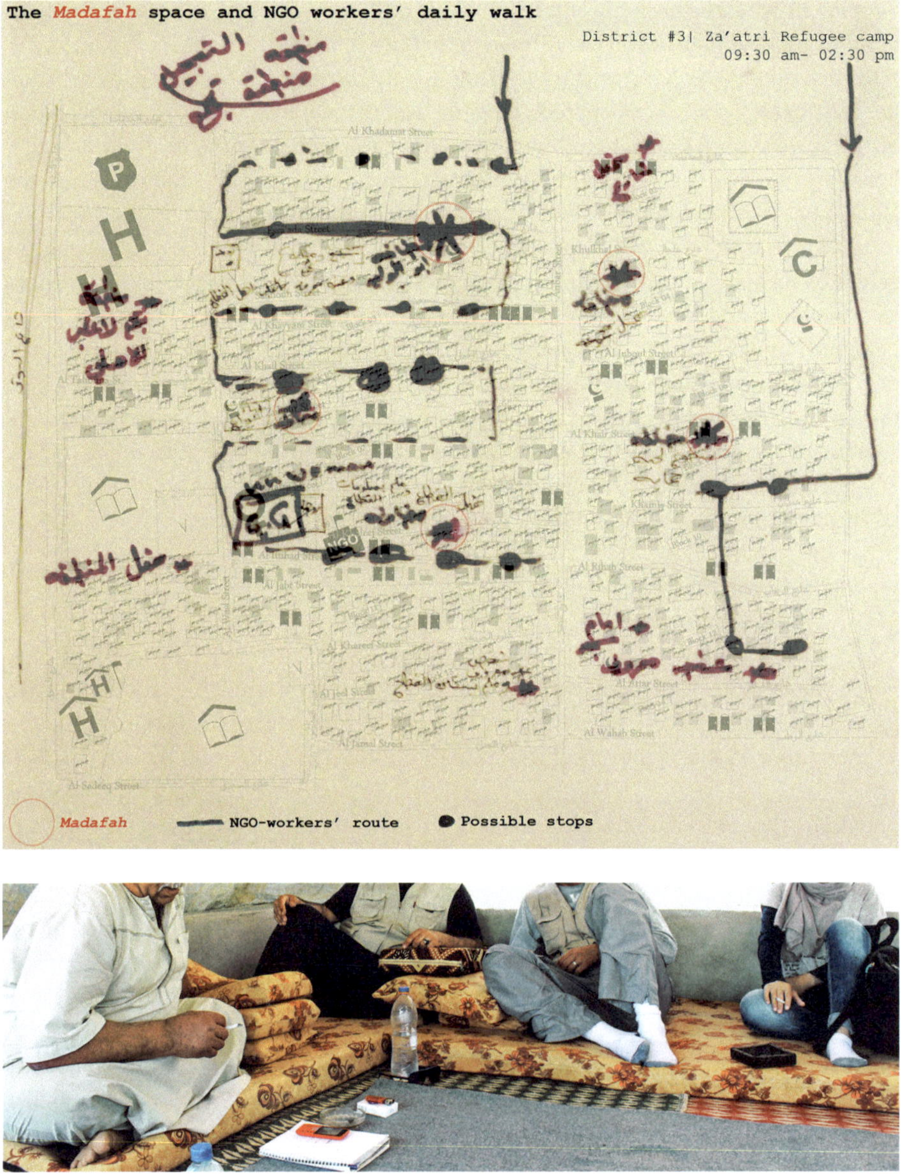

Figure 6. Based on a UNHCR map, this sketch is drawn by one community mobilizer, showing the different *Madafahs* that he visits through his everyday walks in District Three. He makes a distinction between four types of *Madafahs*: 1) one was for one man that is morally respected by the district; 2) one was for a street leader; 3) one *Madafah* was for the mosque imam; 4) another for an NGO volunteer that people in the district were familiar with. Source: Author

place where they can sit with people first. With time, they help people or help people to help themselves by contributing to solving a problem.

To Abu Saleem's

> We only ever speak one language – and, since it returns to the other, it exists asymmetrically, always for the other, from the other, kept by the other. Coming from the other, remaining with the other, and returning to the other (Derrida 1998, 40).

In Arabic language and culture, *Madafah* denotes a place where the cultural ethic of "hospitality" (*Deyafah*-ضيافة) is performed and mediated upon the principle of helping those in need of help. In fact, the ethic of *Deyafah* in the Arabic language pre-existed the Western syntax of hospitality (Shryock 2008). Unlike the Latin stem verb "host" and the complex taxonomy of derivations that Derrida navigates through to comprehend the politics of cosmopolitan conditional hospitality (Derrida and Dufourmantelle 2000), the Arabic stem verb (Daf-ضاف) contains an unequivocal relationship between the host and the guest. In this relationship, as structured in language, it is the subjective request of the guest (or the traveler) to be offered hospitality from the host (the requestee) that necessitates hospitality. In this relationship, the host/requestee is ethically responsible to respond to the guest/traveler's request. Thus, hospitality in this relationship is not juridical, but rather ethical.

The ethic of hospitality (*Deyafah*-الضيافة) originates from pre-Islamic Arabia tribal "virtues of welcome and generosity" that took form in the harsh desert environment (Siddiqui 2015, 10–11). Pre-Islamic Arabia tribes did not ask their hosted guests about their names and their families. Then hospitality (*Deyafah*-الضيافة) was a communal ethic that ruled over people's social relations; to abstain from the act of hospitality (*Deyafah*-ضيافة) was therefore a shameful act that was denounced by others (Feghali 1997). In Derridian logic, this Arabic hospitality (*Deyafah*-ضيافة) equates the singular law of hospitality insomuch as it is "above" and "outside" of the laws of conditional hospitality (Westmoreland 2008, 8). Despite the manifold historical eras that have passed since pre-Islamic times, the moral structure that is contingent on the exchange of cultural codes that once acted as moral authorities has been perpetuated as authoritative cultural codes that now regulate the social relations of Arab communicational patterns today (Al-Barghouti 2008). For example, although our contemporary deliberation of the ethic of hospitality has been influenced by the economic and political conditions of exchange associated with cosmopolitan hospitality, hospitality as an ethic is discoursed through the everyday social relations of Arab people, both in rhetoric and in practice (Feghali 1997).

The duality of the position that Jordanian community mobilizers occupy – as social subjects who speak the Arabic language and emit its culture, and as NGO authoritative subjects that are caught up in their occupational duties – allows the *Madafah* to function as a space that satisfies their twofold quests, which are to be helped by others and to help others.

"Near to the exit": the "threshold" and the pact.

Not far from where my colleagues and Abu Saleem were seated, I sat on the cushion that lay near the exit.

> Nowadays, a reflection on hospitality presupposes, among other things, the possibility of a rigorous delimitation of thresholds or frontiers: between the familial and the non-familial, between the foreign and the non-foreign, the citizen and the non-citizen, but first of all between the private and the public, private and public law, etc. (Derrida and Dufourmantelle 2000, 47–9).

Abu Saleem did not make me feel unwelcome, yet I felt that to him I was a foreigner. My colleague told me that I was overthinking it when I explained to him my overall concern about the discomfort that I may have caused Abu Saleem, asking if I should not visit his *Madafah* again. "You are just not used to each other," my colleague said. Despite how invisible I was to Abu Saleem, as he moved his sight away from me during my first visit, he still noticed that I was sitting by the exit. "Tell your new friend to come closer to the inside, tell her she is welcome," Abu Saleem said to my colleague – now an insider himself – reminding him of his responsibility to invite me in. Careful not to be more intrusive than I already felt I was being, I insisted on staying where I was already seated, by the periphery of the *Madafah*; nearer to the outside and purposely by the exit. The same exit that I inhabited in search of a margin that would embrace my foreignness was seen by my colleagues as an entrance to the *Madafah*. The red bike that parked parallel to the entrance, the ritual of taking their shoes off at the entrance as they made their way in, and the many pairs of shoes that accumulated there, all seemed to be phenomenological images and performative practices to which my colleagues did not pay attention as they were used to them.

Whereas the boundaries that marked the space of the *Madafah* as a threshold for my colleagues became blurred as they and Abu Saleem became used to each other, the same boundaries were smudged by my foreign trespass. For Abu Saleem, the master of the *Madafah*, I was but a new subject that did not conform to the conditions of his *Madafah*. "Used to" evokes a history of mutual work in building genuine social relations, whereby Abu Saleem and community mobilizers had exchanged a certain understanding of the power positions to which each of them is entitled. According to this mutual understanding each responded to the *Madafah*'s conditions that are drawn by their reciprocal recognition of these power dynamics. Thus, "new" not only lacks this historicity of mutual work in honing social relations with Abu Saleem, but also threatens to transgress the *Madafah*'s laws that were sanctioned by a social contract (or the pact) underlying the everyday contact that Abu Saleem had with community mobilizers (Derrida and Dufourmantelle 2000, 47–49).

> *In my few visits to Abu Saleem, I had the chance to be perceived differently; I spoke more about architecture than I did about research.*

In order for Abu Saleem and me to get used to each other, something necessary for me to be permitted into the *Madafah*'s pact, renegotiating my position and the power to which I was entitled was necessary. Attentive to the association that the term "researcher" had for Abu Saleem, as well as the esteemed position that "architect" denotes more generally in our shared understanding of certain relationalities (such as class and social ranking), substituting "researcher" for "architect" was key for this access.

> *"I have never needed an NGO to provide me with aid and I will not ask for it. They owe me, I do not owe them. I know how to sustain myself and keep my extended family sustained too."*

> There is no hospitality, in the classic sense, without sovereignty of oneself over one's home, but since there is also no hospitality without finitude, sovereignty can only be exercised by filtering, choosing, and thus by excluding and doing violence (Derrida and Dufourmantelle 2000, 55).

For Abu Saleem, what the UNHCR and other international NGOs represented was a demeaning debt for which refugees, who are dependent on humanitarian aid, are supposed to be grateful. Correlating the politics of "aid" distributed by UN humanitarian agencies, where he, as a refugee, is assumed to be "helpless" on the one hand (Harrell-Bond 1986), and the war in Syria which caused the uprooting of millions of Syrian citizens turning them into refugees all over the world on the other hand, Abu Saleem's dispensation of aid relays his criticism of the political basis of the humanitarian response, according to which refugee camps are established and governed (Agier 2011). Abu Saleem as well as many of the men and women that I encountered in the camp described management figures from the UNHCR and international NGOs as "blue-eyed, white, and blond European foreigners" who usually speak another language rather than Arabic.[11] This image of the foreigner echoes their image of the "colonizer", a figure who had ultimate control over the lives of the colonized (Duffield 2007).

To give an example, in one of the meetings which refugees were urged to attend in order to speak to delegates from the US Congress, I was tasked with translating. As one of the American delegates in his mid-50s asked the group of refugees about "their needs," one refugee man, also in his mid-50s, stood and responded to the question by saying:

> "May I tell you a short story to answer your question? It is about a man, maybe of our age, who visited Mecca to perform the Islamic duty of Haj. He was a man that was in need of Allah's mercy. When he was in the grand mosque of *Mecca*, he raised his hands to *Allah* in prayer to tell *Allah* about his needs. He was so puzzled and confused about where to start his prayers: his health, his children, his livelihood, or his future. At the peak of his confusion, he looked up to the sky, raising his hands high and said, 'Oh *Allah*, you know it all, why should I be saying what I need? You know it all.' So, my sir, do you. Like *Allah* you know it all; so why are you asking?"

Aligning the US congressman with *Allah,* the ultimate sovereign power in everyday Islamic-cultural discourse, indicates how refugees perceived the power to which UN humanitarian agencies are entitled. The confrontational moment when the man stood to tell the story and the ironic question with which he decided to conclude his story, is similar to Abu Saleem's serious comprehension of humanitarian aid. Both point to another form of sovereignty that refugees claim through resistance.

Recognizing the moral power that Abu Saleem was entitled to as a *Sheikh* within his *Madafah* (or as the master of the household in Derrida's terms) necessitated that community mobilizers, while situated in the *Madafah*, abstained from exerting their power positions held by way of their formal affiliations with UNHCR or other international NGOs. Whereas it was mutually understood that abstaining from their formal power positions as humanitarian representatives did not translate into a change in their interests to achieve their everyday duties through the *Madafah*, performing this abstention was key to maintaining the genuine exchange of help through the *Madafah*'s pact. Community mobilizers in the *Madafah* dissociated themselves from their management. To illustrate, when refugees made cynical comments about NGO managements' "uninformed decisions," "big-headed attitudes," and "real concerns" that do not include refugees, community mobilizers responded with humorous jokes that implied a similar level of cynicism and helplessness about any possible change. In other words, "we are only employees that do what we can do." Community mobilizers themselves are vulnerable and helpless, something which brings them together with refugees beyond the formality of their uniforms. Indeed, dwelling on the *Madafah* pact generated certain social intimacies between Jordanian community mobilizers and Syrian refugees through which they shared certain socio-political and economic precarity. As one community mobilizer said, "they trust me because they feel I am one of them, and this is how I really feel, like I am one of them.[12] We speak the same language, share similar history, belong to the same religious, cultural, and traditional values, it is only the NGO uniform that marks my difference. Sometimes I wish I could just take it off."[13]

The decline of the *Madafah*: dressing up the ethic code of hospitality

Through the camp's emergency phase, parallel to the rise of the *Madafah* as a node through which power was negotiated between the host and the guest (see Musmar 2017), arose a form of informal networks headed by "street leaders"; these networks disrupted the humanitarian response, affecting the distribution of humanitarian aid. One of the community mobilizers who worked across the different phases of the refugee camp attributed this disruption to the lackluster performance from the UNHCR and its partnering humanitarian NGOs in the earlier phases of the refugee camp.[14] Among other types of *Madafah*, and unlike Abu Saleem's, many of the *Madafahs* in the district were found, used, and facilitated by street leaders to serve their personal interests (see Fig. 6 for other types of *Madafah*). The street leaders were male figures who claimed certain powers during times of emergency. More often than not, the term denotes a corrupted informality that misused its proclaimed powers. Killian Clarke draws on the link between the street leaders' rise to power and the poor management and coordination of the camp governance at earlier phases of the camp (2018). He argues that when the UNHCR and its partnering humanitarian NGOs were still getting their head around managing the camp and mobilizing it for its humanitarian ends, the refugee camp was already being mobilized to serve the ends of the street leaders (Clarke 2018). Community mobilizers' responsibilities implied that they would demobilize the community before mobilizing it for the humanitarian NGO ends.

Through the post-emergency phase, the *Madafah* had come to prominence even more and was attended recurrently by community mobilizers and other NGO representatives. Demobilization meant that community mobilizers dwelled on the informal networks that refugees had founded and grown among themselves in order to dismantle them later on. Community mobilizers were encouraged by their management, albeit orally and indirectly, to utilize these networks and acknowledge the authority claimed by the street leaders. For community mobilizers, the *Madafah* pact provided the space where a process of demobilizing the informal networks and a process of mobilizing the refugee community towards humanitarian ends were simultaneously performed. For refugees, developing the *Madafah* pact had allowed them to maintain their exercise of power while at the same time providing them with a margin through which they seek the protection of the humanitarian NGO. A community mobilizer reflected on the ways refugees negotiated their power in the camp by mentioning refugees' fear of governmental authorities. Refugees did not have a choice; they knew that governmental authorities can apply their regulations forcefully. Therefore, negotiating their power with the humanitarian NGO was a compromise that they willingly made before the inevitability of an authoritative governance.

Later on, through the development phase, when the UNHCR and its partnering humanitarian NGOs claimed the accountability (power) that they had failed to achieve through earlier phases, the *Madafah* pact not only became dispensable for the camp management, but also implied risking the humanitarian codes which they assumed to be inviting. Furthermore, the social intimacies exchanged between Jordanian workers and Syrian refugees interwove an infrastructure of relations (see Simone 2004) that intimidated humanitarian governance's recently claimed accountability.

The *Madafah* pact codes, through which NGO community mobilizers and Abu Saleem became allies, destabilized many of the principles that the UNHCR and other international NGOs sought to implement through their code of conduct during the development phase. For example, one of the UNHCR's fundamental principles to which their representatives and those from other international NGOs are expected to adhere, according to the *UNHCR Code of Conduct (CofC)*, is "to respect the cultures, customs and traditions of all peoples," promising to "strive to avoid behaving in ways that are not acceptable in a particular cultural context" (UNHCR 2010, 10). However, this respect to the cultures is quickly devalued once it is thought to oppose humanitarian standards; the same principle goes on to denounce the same culture for which it required respect "when the tradition or practice is considered by the relevant organ of the UN to be directly contrary to an international human rights instrument or standard" (UNHCR 2010, 10). Therefore, to stop by the *Madafah*, to accept a coffee, and/or to build social relations with refugees, are all behaviors that contradicted the core values of international human rights. From the summer of 2016, having coincided with a change in NGO management, the *UNHCR CoC* was strictly applied, prohibiting many of the negotiations that their representatives were previously used to while being in the field. Since then, NGO representatives' behaviors have been translated in such a way that delegitimizes them as humanitarian actions. For instance, accepting coffee or any type of food when at refugees' places is considered a violation of the refugee right to their monthly calculated share of food. The seventh principle in the *UNHCR CoC* "prevents, opposes and combats all exploitation and abuse of refugees and other persons of concern" (UNHCR 2010, 9). Also, stopping by someone's place or *Madafah*, or building social relations with certain people in the community, violates the first principle in the *UNHCR CoC*, which is to "treat all refugees and other persons of concern fairly, and with respect and dignity." This contributes to unjust communal power structures whereby those with the least visibility are marginalized by the visible (UNHCR 2010, 5). Jordanian community mobilizers were asked to stop their informal contact with refugees, which required them to decentralize the *Madafah* by revoking its pact.

The pact of the *Madafah*, where the cultural ethic of hospitality was transfused by laws outlined by Abu Saleem, was replaced by another, the pact of Community Gatherings. For the NGO, the emergent need to subvert the informal networks that grew between refugees, within which many community mobilizers were identified, became more urgent. In response to the persistent necessity to construct alternative networks that were overseen and organized by community mobilizers, Community Gatherings aimed to provide a platform through which they could participate in addressing and contributing to solve their communal problems on the district level.

Community Gatherings changed the pact of hospitality which refugees, as well as Jordanian community mobilizers, had been previously used to. Dislocated from the *Madafah*, meetings between community mobilizers and refugees were conducted in NGO Community Centers (large service compounds that existed in five districts) and Service Units (individual units that existed in six districts).

The *Madafah*'s pact was reversed in Community Gatherings; community mobilizers became the hosts and refugees the guests. Community mobilizers, as hosts, are responsible for inviting refugees to attend the planned Community Gathering, inviting other NGO representatives who could help refugees with their general queries, managing the logistics of refreshments distributed through the meeting, facilitating the discussion between refugees and other NGO representatives, and reporting the meeting minutes to their management. While community mobilizers thought that there were certain qualities of *Madafah* meetings that were lost in Community Gatherings, they also thought that reversing the role of the guest-host had displaced the power structures associated with the emergence of the *Madafah*. At least, street leaders could not claim moral authority over other refugees and so refugees had equal access to humanitarian resources like everyone else.

The reversed pact of hospitality and the spatial shift that it entailed – substituting the *Madafah* (curated by refugees) for the community center or the service unit (owned by the humanitarian NGO) – stripped refugees, who had previously occupied a moral power position in their district, of the agency that they claimed within the settings of their *Madafahs*. Caught by their resistance to perform their powers while at the same time by their willingness to negotiate and even dispense this moral authority, *Sheikhs*, who had been at the center of their *Madafahs*, performed their "host" role otherwise. In the first Community Gathering that I witnessed in 2014, those that had long identified themselves as *Sheikhs* came dressed in Arab white garments, a *Thobe*, covered by a loose black gown, an *Abaya*, and a patterned *Kufiya*. This is the same dress code that refugees would then follow in significant traditional events.

Conclusion

The few times I shared my research with others, locating it in the boundaries of the architectural discipline, I was often asked, "Architecture in the refugee camp? How?" This chapter is an attempt to resolve the tension between our conventional understanding of what an architectural practice is and what it can be when applied in the refugee camp. By displaying my encounter with the *Madafah* in Za'atri refugee camp from my dual positions of researcher and architect, I have aspired to show the possibility for another architecture, which escapes the capitalist, gendered, and classed connotations and accounts for the ethical intricacies implied in the refugee camp encounter.

From the multiple social, political, and legal layers that shape the refugee camp materializes an architecture, yet another layer that hosts, mediates, and mobilizes the complex power positions existing within the governance structure within the refugee camp. Analyzing how certain spaces are being used, attended, and socialized permits an understanding of the different ways in which the refugee camp is inhabited. Beyond our understanding of the refugee camp as a heavily governed and administered space in which refugees are stripped of their agency, the *Madafah* encounter demonstrates a space where refugees perform their agency. The way Abu Saleem perceives the *Madafah* as a space where he and others enact the ethic code of hospitality that they had enacted back in Dara'a performs the sense of ownership that Abu Saleem, as well as other refugees, claim over the extraterritorial territory of the refugee camp. It is a sense of ownership that defies the legal layer that locates refugees in a precarious position, where they can own barely anything in their ephemeral state of being in their host country.

This chapter was originally published in my PhD dissertation, "Witnessing as a Feminist Spatial Practice" (Musmar 2020, 137–53).

---

1 In *The Guests' Guests* (2008), Adam Ramadan writes about how Palestinians in refugee camps in Southern Lebanon hosted Lebanese people fleeing the war between Israel and Hizbullah in 2006. During the war, Palestinian refugees, themselves hosted by the Lebanese, became the hosts of their hosts. Ramadan interrogates the contrasting relationship which emerged between the Palestinians as the guests and the Lebanese as the guests' guests. **2** I conducted the fieldwork for my PhD over three months with one of the aid-and-development NGOs working inside the Za'atri refugee camp. **3** In the summer of 2014, I worked in the community mobilization unit with an international NGO in the Za'atri refugee camp. Community mobilization work is field-based. The NGO workers working in the community mobilization unit are known as "community mobilizers." They are responsible for creating links between the camp management and refugees; they deliver the management messages to refugees and channel refugees' needs and questions to their management. The work of the community mobilization unit took different forms through different phases of the refugee camp (emergency, post-emergency, and development). In my work as a community mobilizer in 2014 (post-emergency), I, together with two male colleagues, was responsible for supervising and administering the communal kitchens in District Three. Our walking path was planned in accordance with the locations of the communal kitchens. Our job was to assign kitchen supervisors and to manage the distribution of gas cylinders to kitchens. **4** Base camp is a term that designates one unit of the refugee camp in which humanitarian NGOs set up their compounds. It is a camp in which the humanitarian operations are planned, managed, and organized, and a departure point from which humanitarian activities are carried out in the refugee camp districts that accommodate refugees. **5** The use of concrete to floor caravans after having removed the original wooden floors was a widespread practice in most of the camp districts. Regardless of the assumed duration of their temporal stay in the camp, refugees sought some stability. Most of the households that I visited with my colleagues, like Abu Saleem's, had replaced their shaky wooden floors, as they wanted, at the very least, a physically stable stay. It is also common for refugees to upcycle the wooden boards from the original floors of their caravans to make their own furniture. In other cases, wooden boards were sold to carpenters who made a living out of making furniture. **6** (*Sheikh*/شيخ) in the Arabic language means a person who has been publicly recognized in his tribe for the knowledge and the experience that he has acquired throughout his life. Whereas this recognition is conditioned by the *Sheikh* morals and morale, it is also associated with his age (Almaany 2010–18). The *Sheikh* denotes the category of elders who have reached their 50s. In Islamic terms, the *Sheikh* also means a person who has studied one of the branches of Islam and has therefore become an expert in its field of study (Almaany 2010–18). **7** By official I mean those that are administratively assigned to operate such positions. Before this administrative assignment was withdrawn by a governmental decision in 2015, official district leaders were elected by their district's represented refugees. **8** The Campus in Camps project entitled *Xenia* provides some creative accounts on the geopolitical dimension of hospitality. See: http://www.campusincamps.ps/projects/xenia/ **9** The decline of the *Madafah* was for the following reasons: firstly, the NGO's strict rules prohibited Jordanian community mobilizers from dwelling inside refugees' households (to dismantle the power structure of refugees that challenged the working agendas of NGOs); and secondly, community mobilizers in districts that lacked an NGO-affiliated space for their administrative work were provided with what was called a "community unit." **10** A definition for community mobilization has been clarified earlier. See footnote no. 2. **11** Albert Memmi starts his book with a similar image of the colonizer: "We sometimes enjoy picturing the colonizer as a tall man, bronzed by the sun, wearing Wellington boots, proudly leaning on a shovel – as he rivets his gaze far away on the horizon of his land" (Memmi 1974). **12** It is important to note that community mobilizers did not all share the same sentiment towards the community of refugees whom they are responsible for mobilizing. Whereas some of the community mobilizers that I interviewed, similar to the one mentioned here, had indeed viewed their job responsibility as people-oriented, some other community mobilizers observed their roles in administrative terms (see Musmar 2020, 89–118). **13** From a formal interview with a female Jordanian community mobilizer. The interview was conducted in 2016, before the NGO substituted most of its Jordanian staff for Syrian volunteers. **14** From a formal interview with a male community mobilizer. The interview was conducted in 2016.

References

Agier, M. 2011. *Managing the Undesirables: Refugee Camps and Humanitarian Government*. Cambridge: Polity Press.

Ahmed, S. 2006. *Queer Phenomenology: Orientations, Objects, Others*. Durham, NC: Duke University Press.

Al-Barghouti, T. 2008. *The Umma and the Dawla: The Nation-State and the Arab Middle East*. London: Pluto Press.

Butler, J., Z. Gambetti, and L. Sabsay, eds. 2016. *Vulnerability in Resistance* [Kindle edition]. Durham, NC: Duke University Press.

Campus in Camps. 2017. "Xenia." *Campus in Camps Collective Dictionary* [blog], March 24, 2017. http://www.campusincamps.ps/projects/xenia/.

Clarke, K. 2018. "When Do the Dispossessed Protest? Informal Leadership and Mobilization in Syrian Refugee Camps." *Perspectives on Politics* 16, no. 3: 617–33.

Derrida, J. 1998. *Monolingualism of the Other; or, The Prosthesis of Origin*, translated by P. Mensah. Stanford, CA: Stanford University Press.

Derrida, J. 2002. "Hospitality." In *Acts of Religion*, translated and edited by G. Anidjar, 358–420. New York: Routledge.

Derrida, J. and A. Dufourmantelle. 2000. *Of Hospitality: Anne Dufourmantelle Invites Jacques Derrida to Respond*, translated by R. Bowlby. Stanford, CA: Stanford University Press.

Dikeç, M., N. Clark, and C. Barnett. 2009. "Extending Hospitality: Giving Space, Taking Time." *Paragraph (Modern Critical Theory Group)* 32, no. 1: 1–14.

Duffield, M. R. 2007. *Development, Security and Unending War: Governing the World of Peoples*. Cambridge: Polity Press.

EOD. 2018. "Aporia | Definition of Aporia in English by Oxford Dictionaries." *Oxford Dictionaries*, 2018. https://en.oxforddictionaries.com/definition/aporia.

Feghali, E. 1997. "Arab Cultural Communication Patterns." *International Journal of Intercultural Relations* 21, no. 3: 345–78.

Graham, S., and C. McFarlane, eds. 2014. *Infrastructural Lives: Urban Infrastructure in Context*. Abingdon, UK: Routledge.

Haddad, E. 2008. *The Refugee in International Society: Between Sovereigns*. Cambridge: Cambridge University Press.

Harrell-Bond, B. E. 1986. *Imposing Aid: Emergency Assistance to Refugees*. Oxford: Oxford University Press.

Memmi, A. 1974. *The Colonizer and the Colonized*, translated by H. Greenfeld. London: Earthscan Publications Ltd.

Mommersteeg, B. 2014. "Space, Territory, Occupy: Towards a Non-Phenomenological Dwelling." Electronic Thesis and Dissertation Repository, no. 2510, 121, The University of Western Ontario.

Musmar, A. 2017. "Environmentalizing Humanitarian Governance in Za'atri Refugee Camp: A Posthuman Approach." In *Architecture and Feminisms: Ecologies, Economies, Technologies*, edited by H. Frichot, C. Gabrielsson, and H. Runting, 181–91. London: Routledge.

Musmar, A. 2020. "Witnessing as a Feminist Spatial Practice: Encountering the Refugee Camp Beyond Recognition." PhD dissertation. University of Sheffield. http://etheses.whiterose.ac.uk/25927/.

Ramadan, A. 2008. "The Guests' Guests: Palestinian Refugees, Lebanese Civilians, and the War of 2006." *Antipode* 40, no. 4: 658–77.

Rosello, M. 2001. *Postcolonial Hospitality: The Immigrant as Guest*. Stanford, CA: Stanford University Press.

Shryock, A. 2008. "Thinking about Hospitality, with Derrida, Kant, and the Balga Bedouin." *Anthropos, Bd. (Nomos Verlagsgesellschaft mbH)* 103, no. 2: 405–21.

Siddiqui, M. 2015. *Hospitality and Islam: Welcoming in God's Name*. New Haven, CT: Yale University Press.

Simone, A. 2004. "People as Infrastructure: Intersecting Fragments in Johannesburg." *Public Culture* 16, no. 3: 407–29.

UNHCR. 2010. "UNHCR Code of Conduct and Explanatory Notes." *UNHCR* 50.

Westmoreland, M. W. 2008. "Interruptions: Derrida and Hospitality." *Kritike* 2: 1–10. https://doi.org/10.25138/2.1.e.1.

Between Securitization, Appropriation, and the Right to Dwell: A Multiscalar Analysis of Azraq Camp

Ayham Dalal, Petra Heber, and Leticia Palomino

Refugee camps are dispositives of care and control. While they offer refugees shelters, they also suspend them from inhabiting them. In this paper, and using the case of Azraq camp in Jordan, we will show how notions of securitization, appropriation, and dwelling are interlinked. By applying a multiscalar approach, we will demonstrate that refugees' appropriation will always be present from below regardless of how advanced the technologies of discipline used to hinder it are. Taking this tension between securitization and dwelling as a starting point, we situate dwelling as a cursor for exploring these spatial practices. While securitization prevents refugees from dwelling, appropriations fight to enable it. In that sense, not only will the power to appropriate and to inhabit be always present in camps whether planned or not, but it is within these cracks of thinking from above that moments of organic reorganization from below happen and a "right to dwell" can be called for.

Introduction

Since its opening in April 2014 in Jordan, Azraq camp has provoked multiple controversies. On the one hand, its layout utilized years of humanitarian expertise in camp planning, and its shelter was designed specifically for the site, taking into consideration innovative measures and experiences from other camps. The result was described by a UN official as "one of the best planned refugee camps in the world" (Oddone 2014). On the other hand, researchers have criticized this model for various reasons. In another paper, for instance, we have shown how the planning of Azraq camp, its layout, design, and planning strategies all contributed to camouflaging control over refugees while claiming the opposite (Dalal et al. 2018). Other researchers suggested that its planning ignored the actual "lessons learnt" from Zaatari camp (Gatter 2018), and some considered it as a new experiment where the agendas of the nation-state, humanitarianism, and neoliberalism all blurred into each other, while putting refugees' need for a dignified living on hold (Herscher 2017; Hoffmann 2017).

In this paper, we will extend the previous debates by showing how refugees responded to the securitization of the camp and appropriated the space for their personal needs. These appropriations were mapped on three interlinked spatial levels: the camp, the plot, and the shelter. To do so, we will first illustrate how the securitized planning of Azraq camp was influenced by two main objectives – distancing and sheltering. Then we will show how on a camp-level, refugees overcame the panopticon-like design by producing informal routes cutting through the original layout of the camp and by dismantling the empty shelters at different parts of the camp. The appropriations on the plot- and shelter-levels are interlinked as well and serve the purpose of dwelling.

Dwelling, habiting, home-making, and the camp

Following Heidegger (1971), we understand dwelling as an existential need, a mode of existence and *being* on earth that is prior to any other human condition. This phenomenological approach allows us to see dwelling as a force, a creative process (Heidegger 1971) that transcends in its immediacy and spontaneity any structured and top-down translations of this need, whether in the form of housing or shelter. This phenomenological understanding was carried further by Lefebvre who recognized a tension in between what he calls "habitat" and "habiting". He argues:

> Habitat, as ideology and practice, repulsed or buried habiting in the unconscious. Before habitat became commonplace, habiting was an age-old practice, poorly expressed, poorly articulated linguistically or conceptually, seen sometimes as vital and sometimes as degraded, but always concrete, that is, simultaneously functional, multifunctional, and transfunctional. During the reign of habitat, habiting disappeared from thought and deteriorated strongly in practice (Lefebvre 2003, 81).

This tension between habitat and habiting we incorporate into our understanding of dwelling. In fact, it might be difficult to distinguish "habiting" from "dwelling" for the words refer to the same act. Yet, we still consider Heidegger's phenomenological approach to dwelling as particularly important and relevant in the context of camps.

In other studies, refugees' attempt to dwell in camps was interpreted as home-making. In this study, we understand the importance of the term, yet we also cannot look far for its limitation. Home is a concept that is argued to be multiscalar and expressed on different levels: national, personal, societal (Brun and Fábos 2015; Hart et al. 2018). But can a tent be called a home? In fact, the emotional dimension that the term "home" carries with it takes us from the realm of the phenomenological, the direct, the immediate, the present, to the constructed, the mind-made, the imagined, and the articulated. This does not mean that dwelling does not implicitly incorporate a search for a home, but by insisting on the use of dwelling as a human phenomenon, we draw on the right to dwell as an important and neglected human need that is often compromised in the context of camps.

Refugee camps are built to deter dwelling, to prevent it from happening by suspending refugees' lives and producing a permanent temporariness. This is because camps are special types of spaces. They are "dispositives," an orchestration of elements, laws, architectures, and regulations, that come together at a given historical moment, aiming to respond to an "urgent need" (Foucault 1979, 195). By doing that, they subvert the rhythm of ordinary life (Agamben 1998). The shelter here cannot be seen as habitat in which habiting occurs. Beyond the emergency phase, a tent or a shelter is a suspension of the human need to dwell, and therefore a means to control and discipline. Having to live in a camp and in a shelter entails a form of disciplining for disobeying a globally constructed dispositive of mobility and borders.

In this paper, we understand refugees' response to all forms of disciplining in camps, across the medium of space as appropriations. According to Feldman and Stall (2004, 184), "appropriation" means "individuals' and groups' creation, choice, possession, modification, enhancement of, care for and/or simply intentional use of a space to make it one's own." In the Lefebvrian tradition, appropriation practices are regarded in the context of different actors, negotiating about power and control. Differently empowered actor groups compete for space (De Haan 2005). The focus in this study, however, lies on the refugees and specifically their suspended need to dwell manifesting in spatial structures. Appropriations can be an active choice as well as passive or even unconscious everyday behavior; they can be conducted by individuals as well as by groups of people (Feldman and Stall 2004).

Following this approach to appropriation, we see it as a force, a tactic, that embodies resistance to the dispositive of the camp. Many studies have addressed the agency of refugees through appropriation (Sanyal 2010; Ramadan 2013; Maqusi 2017). In this paper, we add to this by looking at their spatial impact on the camp as a whole and the shelter in particular. We will show that these appropriations are interlinked. Locally, they appear as responses and ad hoc solutions to challenges as they arise on the ground in refugees' everyday lives. But their sum reveals a tension between the securitized camp and the shelter on the one hand, and the need to dwell on the other. Between this suspension of ordinary life through the dispositive of the camp and the human need and power to dwell lies our understanding of appropriation.

Along these lines, we will present our findings. First by giving a background on our research methods and fieldwork, and then by exploring and juxtaposing the notions of "securitization" and "appropriation" within three interlinked scales: the camp, the plot, and the shelter.

Methodology and field limitations

The findings presented in this paper are influenced by the conditions of the field and its limitations. As mentioned earlier, Azraq camp is a refugee camp with high security measures that work in favor of hindering researchers from gathering data from the field. This is enforced by long waiting periods to obtain permissions to visit the camp; the hassle of organizing the trips with "anchor points," who are the relief organizations that would be responsible for the researchers in the field; and the challenge to be alone in the camp without being escorted by a police officer during the trips. For that purpose, the findings presented here are the result of two overlapping periods of research. The first was conducted by Dalal between 2017 and 2018 and was preparatory in nature. During 2017, Dalal was visiting the camp as a consultant for an NGO, and therefore, was able to learn about the camp through participatory observations. These were combined with various interviews with experts (site planners, shelter specialists, etc.) and refugees. However, the collected data were aimed at acquiring a general understanding of the camp and its planning. By the end of 2018, a trip to Azraq camp for research purposes allowed Dalal to map the appropriations made to plots and visit shelters. In 2019, Palomino and Heber extended the previous findings during three visits to Azraq camp. The initial observations were explored further through interviews with two households (belonging to an extended family from Dara'a) living on the same plot, participatory observations, walk-along interviews, and photo documentation. These observations were contrasted with official documents made public by the United Nations High Commissioner for Refugees (UNHCR) and other NGOs. Additionally, Palomino conducted an extensive study of the camp using Google Earth. During that field visit, the interviews were conducted in Arabic.[1] The collected visual data were then translated into architectural analytical drawings presented in this paper.[2]

The "securitized" planning of Azraq camp

In order to cope with a most-likely-to-occur "mass displacement" towards Jordan (Al-Rai 2013) in March 2013, the Jordanian government approved the plan to build a new camp in the area called Azraq (UN 2014). While this decision was taken in response to the waves of refugees arriving in Jordan on a daily basis, 2013 saw a gradual decrease in refugee counts. Therefore, the camp was kept in a "state of readiness" until the decision to officially open it was taken on April 30, 2014 (Oddone 2014; UN 2014, 4). In contrast to the stereotypical case, where refugee camps are built and planned rapidly and in an emergency situation, Azraq camp took around a year of "careful planning and attention" (Oddone 2014). According to the UNHCR representative in Jordan, Azraq camp was perceived as a role model in camp planning and implementation. It was described literally as "one of the best planned refugee camps in the world" (Oddone 2014). Thinking about mass-displaced populations, the camp was massive in size, stretching over a vast area of about 14.7 km². The camp was planned by the United Nations High Commissioner for Refugees (UNHCR) with the support of the Jordanian government and the Syrian Refugee Affairs Directorate (SRAD).

The planning of Azraq camp is distinctive for its restrictive spatial organization and militarized architecture. The securitization of the camp was enforced through planning, which utilized technology and discipline. For instance, in his book *Discipline and Punish*, Foucault (1979) suggests that a disciplinary space is one that is partitioned, enclosed, and cellular at the first place; a space that situates bodies vis-à-vis relations of power. The relationship between power and bodies results in what he calls an "analytical space" in which circulations are controlled, bodies are "fixed" in place, ranked, registered, and controlled through tables, and where unwanted groupings and contact are reduced to the minimum. All these aspects are reflected in the way Azraq camp has been planned. For instance, the camp has been divided into four "villages."

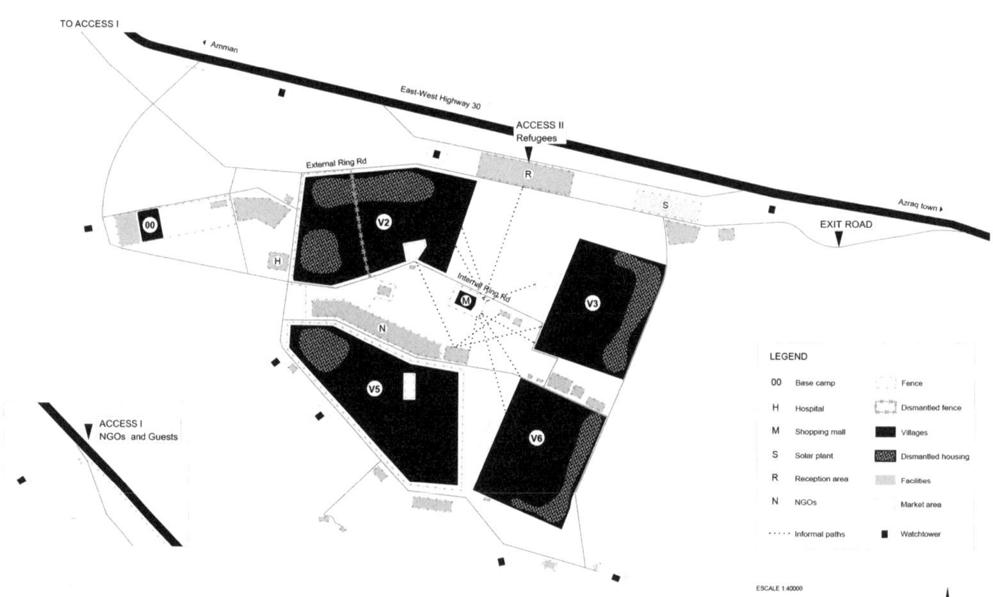

Figure 1. A map of Azraq camp showing the spatial strategies and military architecture used in its production.
Source: Authors

or sub-camps. Each of the villages is divided further into districts, and districts into plots, and each plot into an identical set of shelters. Arguably, this "village-based approach aims to foster a greater sense of ownership and community among residents" (UNHCR 2019, 2). However, what it actually does is locate and fix refugees in space, making them easily locatable through a numeric system containing the numbers of the village, plot, and shelter where they live. These data are stored in tables and lists and kept at the disposal of the camp's management when needed. This systematic division of space does not only fix refugees in place, but also reduces contact and possibilities for riots or resistance. This is achieved by placing the villages apart from each other, from the main road, and from the base camp where the management of the camp is located. This technique prevents big groupings and, according to the site planner, ensures that refugees would need at least 20 minutes to reach the base camp in case of riots.

Figure 2. Cars in Azraq camp used as a modern technology that enhances the securitization of its planning. Source: Authors

The disciplining of space in Azraq camp relied on technology, too. Particularly, the use of the car and mobility networks produced a panopticon-like effect where refugees remain under the gaze of those who manage the camp. As explained by Foucault (1979), a panopticon is a space where prisoners are placed in cells, elevated, all facing a central tower. This particular design allows the officer who is located at the center of the panopticon – on the tower – to constantly observe what prisoners do in their cells. The *gaze* of the officer, therefore, controls the prisoners and ensures that the space is disciplined (Foucault 1979). This panopticon effect was produced through the arrangement of shelters, plots, villages, and the organization of the street network in Azraq camp. For instance, the shelters were fixed and distanced from each other, allowing the gaze to reach between the shelters – in contrast to the crowded Zaatari camp. According to a refugee resident of Azraq camp, they were warned by the camp manager saying, "I want to stand between shelters and be able to see the end of the camp." This humanitarian gaze on refugees, which is practiced also by the Jordanian police, was enhanced through the mobility network and the use of the car. The four villages were distanced from each other and connected only using street networks, which comprised an external and an internal road (Fig. 1). Accessing this mobility network is made possible only for those visiting or managing the camp because refugees in Azraq camp are deprived of the possibility to drive or own cars. This means that the use of the car and the planning of the camp made parts of the camp distanced from each other for refugees, and easily accessible for humanitarian workers and Jordanian police. Moreover, the arrangement of the villages around an internal and external road network makes spotting refugees within the space of the camp easier, especially if they attempt to cross the no-man's land between the villages. In that sense, the street structure with the help of a technological invention, namely the car, produced a panopticon-like effect where refugees cannot escape the gaze of those roaming the camp in their cars (Fig. 2).

In addition to distancing (using cars and street networks), the camp is also securitized by the extensive use of fences and watch towers. Chain-link fences topped with razor wire and bent outwards are the most common. They enclose every NGO facility, community center, playground, and infrastructure. Some important facilities like the base camp are even double-fenced using materials of better quality such as steel profiles of larger section (IPE or similar), building sturdier fences. Fencing is also used at the checkpoints and for enclosing Village 5 and Village 2. These villages hosted refugees suspected of having lived in areas controlled previously by ISIS and thus, considered to be a threat. Refugees stay at Village 2 while they are being screened through a security check and their identity is clear. Once they are not considered suspects anymore, they can apply to relocate to another village. Otherwise, they will permanently move to Village 5, which is double-fenced inside the camp and has its own infrastructure. Watch towers are situated around the camp overlooking strategically sensitive areas such as the entrance and the exit of the camp, the base camp, and specially Village 5 (see Fig. 2).

T-shelter and plot design

The so-called T-shelter (short for "transitional shelter") was designed specifically for Azraq camp, taking into consideration the climatic, financial, and cultural constraints. The size of the shelter adds up to 32 m² with a spacious all-purpose room of 24 m² and a belatedly added kitchen of 8 m². In total, it takes four people between 12 and 16 hours to set up a T-shelter (UNHCR 2016). The standard allocation in Azraq camp comes to six people per shelter. If a family has more members, a second shelter is allocated. The peculiarity of the T-shelter is its fixed foundation. This limits the possibilities of spatial variations, unlike at Zaatari camp, where the caravans were movable and modifi-

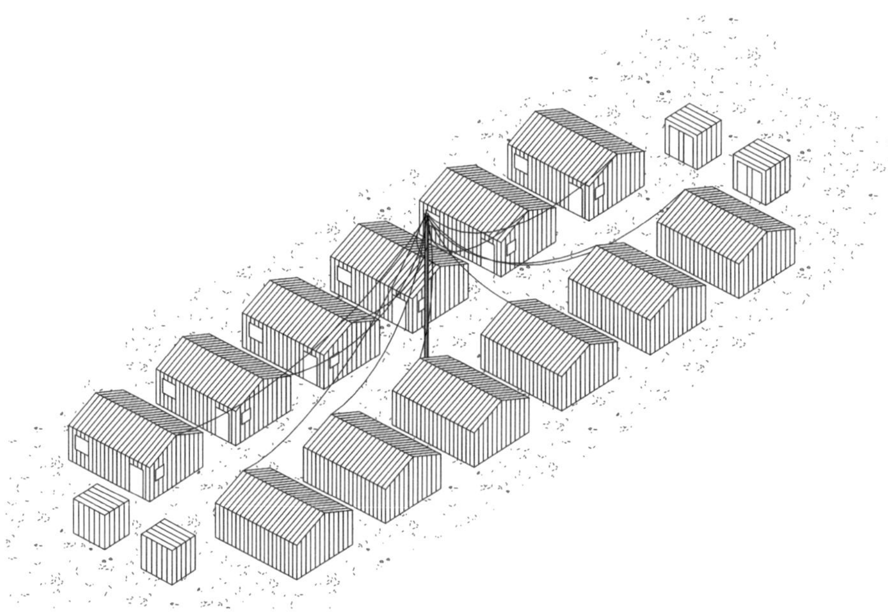

Figure 3. The planned plots in Azraq camp consisting of 12 shelters and four WASH facilities. Here, the entrances are as planned on the side of the T-shelter. Source: Authors

Figure 4. Refugees crossing the empty no-man's land between the villages along an informal route. Source: Authors

able. The allocation of T-shelters within the plots attempts to create smaller residential units. For that purpose, six T-shelters are placed facing each other across a rectangular communal space measuring 4 to 45 meters ending with two WASH (Water, Sanitation, Hygiene) facilities (one washing facility for men and one for women on each side). This structure is often repeated six times along the plot, which is thus composed of 12 T-shelters (Fig. 3). Additionally, the design of the T-shelter was initially enhanced with a tilted entrance to increase the privacy for its residents. However, this option was not implemented due to financial restrictions. Together with the security restrictions mentioned above, this adds to the idea of producing a securitized camp from the perspective of its management (UNHCR and SRAD). The following section shows how refugees took part in carving out the space of the camp by appropriating on three levels: the camp, the plot, and the shelter.

Appropriating the camp

The securitized and disciplinary planning of Azraq camp resulted into two main practices: the emergence of informal routes and the dismantlement of shelters. Those practices were observed during field visits and mapped using Google satellite images. (Obviously there is a limit to these data, dependent on when they were taken and their resolution. However, comparing the digital data with the data from the field visits confirmed the situation.) The allocation of vital facilities such as the central mall and the main hospital apart from villages and the main access resulted in the emergence of an informal transportation network crossed by foot or bicycles that links these elements together (Fig. 4). This network demonstrates refugees' attempts to live in the camp beyond security measures – to experience it as a living environment. The failure of the camp's planning to embed this notion reminds us of Modernist planning that can still be traced within humanitarian planning and management even today. This approach is still visible within the UNHCR manuals despite the call to shift towards "sustainable" and "integrated" planning (see UNHCR 2014).

The second example is dismantling empty T-shelters. Azraq camp was initially planned to host around 120,000 refugees but its current population is about 35,000

(UNHCR 2019). This has left many empty T-shelters dispersed around the camp, especially on the outskirts of Village 3 and Village 6. The dismantled zinco sheets are often detached from the metal skeleton of the T-shelter and the concrete slab and are used to enhance inhabited shelters. While policing during the first few years of the camp restricted this process, it became less effective later on. Generally, this process results in the production of zones filled with dramatic ruins within Azraq camp, standing as material manifestation of its gradually eroding bio-power and disciplinary planning (Fig. 5).

Appropriating the plot

In contrast to the bigger scale of the camp, appropriating the plot reveals a variety of spatial practices. The purpose of these practices is to give new meanings to the empty space around shelters, and by doing so, to enhance the social and functional quality of the plot. Two main practices were observed: the expansion of shelters and the reuse of shared spaces and WASH infrastructures such as shared toilets located on the sides of each plot. Those were mapped on a studied plot in Village 3. The plot was inhabited by extended families from Dara'a who arrived at Azraq camp in 2014 (Fig. 6).

Expanding the space of the shelters was the most observed practice during fieldwork. It was implemented by either closing the gap between two adjacent shelters with zinco sheets; adding spaces towards the back (outside the plot); or stretching towards the shared WASH facilities. Those expansions are constructed by metal sheets (from dismantled shelters), wooden beams, and textiles. They prevent unwanted gazes, protect from wind and dust, and allow refugees to create useful spaces like storage rooms, kitchens, washing facilities, and fenced courtyards. Filling the gap between two adjacent shelters was the most common as it is easily constructed and less visible in contrast to expansions towards the back which can be noticed from outside the plot. Similarly, the expansions towards WASH facilities can be easily noticed; however,

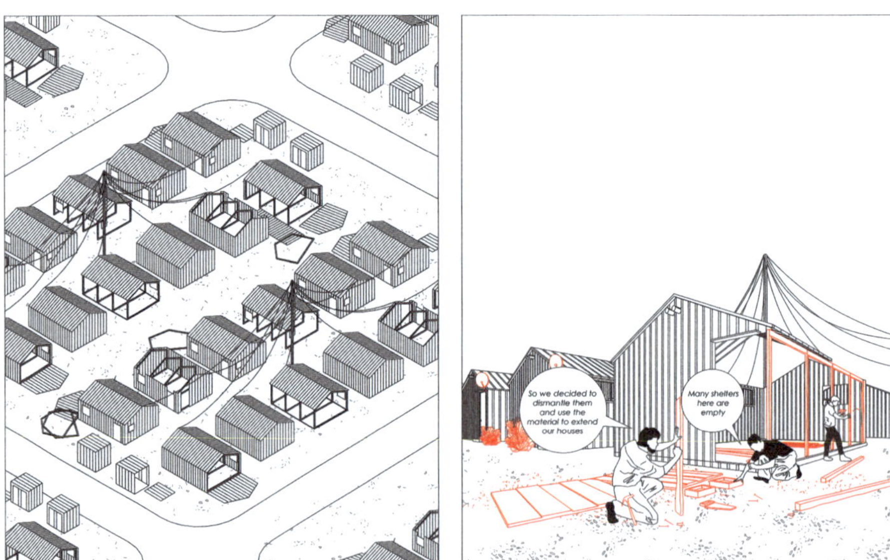

Figure 5. A perspective showing the zones of dismantled T-shelters. Source: Authors

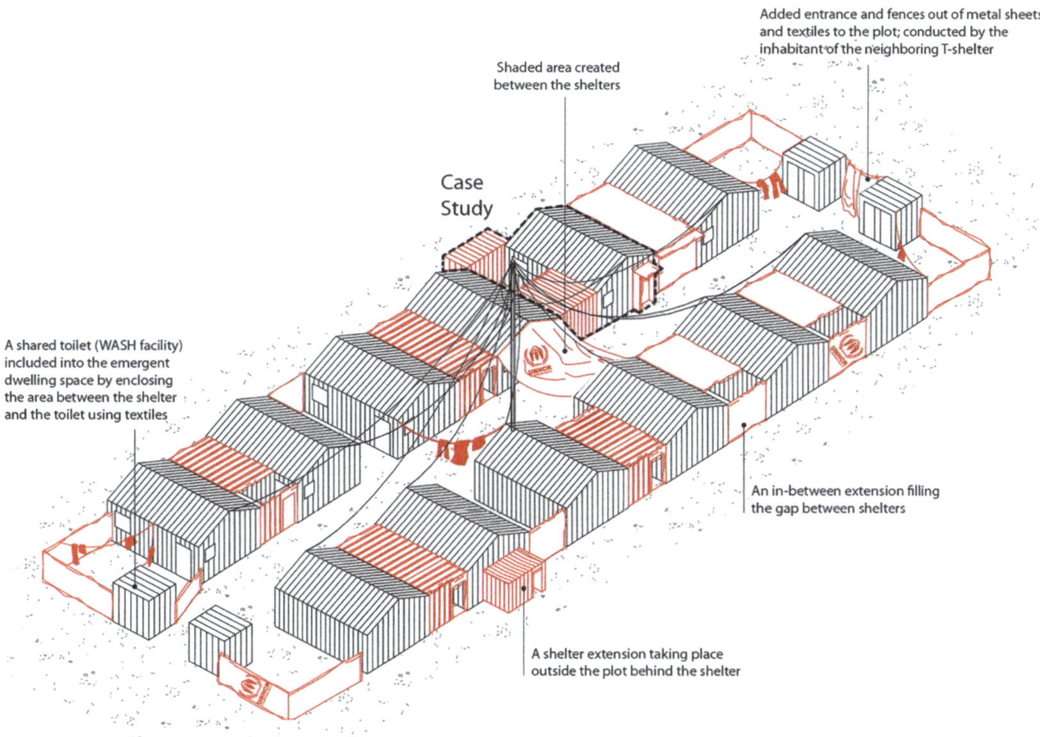

Figure 6. The mapped practices on the examined plot showing how it was transformed from a restrictive plan into a lively neighborhood. Source: Authors

they are often constructed with textiles as to suggest that these appropriations are temporary. They are often used as courtyards and seating areas for the adjacent shelters.

In addition, refugees appropriate the rectangular nucleus of the plot including its shared space and infrastructures. For instance, in the studied plot, some families extended their shelter expansion to include one of the shared bathrooms so it can be used by members of this family only. Such rearrangements require consensus and internal negotiations between the inhabitants of the plot. Other changes to the shared space within a plot include creating an entrance to the plot (by adding a fabric door between the WASH facilities), adding washing lines between shelters, planting herbs, creating a raised step next to the shelters to prevent rainwater from entering shelters, and adding shading between shelters (Fig. 7). All these practices not only enhance the social and environmental quality of the space, but they also effectively help in transforming the strictly planned identical plots into diverse, lively, and slightly more humane neighborhoods. Such appropriations extend to the inner space of the shelter as well.

Figure 7. The appropriation of the shared space between shelters within the studied plot. Source: Authors

Appropriating the shelter

The appropriation of shelters means that refugees have to negotiate, on the one hand, the daily needs of their families (social, cultural, habitual), and on the other hand, the spatial-material settings in which the shelters are constructed (their dimensions, spatial organizations, and location within the plot). This has resulted in various forms of shelter appropriations. To give an example, we will take a closer look at one of the shelters within the same studied plot.

The studied shelter was inhabited by a family of six from Dara'a: a mother in her mid 30s, a husband in his 40s, and four children (two teenage boys and two infant daughters). They entered Jordan in 2013 and were initially hosted in Zaatari camp for one day. Afterwards, they moved to the suburbs of Amman (Khirbet El Souq) where they soon settled with other Syrian refugees. Later on, however, they were moved by the Jordanian authorities to Azraq camp where they have been living since 2014.

Upon arrival, the family lived in the single space of the shelter, used its built-in kitchen, and relied on the communal bathrooms/toilets constructed on the sides of the plot. To protect the shelter from wind and dust, and to increase its privacy, the family started to enclose the gap between their shelter and the neighboring one, using metal sheets extracted from the empty shelters. Once the gap was partly closed, the space in between became more private and was used by the family to store things and dry clothes. Over time, they appropriated that newly created space and used it as a kitchen. Simultaneously, and because the original entrance of the shelter was now blocked, they added a new entrance door facing the shared space between the shelters. To increase its privacy, a small metallic cantilever was added around it. By doing so, the original space of the kitchen functioned as a lobby during the day and a sleeping room for the children during the night – where mattresses could be easily added and removed (Fig. 9). It also functioned as a dry area to store mattresses, blankets, and other belongings, in contrast to the open court in the appropriated gap space, which was used to dry clothes, store gas cylinders and building materials, and to install a ventilation mechanism called the "Desert AC." The Desert AC (air conditioner) resembles a form of modern *Malqaf* (windcatcher), which is an important element in Islamic architecture used for improving the thermal conditions of buildings and cleaning the air of dust. Instead of the long empty neck attached to a building and ending up with a small pool of water, however, the device is composed of a fan, placed on a tray filled with water, and inserted into the wall of the shelter, facing – or surrounded by – a coconut mesh to clear the air of dust (Fig. 8). It plays an important role in improving the thermal quality of the shelter during hot summers. Consequently, the Desert AC was observed in most of the examined shelters and was built with

Figure 8. The Desert AC as it appears from the back, inside the open court and within the shelter space. Source: Authors

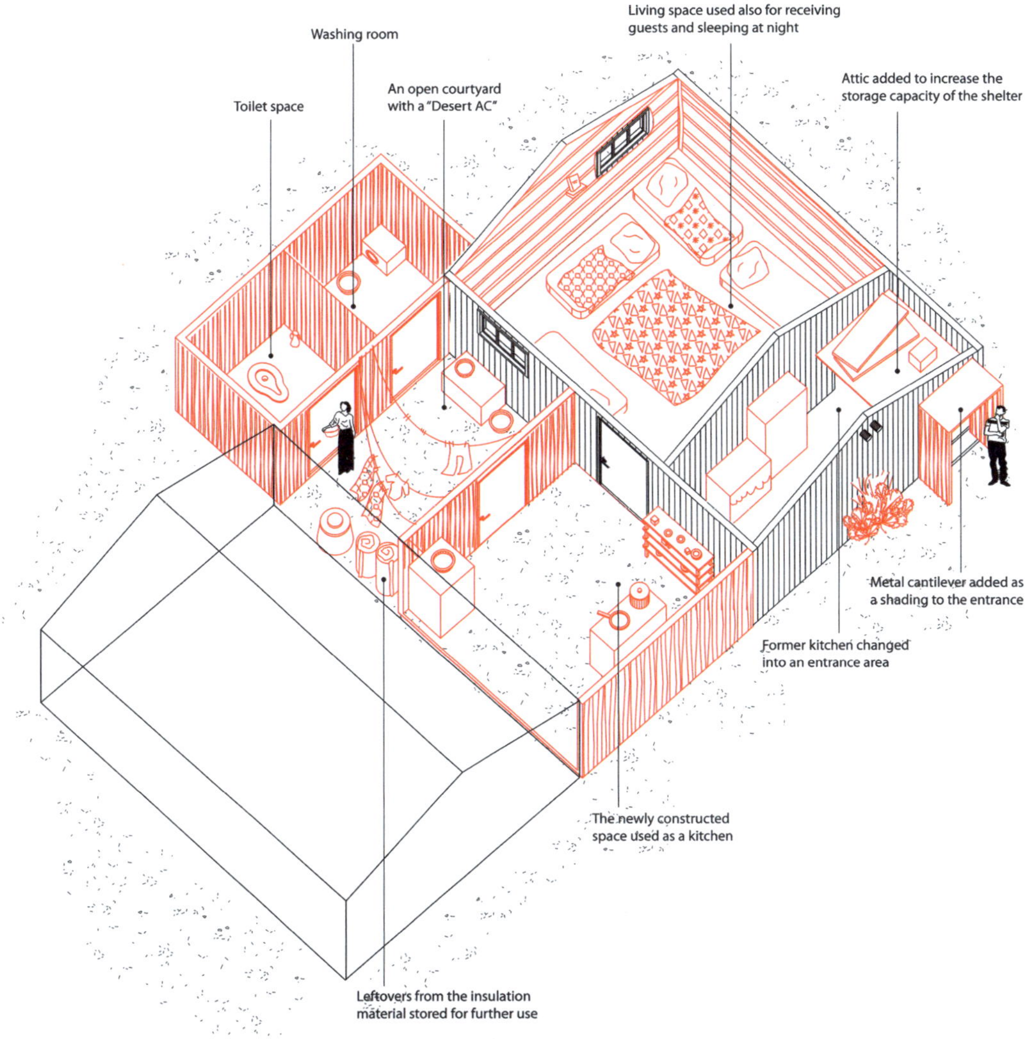

Figure 9. An example of an appropriated shelter in Azraq camp showing the added spaces and their functions. Source: Authors

the help of refugees with construction experience in the camp for about 40 Jordanian dollars (around 50 euros).

Over time, the family felt the need to increase their privacy, and thus decided to construct their own bathing area at the end of the space between the shelters. Using metal sheets extracted from empty shelters, the space was divided into a washing room and a bathing/toilet space. The main space of the shelter kept its central role as the space for daily activities. It can be transformed into a living room, a dining room, a salon for guests, or a main bedroom for parents at the end of the day. The floor is covered with carpets and laid out with several mattresses. These mattresses can be used for different purposes; when a purpose changes, residents simply add or remove items. Textile curtains at the windows impart a warm feeling in the room and protect from sunlight as well as unwanted gazes. Pillows welcome the visitors and inhabitants to sit comfortably on the low mattresses during the day and can be assorted in various ways. A small bookshelf next to the window stores a few personal items (Fig. 9).

While these practices transform the empty space of the shelter into a more livable space, this does not immediately transform the shelter into a private house or a dwelling. Looking inside the shelters, one could see the odd-looking insulation material with its shiny silver color covering the inner surface of the shelter, as if reminding refugees of the temporariness of this space and its humanitarian and emergency nature. Adopting these different mitigating measures, refugees try to give meaning to the spaces in which they suddenly find themselves by appropriating them, even if temporarily (Fig. 10).

Figure 10. Insulation added to the inner surface of shelters reminding refugees of their temporariness. Source: Authors

From securitization to discipline, and from appropriation to dwelling

Despite being praised for its planning and innovation, Azraq remains one of the more understudied refugee camps. Access for researchers is made difficult by the complex procedures to enter the field; and collecting data is made problematic as researchers are escorted by a police officer whose gaze could interfere with what is being said and looked at. In this research we tried to take these aspects into consideration, and to maneuver the field by relying heavily on participant observations, visual analysis (of satellite images and architectures), interviews with experts and relief workers in and outside the camp, and by reducing interviews with refugees to the minimum. The data collected and presented in this paper, were therefore, the result of extended and dispersed visits to Azraq camp between 2017 and 2019, and the findings aimed to reflect on two pairs: securitization and discipline, and appropriation and inhabitation.

Securitization in refugee camps can be a blurry notion, allowing different agendas to meet and manifest. This was shown in the ways in which state security has met with humanitarian and neoliberal agendas in Azraq camp (Hoffmann 2017). Nonetheless, the examination of space – that is, the planning of the camp and its spatial arrangement – reveals an important element that helps securitization to materialize, which is discipline. In Azraq camp, discipline is not enforced by sets of regulations, but is as Foucault suggests "a game of mind," where the organization of space and its elements seeks to control refugees and their bodies. The placement of shelters, plots, districts, and villages helps to fix refugees in place; prevent groupings, riots, and unwanted contacts; make refugees easily locatable through an address system and therefore screened and listed; and most importantly produces a panopticon-like effect where refugees are constantly under the gaze of relief workers and policemen roaming the camp with their cars. The use of the car and mobility network in this particular case show a rather modern and new typology of the panopticon in contrast to its traditional form, underlining the importance of planning and its ability to reproduce power relations and to utilize knowledge and technology for that purpose. Particularly here, the use of the car and mobility network presents a new way in which distancing is produced, and the panopticon is put into practice. This means that discipline in refugee camps is fundamentally spatial in nature. Further research on how this is manifested and practiced in other contexts is needed to advance the scholarly perspective on this notion. Foucault's writings in this regard can be a suitable starting point.

Securitization and discipline are faced with appropriation and dwelling in Azraq camp. Although the camp was declared as one of the best planned in the world and presented itself almost as a fortress of security and discipline, refugees have managed to appropriate its various spaces. On the one hand, this underlines the fact that, no matter how much discipline is sought in a refugee camp, refugees will always appropriate the space. This message is important for planners and architects, as well as to humanitarian workers, whose responsibilities entail planning camps. Despite all the attempts to restrict refugees and fixate them in space, they manage to find ways in which they humanize the space of the camp, interacting with its various elements. It is clear that the agency of refugees cannot be buried or ignored through planning tricks and technologies. It is time to give space for these appropriations to take place within the given frames of any planned camp around the world.

Moreover, in this paper we showed that the appropriation of refugee camps is a multiscalar process, and its purpose is to make dwelling possible. Aspects like the emergence of informal routes, the dismantling of empty shelters, and the enclosure of spaces around the shelter might appear random if observed separately, yet considering them together changes the way in which the camp is lived and experienced. Through incremental and tactical acts, these appropriations defy the contours of disciplinary powers on one hand, while enabling refugees to occupy the space and dwell on the other. For that purpose, refugees have utilized various resources. The shelter was not used as planned – a "container" of complex social relations and therefore, an abstract space (Lefebvre 1991); but it was occupied with complex and dynamic social relations. Notions of privacy, family structures, functions, and boundaries are brought into that abstract space of the shelter. Through negotiating and spatializing these relations, the shelter is not just being appropriated; it is being dwelt.

Consequently, the Heideggerian notion of dwelling is strongly linked to appropriations in refugee camps. By appropriation we not only addressed the ways in which refugees personalize the space and make it enjoyable (see Lefebvre 2014); but we also understood it as a form of resistance to disciplinary powers, a manifestation of a universal need to dwell (Heidegger 1971). Similar results were found in other camps like Zaatari in Jordan (Dalal 2020), and Tempohomes in Berlin (Dalal et al. 2021). This means that no matter how well-planned or disciplined the space of the camp is, it will inevitably be appropriated. The purpose of these appropriations is to allow refugees to dwell. Until there is a universal "right to dwell," the planning of refugee camps needs to embrace appropriations for they enable refugees to dwell creatively. Dwelling needs to be given as a right (from state actors to planners and architects, etc.) to the refugee. The power to dwell, the power to inhabit and alter, the power to appropriate is always present from below. It is the problem of institutions from above (state, planning and design practices, etc.) that have tried to control and regulate this already existing right that have given rise to this problem. It is actually within the cracks of thinking from above that moments of organic reorganization from below happen. Perhaps the issue is how we define rights in the modern sense – in this case, the spatial right to appropriate – while appropriation of space will happen regardless, planned or not. This approach does not only underline dwelling as an important drive towards the spatial transformation of refugee camps, but also urges us to think of our dwelling practices beyond the restrictive boundaries of the camp.

This article emerged out of a shorter version called "Appropriating Azraq Camp" appearing in Camps: A Genealogy of Refugee Camps in the Middle East, edited by Ayham Dalal and Kamel Doraï (forthcoming). We are grateful to the editors for their encouragement to explore the theoretical notions behind this work. We would also like to thank Veronika Zaripova for her support in producing the final illustrations. Finally, we would like to mention that this research was made possible through the financial support of the Deutsche Forschungsgemeinschaft (DFG, German Research Foundation) – Projektnummer 290045248 – SFB 1265 and Erasmus+ Mobility Fund (KA 107).

1 The authors would like to thank Sara Nowar, a master's student at TU Berlin – El Gouna campus, for her support during the fieldwork and for helping in translating the interviews from Arabic to English. **2** It should be mentioned that the findings of this research in Azraq camp were compared and contrasted with those gathered within the framework of the research project "Architectures of Asylum" at the Technische Universität Berlin. The research project was hosted at the Collaborative Research Centre "Re-Figurations of Space" (SFB1265), which aims to examine the appropriation of camps in Jordan and Berlin (Tempohomes). Palomino and Heber's research stay in Jordan was also assisted by the Erasmus+ funds, through an exchange program between Jordan and Germany.

References

Agamben, G. 1998. *Homo Sacer: Sovereign Power and Bare Life.* Stanford, CA: Stanford University Press.

Al-Rai. n.d. *Rabaa Al-Sarhan: a transit center soon to receive Syrian refugees* [in Arabic]. Accessed January 5, 2021. http://alrai.com/article/568948.html.

Brun, C., and A. Fábos. 2015. "Making Homes in Limbo? A Conceptual Framework." *Refuge: Canada's Journal on Refugees* 31, no. 1: 5–17.

Dalal, A. 2020. "From Shelters to Dwellings: On the Construction of Dwellings in Zaatari Refugee Camp, Jordan." PhD dissertation. Technische Universität Berlin.

Dalal, A., A. Darweesh, P. Misselwitz, and A. Steigemann. 2018. "Planning the Ideal Refugee Camp? A Critical Interrogation of Recent Planning Innovations in Jordan and Germany." *Urban Planning* 3, no. 4: 64–78.

Dalal, A., and K. Doraï, eds. Forthcoming. *Camps: A Genealogy of Refugee Camps in the Middle East.* Beirut: Presses de l'Ifpo.

Dalal, A., A. Fraikin, and A. Noll. Forthcoming. "Appropriating Tempohomes." In *Spatial Transformations: The Effect of Mediatization, Mobility, and Social Dislocation on the Re-Figuration of Spaces*, edited by A. Million, C. Haid, I. Castillo Ulloa and N. Baur. Routledge.

De Haan, H. 2005. "Social and Material Appropriation of Neighborhood Space: Collective Space and Resistance in a Dutch Urban Community." Paper presented at the international conference *Doing, Thinking, Feeling Home: The Mental Geography of Residential Environments.* Delft University of Technology, October 14–15. Wageningen: Wageningen University.

Feldman, R. M. and S. Stall. 2004. *The Dignity of Resistance: Women Residents' Activism in Chicago Public Housing.* Cambridge: Cambridge University Press.

Foucault, M. 1979. *Discipline and Punish: The Birth of the Prison*, translated by A. Sheridan. New York: Vintage Books.

Gatter, M. 2018. "Rethinking the Lessons from Za'atari Refugee Camp." *Forced Migration Review* 57: 22–24.

Hart, J., N. Paszkiewicz, and D. Albadra. 2018. "Shelter as Home?: Syrian Homemaking in Jordanian Refugee Camps." *Human Organisation* 77, no. 4: 371–80.

Heidegger, M. 1971. *Poetry, Language, Thought*, translated by A. Hofstadter. New York: Harper & Row.

Herscher, A. 2017. *Critical Spatial Practice 9: Displacements – Architecture and Refugee*, edited by N. Hirsch and M. Miessen. Berlin: Sternberg Press.

Hoffmann, S. 2017. "Humanitarian Security in Jordan's Azraq Camp." *Security Dialogue* 48, no. 2: 97–112.

Lefebvre, H. 1991. *The Production of Space*, translated by D. Nicholson-Smith. Oxford: Blackwell Publishing.

Lefebvre, H. 2003. *The Urban Revolution*, translated by Robert Bononno. Minneapolis, MN: University of Minnesota Press.

Lefebvre, H. 2014. *Toward an Architecture of Enjoyment*, edited by Ł. Stanek. Minneapolis, MN: University of Minnesota Press.

Maqusi, S. 2017. "Space of Refuge: Negotiating Space with Refugees Inside the Palestinian Camp." *Humanities* 6, no. 3: 1–9.

Oddone, E. 2014. "Azraq Refugee Camp Officially Opened', *Jordan Times*, April 30, 2014, http://www.jordantimes.com/news/local/azraq-refugee-camp-officially-opened.

Ramadan, A. 2013. "Spatialising the Refugee Camp." *Transactions of the Institute of British Geographers* 38, no. 1: 65–77.

Sanyal, R. 2010. "Squatting in Camps: Building and Insurgency in Spaces of Refuge." *Urban Studies* 48, no. 5: 877–90.

UN. 2014. *Syria Regional Response Plan: Jordan.* https://data2.unhcr.org/en/situations/syria.

UNHCR. 2014. *Shelter and Settlement Strategy, Syrian Refugee Crisis, Shelter Working Group – Jordan*, 1–15.

UNHCR. 2016. *Shelter Design Catalogue,* UNHCR Shelter and Settlement Section, https://reliefweb.int/report/world/shelter-design-catalogue.

UNHCR. 2019. *Azraq Camp – Facts Sheet November 2019,* UNHCR Amman. https://reliefweb.int/report/jordan/unhcr-jordan-factsheet-azraq-refugee-camp-november-2019.

PART II
INHABITING THE "CITY"

Interview with Gregor Brune, a Practicing Architect

Shahd Seethaler-Wari

In June 2018, Dr. Shahd Seethaler-Wari interviewed architect Gregor Brune from the city of Göttingen about his building project Integrated Refugee Accommodation and Meeting Center (IFUB).[1] The project aimed at transforming an old hospital in Hann. Münden, a town in the district of Göttingen, into a refugee accommodation. It consisted of two phases: an analytical study and a design-and-construction phase.

The project started in early 2016, a time linked to fast, unpredictable geopolitical events and decisions in response to the increasing number of asylum seekers arriving at European borders followed by the so-called EU-Turkey Deal. The interview aimed to understand the main challenges for architects while working on refugee accommodation projects during such uncertain times. The interviewer also asked Mr. Brune about his opinion as a practitioner on the response of German cities and the readiness of urban planners, and designers in general, to react effectively in emergency situations.

Shahd Seethaler-Wari: Mr. Brune, I am interested in learning about the challenges that urban planners and practicing architects have been facing when working on refugee accommodation and housing projects in such a fast-changing geopolitical environment. Maybe you can start by telling me a little bit about the IFUB project.[2]

Gregor Brune: Of course. The IFUB project started at the peak of the *refugee crisis,*[3] in November 2015, when the head of the social services department of the Göttingen region at the time contacted us, looking for an architect to analyze the possibility of transforming the former hospital Hann. Münden into a new type of refugee accommodation. This new type was intended to facilitate a stronger and faster integration of refugees into the regular labor market through various offers. Hence the title Integrated Refugee Accommodation and Meeting Centre. Furthermore, the goal was to plan future uses involving the neighborhood, which would transcend the medium-term use as refugee accommodation.

We were directly assigned by the district to conduct a study to elaborate the necessary steps of the transformation, analyzing the whole complex of buildings, which the district had to take over after the hospital had gone bankrupt. Some of the buildings were not fit for further use and, therefore, needed to be torn down. Furthermore, the task was to elaborate a concept for both short-term (that is, refugee accommodation) and long-term use (possible subsequent uses).

Our study started, on the one hand, with a basic analysis of the building structure, and, on the other, with the dynamics of the ongoing *refugee crisis*, which might influence our design process. This project phase was accompanied by a series of public discussions with local and regional actors, including the MPI.[4] After the study, there was a public call for the realization of the project, as the sums involved were too big to be given directly to one office. Our office won the tender. Both the study and the main project were financed by the district of Göttingen. This was a rather unusual situation, as the public authorities mainly tried to invest in temporary settlements (mostly container villages) at the time.

You have mentioned that the developments on the ground affected the character of the project. Can you elaborate on that?

In the beginning, as many asylum seekers were arriving daily, the aim of the project was to create an emergency shelter. The standpoint of the district at the time was to house as many people as possible in the building complex, resulting in a hostel-like character rather than a permanent housing typology. Then the *refugee crisis* took a different turn in Germany when the majority of refugees were stopped in Turkey.[5] This resulted in a significant decrease in new arrivals, which had a considerable effect on our planning. The district then communicated that the refugees who still needed to be housed were not asylum seekers anymore; they had a residency permit. Therefore, it could no longer be expected of them to remain in district-run hostel-like refugee accommodations. They now had the right to choose their own housing situation. So, we had to change the project's short-term aim because no one would voluntarily stay in a hostel room with many other people unless they would otherwise have no roof over their heads. If there were enough affordable housing available, one would look for an apartment elsewhere. It was then that we decided that we needed to make sure that the project offered apartments of a certain type. The process dragged on in 2016 and 2017 and took a very long time, during which we had to revise the project several times due to changed settings. So now, we took a shift towards more common housing typologies with an apartment-like structure. For this, we had to redesign most of the floor plans, which, in the end, turned out to be for the best. The apartments are suitable for permanent housing. The hostel-like structure would have functioned mainly as temporary accommodation.

In our study, we had actually planned this versatility of the structure in the long run. However, we had expected that the change towards permanent housing forms would be implemented in a few years. Instead, the whole design underwent this change while we were still planning, and partly already building.

Originally, we had proposed three phases of development for the building complex. For phase I, we planned almost no structural interventions. The idea was to provide accommodation quickly in the former hospital rooms. We expected this phase to last about one year. Phase II included significant structural interventions including tearing down inadequate buildings. For that step, some of the buildings would have had to be evacuated in order to enable an unhindered construction process, while others would still serve as accommodation. We had expected this phase to last about five years, or possibly longer. In phase II people would have been living in mixed forms of accommodation ranging from family apartments to hostel-like rooms. Finally, in phase III, the building complex would undergo a final transformation to affordable housing units.

However, closing the borders resulted in taking the goal of quickly accommodating as many people as possible off the main agenda, and acted, in a way, as a catalyst in the development. Thus, the project took the exact turn that we had foreseen, but within months instead of years. We quickly reached phase III – long-term accommodation. At the beginning of the project, the building was meant to house up to 260 people by September 2016 (phase I) and around 250 people in the medium term (phase II). Ultimately, the building ended up housing around 70 people in total (phase III).

You mentioned that this shift in the strategy turned out to be for the best in the end, in your opinion, at least with regard to the floor plans. Were there also other, unfavorable consequences?

Certainly, this development did not fail to leave its mark on the project. In fact, it had a variety of effects. For example, we had concerns about the consequences for public procurement law, to which this *refugee crisis* had brought considerable relief. This is especially in the area of public calls, which were otherwise very official, very complicated, very "German," one could say. In this exceptional situation the authorities were saying that we had to respond quickly to get things done. There were many simplifications in the area of public procurement law, for example in the area of the Energy Saving Ordinance. Then, the EU-Turkey Deal was sealed. Consequently, the audit offices, which monitor procurement law as an independent body to a certain extent, suddenly had second thoughts. This led to us not being able to commission companies for the building of heating, ventilation, sanitation, and electrical installations at the beginning of 2017 as was originally planned. Instead, they were commissioned with a 10-month delay, in October 2017. In these months we continued to work, of course, but we had to cut everything down to the minimum, otherwise we would have quickly reached a point where we couldn't go any further.

Altogether, we are quite happy with how the project turned out. I am very proud of my team – we have endured all of this with a lot of patience. Naturally, we also wanted to earn money with the project. It would have been easier for us to earn money if we could have finished the project in one and a half years as planned, instead of three years. But again, I would still say it is OK, because we reduced our efforts to a minimum during the times when we didn't know where this was all going. In the end, this project was actually very much at the mercy of the changing political climate and related factors. What if the laws changed again? What if Turkey changed its mind and opened its borders? Of course, then we would have had to revisit the project and decide how to fit more people in.

Would you please explain the changes that occurred throughout the project?

The main building, also called the *Winkelbau*,[6] is the only one that underwent considerable changes and structural interventions. It proved to be in a worse state than expected. Once we started looking closely into the structure, we found more and more things to do. The foundations had to be improved in some parts; the slabs didn't meet the fire safety requirements, so we had to reinforce them; the plumbing was bad, etc. Due to the rather steep terrain, this building has two ground-floor levels – one on the hillside and one on the valley side. These two levels were planned to accommodate functions that could be used by everybody in the neighborhood as a form of community center. The upper floors were to house the actual private living areas.

Kopfbau[7] is the oldest building in the complex, dating back to 1870. It has been listed as a protected monument. We used it briefly in phase I, after which we sealed it and it is still not in use. It is a beautiful building but restoring it properly would cost a lot. Moreover, due to unfavorable real estate conditions in Hann. Münden and its location, even selling it to a developer doesn't seem to be a viable option.

The *Gartenhaus*, on the other hand, is a fairly well-preserved building, so we were able to quickly transform it into an emergency shelter in phase I. It turned out to be the

Figure 1. Site plan. Source: RSE+

only building ready to be used with minimal changes, and ultimately the only emergency shelter on the compound. It served as an intermediate structure able to house at least a few dozen people while we were renovating the main buildings.

The rest of the buildings were the most recent additions dating back to the seventies and the eighties. They were not in a condition to be preserved and also would have stood in the way of using the *Winkelbau* and *Kopfbau* for residential purposes.

All these twists and turns made the project more complicated than expected, resulting in increased time and expenditure. In order to deal with the consequence of having spent money on unexpected things, especially given that the budget was set, we developed our sufficiency principle. We decided to make a virtue out of necessity and say, this is not a condominium building where people pay a lot of money to live in luxurious apartments with smooth walls, but it's for people with less money, who can do with simpler materials and finishing.[8] This led us to keep the flooring wherever possible, although we would have preferred to replace it. We also left the walls as they were and just painted them instead. So, we called our concept "shabby chic." In Berlin, for example, there are numerous interior design offices that specialize merely in refurbishing fashionable, hipster bars to give them a shabby chic appearance. They basically transform finished, smooth surfaces to give them a deliberately shabby and industrial appearance. In our case, the structure was truly shabby, but it's all done neatly and it's all clean, and one can live in it. People would probably not pay 12 or 13 euros per square meter but renting it for less money is fair.

Figure 2. Sufficiency principle, before and after. Source: RSE+

In order to convey this idea to our client, the district, we showed them pictures of the original state of the building. Then we created visualizations of what we planned to do with it. The images were shown to the two department heads who were involved, and they were quite impressed. It was clear to them that we were not creating high-end housing, but instead, we ended up saving an incredible amount of money, a few hundred thousand euros, which can now be used elsewhere. Otherwise, we would have exceeded the budget and the project might have perished in the long run. This was of course a major investment for the district and the immediate urgency to create accommodation was no longer so evident. In the end, I think it was the right thing to do because the other option would have meant spending more public money on this project rather than on other important projects by the district. Moreover, the whole thing was not that shabby, but rather non-standard in comparison to other, average apartment buildings. The whole project shows a less expensive approach to construction, which is currently a matter of interest, especially in the housing sector.

Indeed, the lack of affordable housing in general is also due to high building costs and complicated procedures. But, back to the building site, when do you expect to complete the project?

Since the companies for the building of heating, ventilation, sanitation, and electrical installations only started in October 2017, everything is delayed now. We will not finish the private living areas until late summer 2018.

Levels Zero and One, that is, the neighborhood and the community center, on the other hand, will probably not be finished until the end of 2018. It is difficult to complete the construction work now, because we commissioned the companies some time ago. They had expected to be fully engaged in summer 2017. Hence, they planned their entire capacities accordingly. However, based on the delays, we had to inform them that we were not able to start yet, so they sent all their workers away. When we tried to get

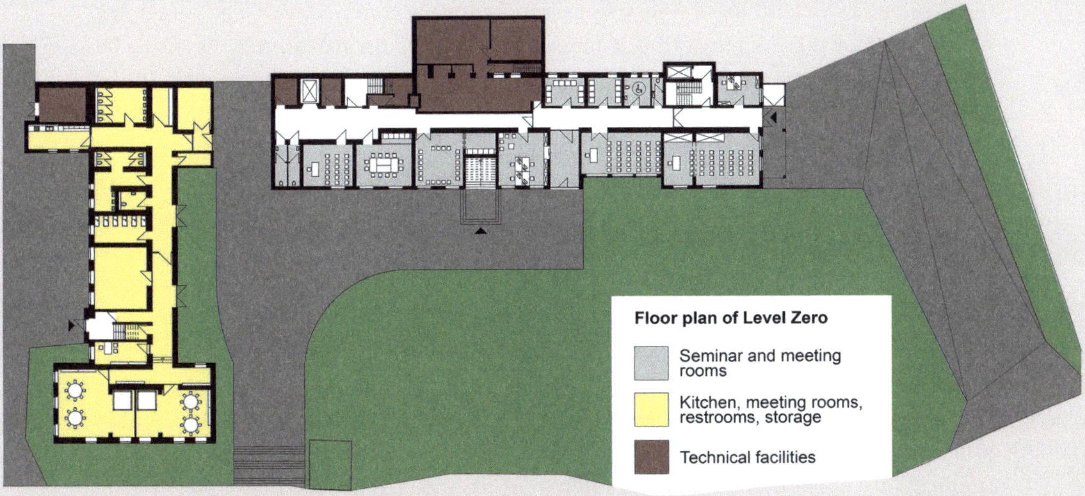

Figure 3. Floor plan of Level Zero. Source: RSE+

them back, it was almost impossible given the current dynamics of the construction market. Sometimes there are only two painters walking around in this large building, so we need to beg the company to send us two more. It is never good for such a project to lose momentum, because all the parties involved get upset, stop taking the project seriously and never come back, as they have so much to do elsewhere. That's why we are far more behind the schedule than we had anticipated.

So, to summarize, the main challenges of working in fast-changing environments together with the sudden change in asylum seekers' arrival rates have altered the size of the project, its design concept, the type of finishing, the flow of work and the power relations with construction workers, in addition to the planned timeline and expected costs.

Yes, and as I said, the character also changed a lot. Curiously enough, however, it turns out that our original concept for the function of Levels Zero and One is actually being implemented. Until a few weeks ago, we didn't know what was going to happen to these two levels, because the client didn't know either. Originally, a large kitchen for cooking classes was planned, now there is only a simple kitchen with a space nearby for a caterer. There was also a kindergarten, but the city of Münden later changed their minds because they thought that they would not be needing it after all. Therefore, the kindergarten area was completely ignored for a long time. Now it has been decided that these spaces will be used for vocational and orientation career training instead. Our original idea was to train refugees with different educational backgrounds, and other unemployed people, to reach a level that allows them to slowly be incorporated into the German labor market. Finally, the building has reached a point where we know for sure how Levels Zero and One will operate. There are various offices, seminar and meeting rooms of different sizes, where German classes, computer courses, and other educational activities will take place. There is a space for the Society for the Promotion of Work and Employment, a subsidiary organization of the district. Ultimately, they are there to support long-term unemployed people. On Level Zero, there is also a café, a social meeting place, storage rooms, restrooms, and so on.

The Levels Two and Three – very similar in layout – accommodate the private living areas. The floor plans changed from a hostel-like design towards simple classic apartments. The plans show how they have different sizes. We had common rooms in the old concept but now we do not need them anymore. Of course, we wanted to reduce the intervention in the structure to a minimum. So, we have small, two-room apartments, but also bigger, three- or four-room apartments. Some have an incredibly beautiful view of the valley. In the plans, we see another example of how we managed to save costs by deciding to locate the bathrooms towards the facade. Indoor bathrooms would give more comfortable floor plans, but building their ventilation system, between the many motors, cables, and suspended ceilings, would have caused unbelievable additional costs, so we settled for less-than-ideal layout solutions.

This example shows that construction can't always be as fast as political developments, especially in the sector of renovation. However, renovation was in my opinion still a better strategy than, for example, tearing down everything, especially since the municipality of Hann. Münden already had been, and still is, facing the challenge of having several non-functioning building complexes and compounds (such as former military barracks, old hotels, empty industrial complexes). Admittedly, it would have been faster to start a new construction from scratch, but the district always has to consider the public welfare of the community as a whole.

Figure 4. Floor plan of Level Two. Source: RSE+

Can you tell us more about the decision to choose this building and transform it into refugee accommodation?

Yes. The building is located in Neu Münden, a residential area in the city of Hann. Münden. This area is somewhat disconnected from economic development, which is why I honestly do not think that the building could have been sold – not even for a symbolic one euro. If the building had remained completely empty, I think this would have led to even more negative consequences for urban development of the area. Regulating services of public interest is one of the district's tasks, and the project is financed by the district, whose aim with this project was also to open up a sustainable prospect for the neighborhood.

How important is the role of urban planners in these decision-making processes in your opinion?

Urban planning has nothing to do with these decisions. They are a product of chance.

Chance, because the hospital was already built, empty and its renovation would be faster than building something new?

Exactly, and because the district had already deposited a large sum as a guarantee on this building. If that had not been the case, I don't think the district would have done anything about it. One could argue that this development is random. The fact that this specific property was chosen in the end was due to the circumstances and not based on conscious urban planning decisions. But of course, it was acted upon from an urban planning perspective in order to take reasonable care of this property. It would have been a beautiful place to live if it wasn't in the middle of nowhere. If this building were in Göttingen or in Kassel, for example, then people would tear each other apart fighting for it, even if it were on the outskirts. However, given its current location and its modest finishing style, nobody would agree to pay 12 euros per square meter for rent.

Indeed, it is a product of chance. After all, as we have explained in our study, the administrative district is already doing something really good compared with some basic refugee accommodation built elsewhere on remote sites, in old supermarkets, or the like.

So, the reality is that city planners and architects have to try to make the most of any circumstances, even though the decisions made for them might not be based on urban planning principles or favorable for urban development.

Yes, but I think that the district of Göttingen is not to blame either. Their hands were tied, too. I think that they have always done the right thing within the scope of their possibilities. Maybe they could have done it a little faster. Admittedly, the original decision to do this project and this study was very quick. It then became tough when it was no longer really clear what was going to happen because no additional refugees were coming. In other words, the district cannot be criticized for that. Of course, the district had not fully prepared itself for such a situation in terms of urban or regional planning, but when the situation was already there, it reacted correctly.

If the task is to project global, political, and uncontrollable processes onto such a building, then yes, of course this can result in a certain level of unpredictability in planning and building.

When you say the decisions about these accommodations were decisions of chance, who actually makes these decisions?

I think that some newly built accommodations have been allocated successfully. Others, in my opinion, are not that successful. To open a U-shaped building to the highway service road in Göttingen, for example, is counterproductive, both in terms of urban planning and urban development. Especially if this refugee accommodation has a long-term plan to be subsequently used as a student dormitory. I can't imagine that a student would want to live in a dormitory close to the highway. The location right on the highway service road would be ideal for a business park for example – there is an industrial and commercial area nearby, so it would work. It would have been different if we started building houses and a residential area in that location. Now as long as refugees live in it, one could argue that it works – as they have no other choice. However, the question is: What happens when they are gone? Who is going to live there? Personally, I'd rather live in a dark room in a tiny shared flat somewhere in the city center instead of moving out there, far away from everything. Maybe the housing shortage will get even worse in Göttingen and then students will also move there.

However, this was also an emergency situation and, at short notice, one reacts accordingly. But that's not urban planning. An emergency should not be the trigger for urban planning. I think this shows that the choice of the location was not a very conscious decision, premeditated from the perspective of urban planning, but probably the city said: "We have space there, so let's do it there."

Do you think the locations were chosen just because these properties belonged to the city?

Yes, that is how I see it. At least with the accommodation close to the freeway. I cannot imagine anyone thinking of it as a great location, especially not for a subsequent use. As long as there is an urgent need to accommodate people and no other options available, it is understandable. But if the necessity is gone, the location has nothing to offer because it is isolated. So, the question arises: Can you blame the planning authorities for having to make a quick decision in an emergency situation? The problem is that urban planning traditionally has very long cycles – probably decades – whereas, during the *refugee crisis,* decisions had to be made in weekly and monthly cycles. This is difficult to reconcile. Hence, I don't know if I would formulate this as a critique.

Urban planners can only take city-owned properties into immediate consideration. It is unlikely that the city would buy additional plots. In the current state of the market, there are hardly any plots for sale suitable for residential development. And if there are some, they are certainly not affordable. In other words, planners can only think about the city-owned land because they need locations where they can quickly build. A complicated inner-city-block development is of course a completely different challenge than setting up container-based refugee housing in the open countryside. That means that the planners have to work with currently available locations and the specific urban planning assessments are probably at the back of the list. The only aspect they might have to consider is whether there is a public transport connection somewhere at a reasonable distance. But further aspects, such as whether there is basic infrastructure in the surrounding area such as a supermarket, a doctor, kindergarten, elementary school, etc. usually cannot be sufficiently assessed. In this situation, I find it hard to criticize planning authorities. The only thing I would criticize is that instead

Figure 5. Construction process. Source: RSE+

of investing money in these temporary projects, they could have created projects that would have a positive effect beyond the immediate crisis. By all means, it was important to quickly provide people with shelter, but what use will these structures be afterwards? Of course, nobody could have predicted how long this crisis would last. If it had been clear beforehand that within a known period of time it would have almost come to a standstill, then perhaps we would have decided right away to create reasonable emergency shelters to be used for a year only, for example, by transforming an old supermarket. That would have cost much less. And then we could do something permanent with the money we had saved. Of course, if the *refugee crisis* had gone on for another two years, then perhaps that would have been another unwise decision. At least we would be able to say that this investment was due to the unpredictable situation. It would have still been a beneficial development for the community.

Society benefits from the creation of long-term jobs for the unemployed, whether they have a migration background or not. But society does not benefit from the current situation: the subsequent use of non-functioning refugee accommodation as a student dorm with unacceptable living conditions. If the main goal was to build student housing in the long term, then it should have been built on the north campus of the University of Göttingen. The university could have been asked to provide a reasonable piece of land to build a student dormitory, which would be made available to the university for a small amount of money after the end of the *refugee crisis*, for example. That would have been a good idea. In that case, nobody would have made a profit, but it would not incur losses, as is the case with temporary structures, or those without a realistic function after the crisis. It would have been much better anyway to take the money and polish up some city-owned empty buildings. Perhaps it is not only a question of urban planning, but also a question of cost-effectiveness. Looking at it from an economic point of view, everyone would immediately ask what we were going to do with the building afterwards.

So, you believe that urban planners should play a different role in making such decisions?

Yes, well, I'd love that in general, but, in my opinion, there is far too little active design in the field of urban planning, at least in this region. Many cities are understaffed, and some outsource a lot of their projects. There are many areas that, in my opinion, have not been sufficiently dealt with from the perspective of urban planning. This becomes evident if we consider the numerous areas without a binding or with an outdated land-use plan. In this case, the decision of what and how much you can build is either made based on Section 34 of the Building Code or the construction is regulated through an urban development contract.[9] But that is, as the name says, urban development, which in contrast to urban planning, is mainly driven by investors who aim to earn money with a project. Hence, main motivations behind these developments are oftentimes financial. This can prove to be negative as the profit-driven developments often lead to increased densities and cheaper ways of building in order to maximize the profit. So, once the impulse to develop a certain area is given by the investors and there is no existing and suitable land-use plan in effect, the trajectory is usually towards density and less towards responsible planning of public spaces. Even though density is nothing negative per se, it could be argued that an existing land-use plan could set certain boundaries that an investor would rather not self-impose.

However, there is a flip side to this kind of development that connects the wider population with all that free-flowing money to the so-called *Betongold*.[10] Many of us are indirectly linked to that money, for example, through large pension funds or real estate funds. They invest our money in real estate to pay for future pensions because other investments do not produce the interest they used to. Of course, that is not the case with every real estate project, but it is an aspect that we should keep in mind while criticizing the real estate market.

Urban planning, in my opinion, is not producing enough land-use plans. As a consequence, many lots do not have a binding plan beforehand. This happens mostly because there are not enough personnel. Moreover, at a time when open lots are scarce, public interest in the existing ones is strong, which sometimes leads to lengthening these developments. People tend to be pro housing, but this is usually on a very theoretical level and not in their own neighborhood. All in all, it's a very complicated market. In my experience, many people become conservative when it comes to real estate – even those who are otherwise progressive. That is, of course, a generalization, but I have witnessed it personally many times.

In my opinion there should be many more land-use plans. The original task of the urban planning department is actually to produce new plans for areas that have none, to check which existing plans still make sense and can be implemented, and which are obsolete and need to be improved to accommodate new developments. But, presumably due to cost reasons and understaffing, this is happening very slowly.

Sometimes it takes an emergency situation for us to realize concrete needs in terms of planning and our limitations in achieving them. These needs, therefore, are not always clear before they become an urgent necessity.

Yes. However, both student and refugee accommodation has a similar concept, in my opinion. It is simple housing for little money, so perhaps we don't have to apply the highest quality standards. A city might not have a concept of what to do when a *refugee crisis* occurs, which, in my opinion, is justifiable, because we cannot be prepared for every thinkable situation. But a city must have a concept of where and how students should be accommodated in the future. And by thinking about it with the right people, one could come up with good solutions for students in the future that would also be ideal for refugees now.

---

1 The interview was originally conducted in German. It was edited by Maja Momić. **2** German: Integrierte Flüchtlingsunterkunft und Begegnungszentrum (IFUB). **3** The increased arrival of refugees to Europe and Germany has been accompanied by the catchphrase "refugee crisis" in media coverage and in the statements of some politicians since 2015. It also became a widespread frequently used term in everyday life. In order to stay true to the interview, the editors of this volume decided to keep the term as it was used throughout; however, the term is italicized to signal its incongruity with this book's perspective on the status of refugees in the world. **4** Max-Planck-Institute for the Study of Religious and Ethnic Diversity in Göttingen (MPI-MMG) launched its research project "Addressing the Diversity of Asylum Seekers," for which Dr. Shahd Seethaler-Wari was a postdoc researcher, around the same time as Mr. Brune's analytical study started. **5** On March 18, 2016, the European Council and Turkey reached an agreement aimed at stopping the flow of irregular migration via Turkey to Europe. According to the EU-Turkey Deal, all new irregular migrants and asylum seekers arriving from Turkey to the Greek islands and whose applications for asylum had been declared inadmissible should be returned to Turkey. Source: https://www.europarl.europa.eu/legislative-train/theme-towards-a-new-policy-on-migration/file-eu-turkey-statement-action-plan. **6** German: L-shaped building. **7** German: "head building," or central building. **8** As opposed to contemporary standards in the real estate development, which are rather high-end (e.g., underfloor heating, fitted kitchens, etc.) and consequently drive housing prices higher and higher. **9** According to Section 34 BauGB, a new construction is admissible if it fits in in its close environment in terms of type, size, construction method, and with regard to the percentage of built surfaces. Urban development contracts serve the implementation and preparation of urban development measures in accordance with the Building Code (see Section 11 BauGB). These contracts regulate the rights and obligations of the investor, on the one hand, and the municipality, on the other. **10** German: "concrete gold," conveying the idea of real estate as a safe investment of assets, especially in times of high inflation or low interest rates.

Inhabiting Refugee Accommodations: A Comparison of Two Temporarily Transformed Buildings

Shahd Seethaler-Wari

This paper brings together different research methods from architecture and social sciences to draw on the empirical findings of a research project (2016–19) in Göttingen, a mid-sized city in Lower Saxony. Through architectural ethnography, the article presents the spatial environments and social spaces of the inhabitants of two existing buildings that were transformed temporarily into collective accommodations for asylum seekers and refugees. By focusing on the interiority of these accommodations, the article showcases the physical and social dimensions of the architectural space and the diverse actors that make these spaces. It demonstrates the fundamental interdependencies of the spatial layouts of refugee accommodations with modalities of their internal transformation and with the inhabitation practices of their inhabitants.

The article highlights how architectural design and spatial layouts result in differential access to services, resources, and social experiences, and exemplifies their role in the levels of exclusion and stigmatization that refugees experience in the first phase after arrival in the host country.

Introduction

Since 2015, asylum seekers and refugees in Germany have been accommodated in a vast variety of accommodation centers.[1] This diversity is not only visible in the different types of centers (that is, initial reception centers, collective and centralized accommodations, or decentralized housing) but also within the same type of accommodations, which have varying combinations of spatial and nonspatial institutional arrangements (Vertovec et al. 2017) that offer a diverse spectrum of experiences and opportunities to their inhabitants.

To best reflect this diversity and its resulting effects on the daily lives of accommodation inhabitants, this article focuses on two comparable collective accommodation centers in the city of Göttingen in Lower Saxony. Both chosen accommodations were existing buildings transformed into temporary, centralized accommodations, with an administrative staff present on a regular basis. Both were located 10 to 15 minutes from the city center, and both closed after their rental contracts expired in 2017 and 2018.

Collective centralized accommodations, like the ones addressed in this article, are usually meant to accommodate asylum seekers temporarily until a decision about their asylum application is made. If granted refugee status, the inhabitants are allowed to look for private housing and move out of the accommodation. At the time of the first fieldwork (2016), asylum seekers who had a good *Bleibeperspektive*[2] were allowed to move to their own housing after spending a minimum of three months in a collective accommodation, even if their asylum process was not yet complete. However, the high demand on – and lack of – affordable housing of the appropriate size made this possibility harder in practice. By the end of 2018, about 1,260 asylum seekers and refugees were still being accommodated in different facilities (Stadt Göttingen 2018).

The two selected accommodations – one with a capacity of 70 inhabitants and the other, 180 inhabitants – were among the biggest accommodations in the city. However, their urban conditions were rather different. One was located in a commercial-industrial area and the other in a middle-class residential neighborhood. Their spatial layouts offered different levels of privacy, different number of inhabitants per room, and different levels of independence and control. Additionally, they had different demographic and social compositions of asylum seekers and different levels of access to management personnel, translators, and volunteers. Due to these differences, the possibilities offered to their respective inhabitants were significantly different, and their needs and aspirations were met rather differently. They had different social positioning as a result of their different experiences and inhabitation practices. These practices include their interaction with the physical space and with the social space, which in the accommodations comprises their relationships with cohabitants, with the administrative staff that manage the accommodation, and with the volunteers on-site.

Research methodology and theoretical framework

In the context of a larger project (Vertovec et al. 2017), a mixture of qualitative research methods were implemented for the study of both accommodations, including participant observation in refugee accommodations and in public meetings and events; focus group discussions; interviews, hanging out, and informal meetings with asylum seekers and recognized refugees; semi-guided interviews with practitioners in different city institutions, social workers, volunteers, and with management staff of selected refugee accommodations. Additionally, participatory research methods like language portraits and photovoice were employed in the research of one accommodation.[3]

I also engaged as a volunteer, translator, and as a sponsor of several research participants.[4] Every research participant, whether refugee, volunteer, or administrative staff member, was informed, and sometimes continuously reminded of my role as a researcher, especially due to the development of informal trust relationships with most informants. Due to these relationships, communication with the contacts and data collection continued until the end of 2018. At the beginning of 2021, contact was reestablished with some research participants – namely, a few refugees and a social worker – to confirm the accuracy of the drawings documenting the inhabitation practices in these spaces.[5]

As an architect, I would have liked to take many photos of the spaces in the different accommodations I visited. However, due to research ethics and out of respect for the privacy of the inhabitants, I ended up taking very few photos of empty spaces before people moved in. These photos did not reflect the social lives that developed in these spaces afterwards. Therefore, the drawings in the article are an attempt to give meaning to the empty spaces I could capture in photos by visualizing the inhabitation practices that took place in them during the fieldwork. A few photos taken by research participants in the context of photovoice were also turned into drawings. These show the inhabitants' perspective of the accommodation space and their activities in it. The text in photovoice drawings was reported by the inhabitants while discussing these photos. These drawings are indicated in the figure captions.

Therefore, the paper is an attempt to bring together multiple research methods from architecture and social sciences. It combines architectural drawing with qualitative, ethnographic, and participatory research methods. In its architectural ethnographic approach (Kaijima, Stalder, and Iseki 2018, Avermaete 2020), the paper centralizes drawings of exterior and interior spaces of two refugee accommodations at different scales: from the neighborhood, through the "public" spaces of the accommodation, to the "private" rooms, visualizing these spaces as a way of analysis. The text in the drawings adds layers of detail, localizes information, or elaborates on the meaning of some spaces for the inhabitants and is therefore an integral part of the paper.

Focusing on the role of spatial layouts and the resulting social relationships, parts of the paper may prompt the Lefebvrian analytical lens and his spatial triad of conceived, perceived, and lived spaces (Lefebvre 1991), Massey's (2013) definition of social space, or Foucault's (1995) power relations within the space and the possibility to change its meaning through social practices that produce that space. Other parts may show the territoriality (Storey 2017) of space users or De Certeau's spatial practices and everyday life (1984), or remind the reader of Newman's concept of defensible space (1972 and 1996), especially due to the blurred limits and meanings of "private" and "public" in the context of large collective accommodations. However, I will deliberately refrain from abstracting or imposing spatial theories, and will let the spatial layouts and inhabitation practices, as I defined them above, speak for themselves as a lens of analysis.

Accommodation A: transformed warehouse

The collective accommodation was opened in March 2016 to accommodate up to 70 men. It was about 15 minutes away from the city center by bus. Although 15 minutes sounds close, for many inhabitants it was perceived far outside the city center. This was also evident in the struggle of the management to find motivated volunteers for the duration of its operation until it was closed at the end of October 2017.

The accommodation was a two-story building originally designed as a warehouse. It was rented by the city (Interview with staff member 2016), and internally modified to temporarily house up to 70 asylum seekers in 15 parcels,[6] until their asylum applications were resolved and they were able to move forward to find housing. The building was surrounded by industrial structures: factories, warehouses, and a bus terminal. It was located at the end of two bus lines that connect it to the city center four times an hour during the day and twice an hour in the evening. Therefore, the bus station was only meters away from the accommodation's entrance.

There were no neighbors or housing in the direct vicinity of the accommodation. Moreover, only young, single males or those who traveled without their families were being assigned to this accommodation. A staff member explained that this specific demographic was chosen due to the lack of facilities (for example, schools or playgrounds) in the neighborhood or along the bus line to the city center (Interview with staff member 2016) typical for residential areas, which would have complicated the lives of families with children. This specificity gave the accommodation a distinct social atmosphere, especially that the only women present were the administrative staff, and a few volunteers.

The inhabitants came from a wide variety of countries and backgrounds. Their ages at the time of the fieldwork ranged between 18 and 50 years old. The accommodation started with 40 inhabitants, mostly Syrians, Lebanese, and Iraqis. For some months – while the European borders were closed – the number remained constant. A few months later, men from different national and ethnic backgrounds started to arrive, more dominantly from African countries like Sudan and Eritrea, and from the Balkans. This changed the socio-cultural and linguistic landscape of the inhabitants, the translators needed, and simultaneously the *Bleibeperspektive* of the inhabitants.

My access to the field happened naturally and spontaneously in this accommodation. On my first encounter with the accommodation, I had a meeting with the manager to introduce the research project. The accommodation had just recently opened. While waiting, I was approached by an inhabitant asking whether I could help translate and fill out a form. In some minutes, while filling out the form, a queue of 12 men had formed waiting their turn. It turned out they thought I was the translator they had been waiting for for two weeks already. Some of these men became research participants. Most of the participants from this accommodation "voluntarily" left Germany, returning to their homelands during or after the end of the research, due to the very slow processing of their asylum applications or difficulties related to family unifications.

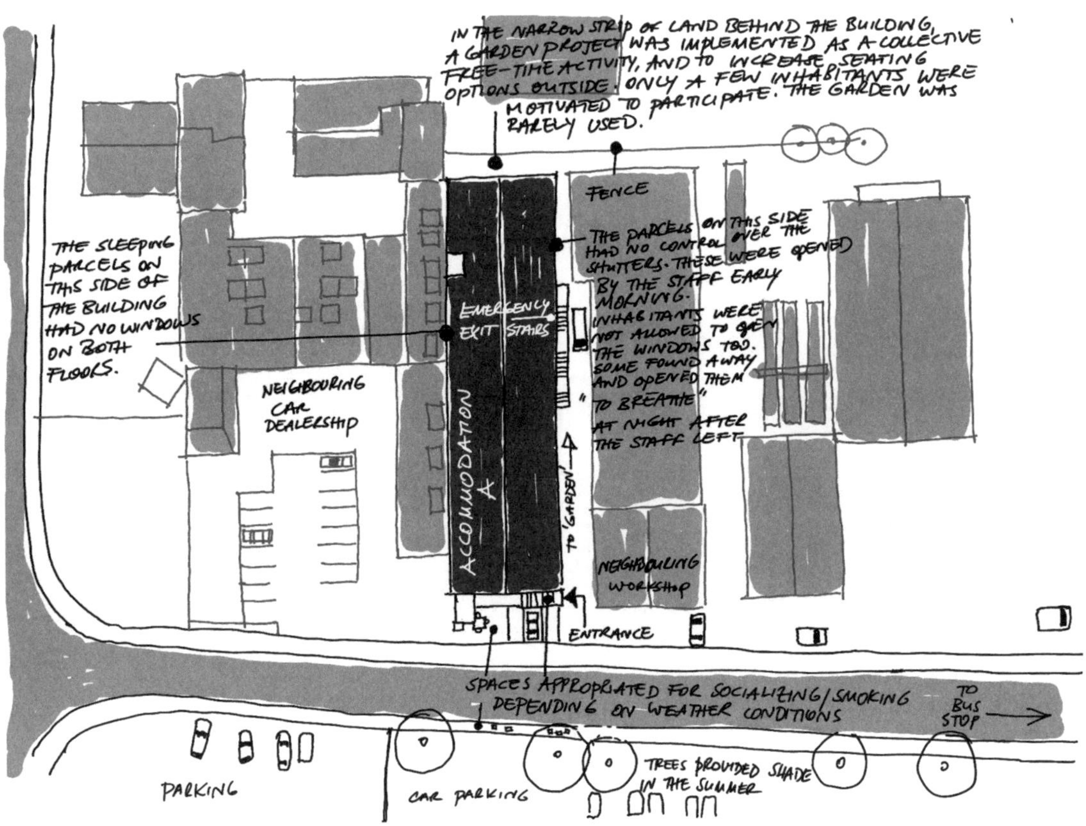

Figure 1. A site plan of Accommodation A showing its direct surroundings in the industrial area.

TREES ON THIS SIDE PROVIDED SHADE WHEN SUNNY
NEIGHBORI
CAR DEALER
BECAUSE SMOKING WAS NOT ALLOWED IN THE ACCOMMODATION AND DUE TO LACK OF OPEN AREAS, THE INHABITANTS APPROPRIATED THE SIDEWALK OPPOSITE TO THE ACCOMMODATION. THIS BLOCKED THE SIDEWALK FOR PASSERS BY WHO MADE THEIR DISAPPROVAL HEARD.

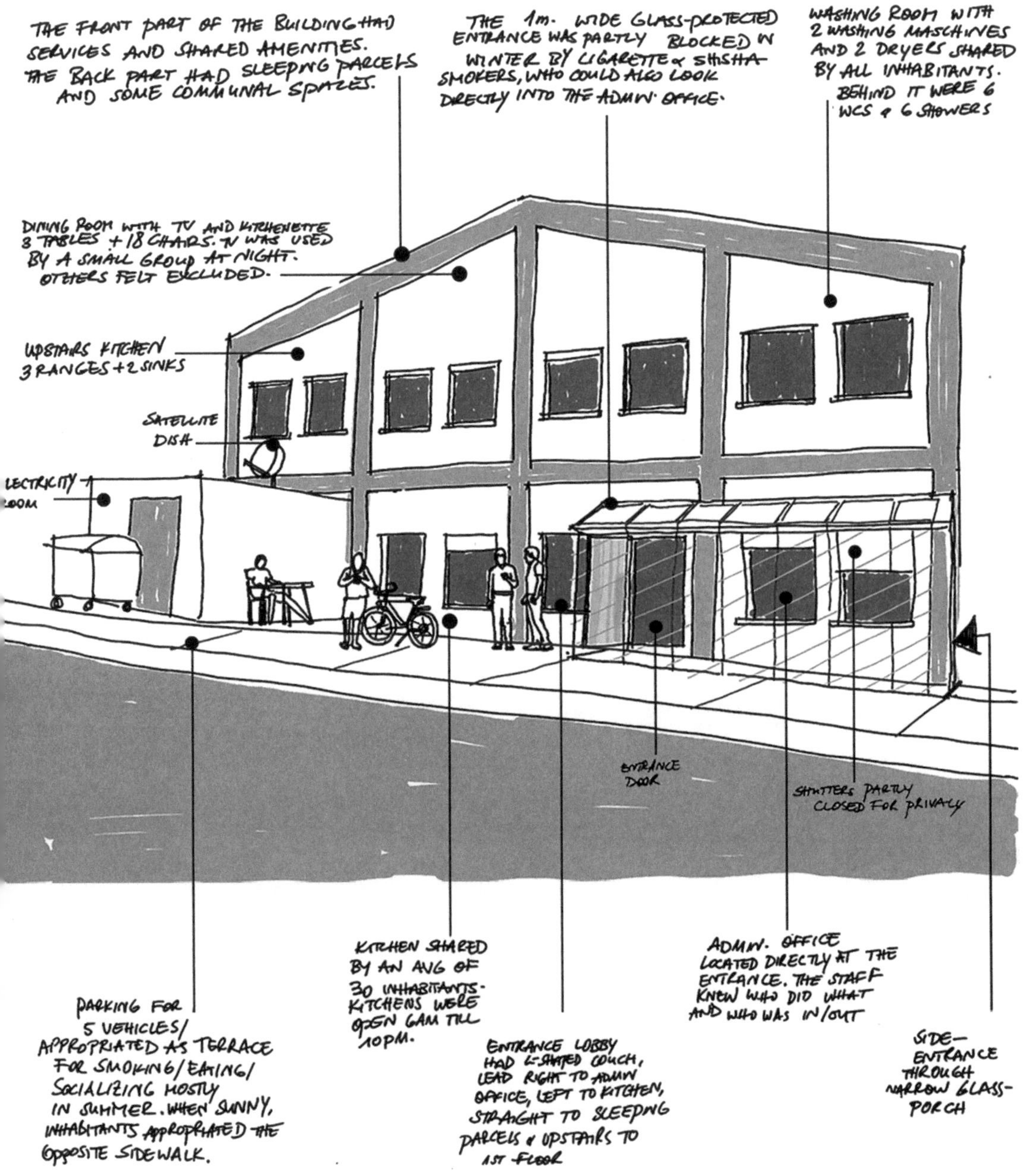

Figure 2. The main facade of the accommodation building and appropriation of spaces in front of it.

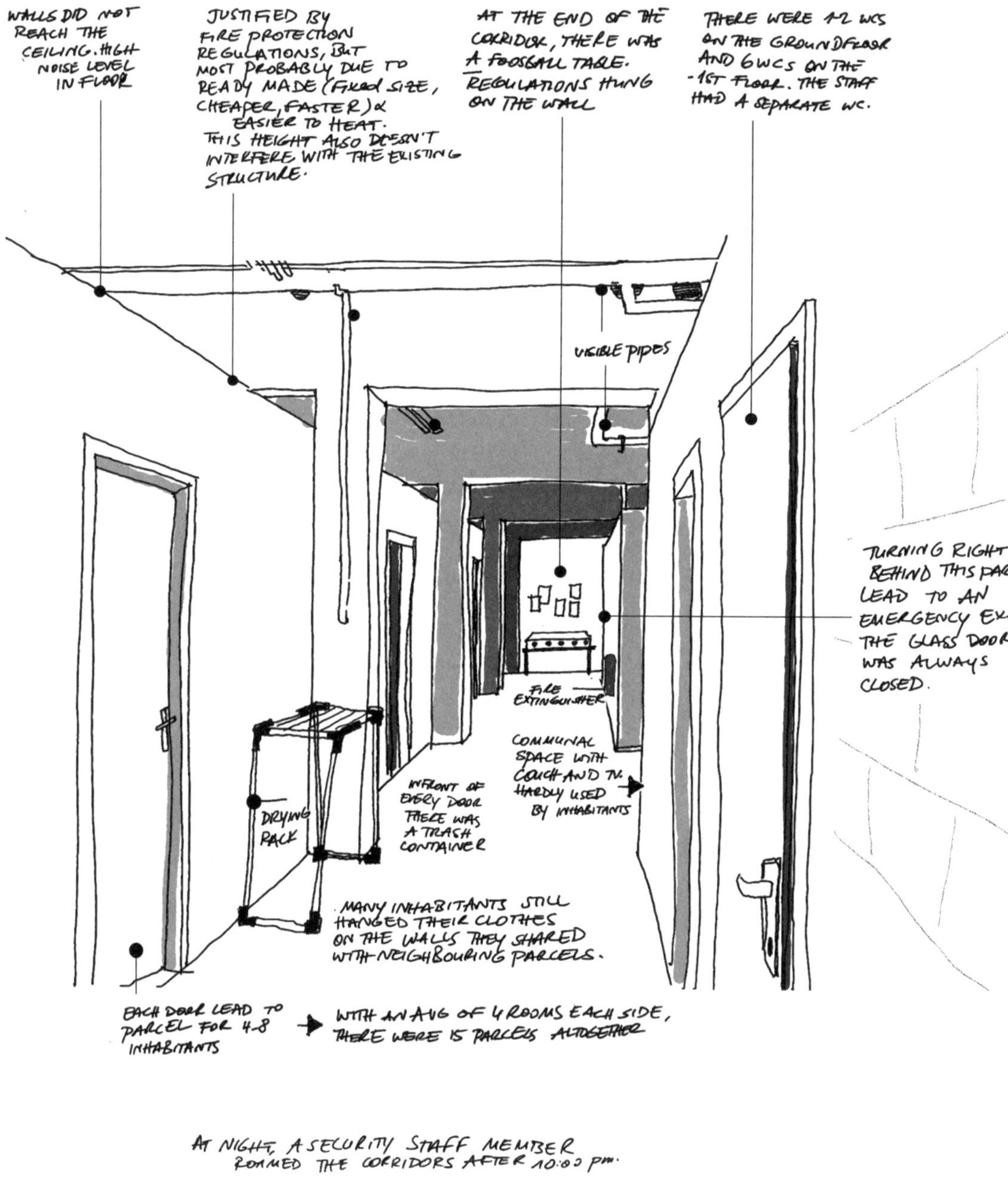

Figure 3. A perspective of the interior of the ground floor.

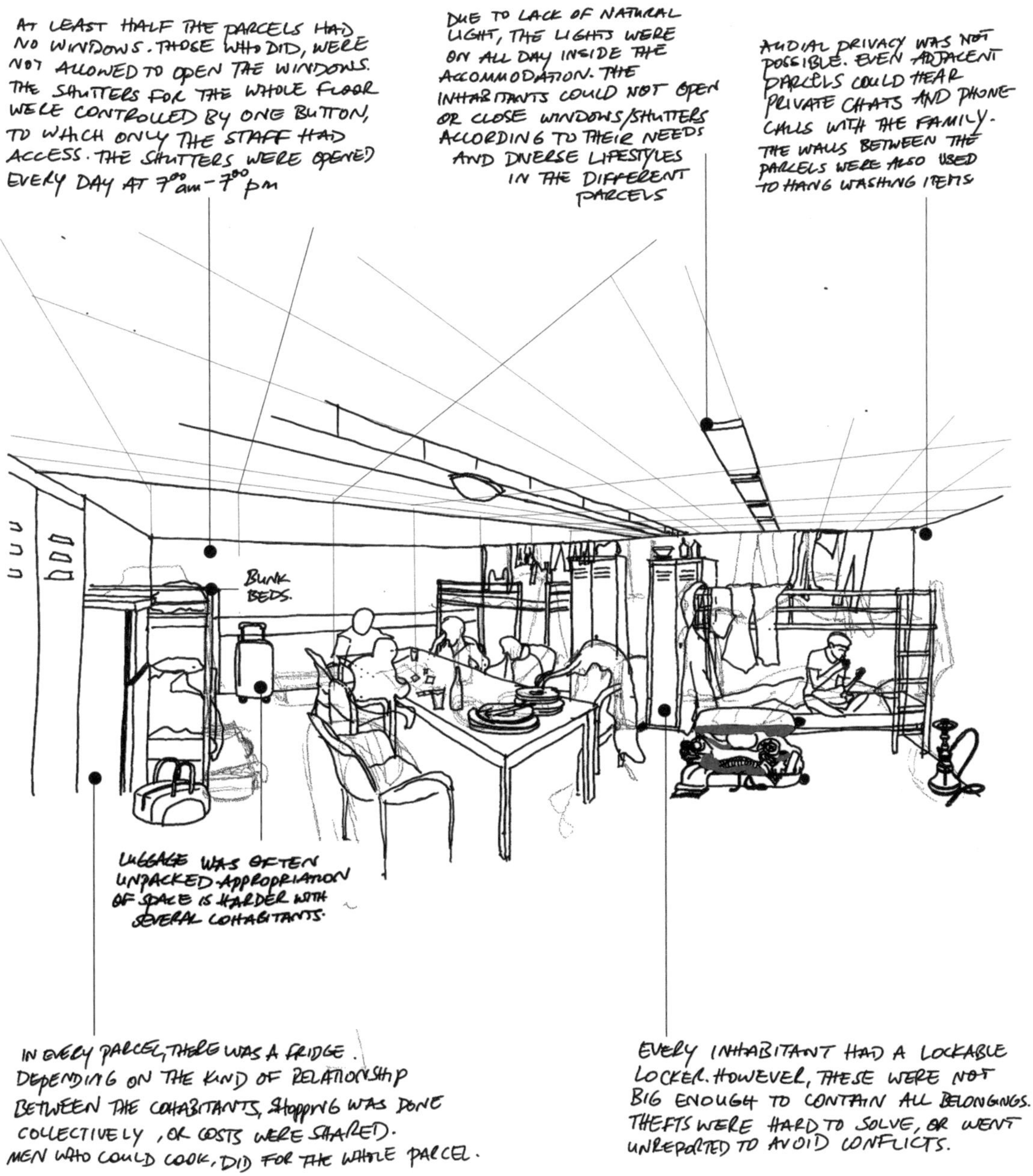

Figure 4. A perspective showing a six-person-parcel on the first floor.

Figure 5. Details of the ground-floor kitchen.

Accommodation B: transformed institute

The second accommodation was a building complex of four connected buildings. It was an institute until 2010 after which it was sold to an investor and stood empty pending construction plans. The city decided to use it temporarily to accommodate a maximum of 150 people. This decision was realized only in November 2015. The accommodation was located in a middle-class neighborhood about 10 minutes by bus from the city center, five minutes walking distance from the next bus stop. This location helped the abundance of volunteers, including a roundtable and a civil initiative, who were engaged as helpers or sponsors, many of whom came from the neighborhood. The building was situated on a main street, so it was immediately visible especially when inhabitants spent time in front of the building, making it easily identifiable as refugee accommodation. The accommodation was closed when its rental contract ended in August 2018.

By early 2016 – the peak of the so-called refugee crisis – 208 asylum seekers from different nationalities were accommodated here. The biggest groups arrived from Syria, Iraq, Afghanistan, and Sudan. After the borders closed, the origin of the groups changed as was the case in Accommodation A. Most research participants I met in this accommodation were either already or later recognized as refugees.

The accommodation's buildings, connected by pathways and corridors, offered rooms of different sizes in five sections. The rooms accommodated two to 12 people according to the media, and two to six people as reported by the staff. Most of the rooms I accessed during the field research accommodated two to four people. The buildings accommodated singles and families, people with diverse demographic and socioeconomic backgrounds. Single men and women were accommodated in shared rooms, separately, and families lived together; an extended family, for example, was accommodated in two adjacent rooms. On every floor, one kitchen with three ranges (stove/oven combinations) and two sinks, four bathrooms and four showers were shared by some 20 to 30 inhabitants depending on the fluctuating number of asylum seekers. This meant that cooking, eating, showering, and washing had to be negotiated among the inhabitants.

The accommodation had a special communication structure that I did not encounter in other accommodations in the city. Each floor had a representative who communicated the needs, problems, or demands of the floor with the management. After being introduced to floor spokespersons, access to the field became easier, since these key people introduced me to interested research participants.

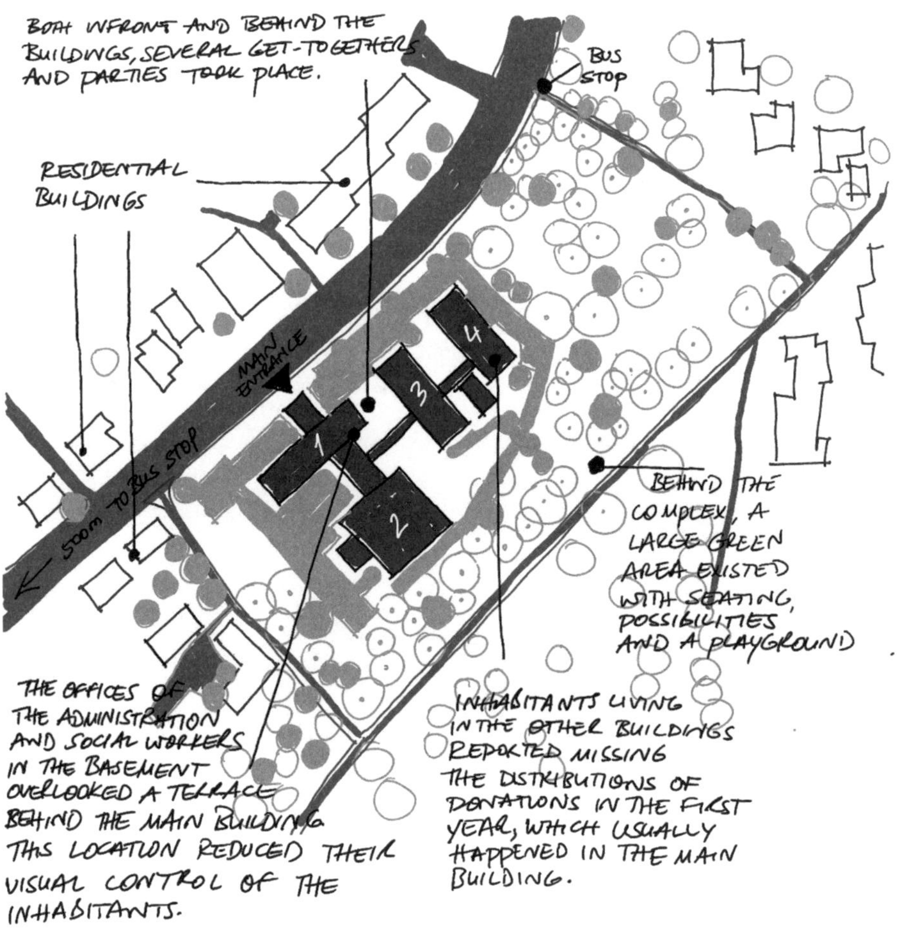

Figure 6. The site plan of the Accommodation B building complex, in a middle-class neighborhood.

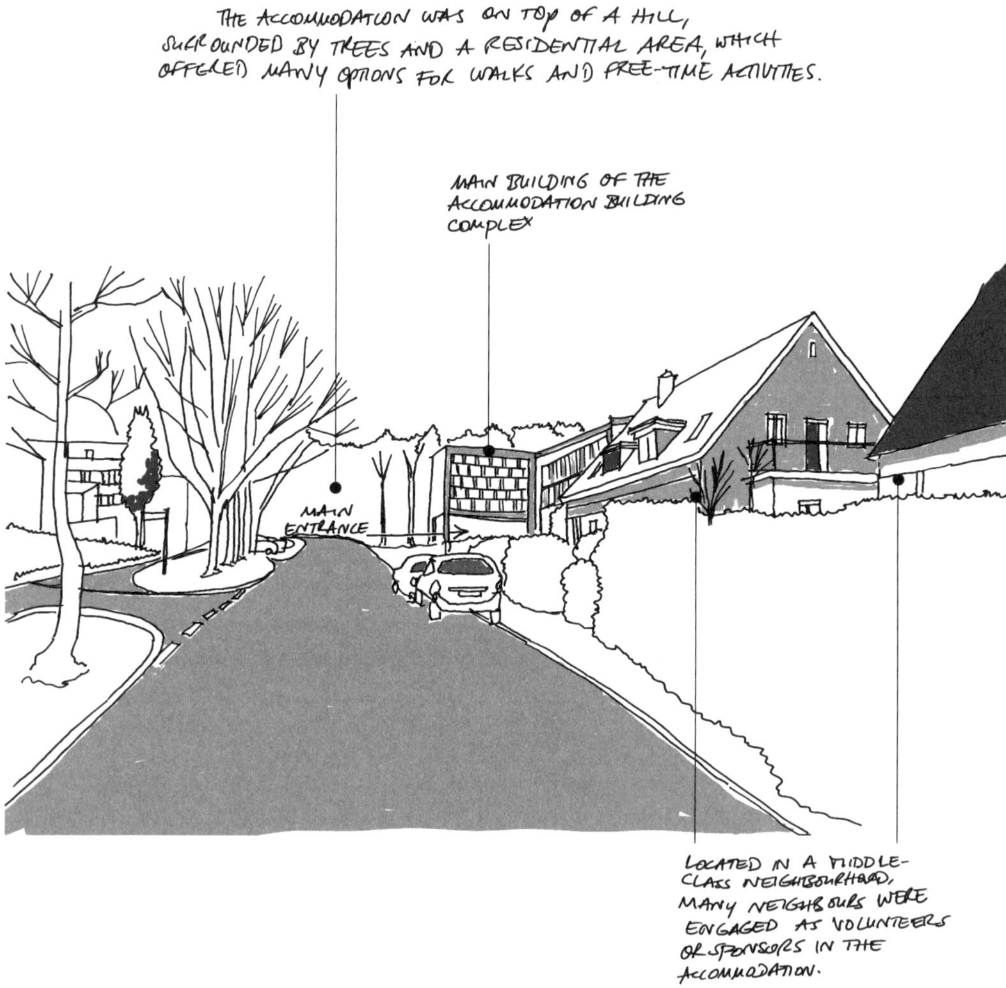

Figure 7. A perspective drawing of the accommodation complex in its surrounding neighborhood.

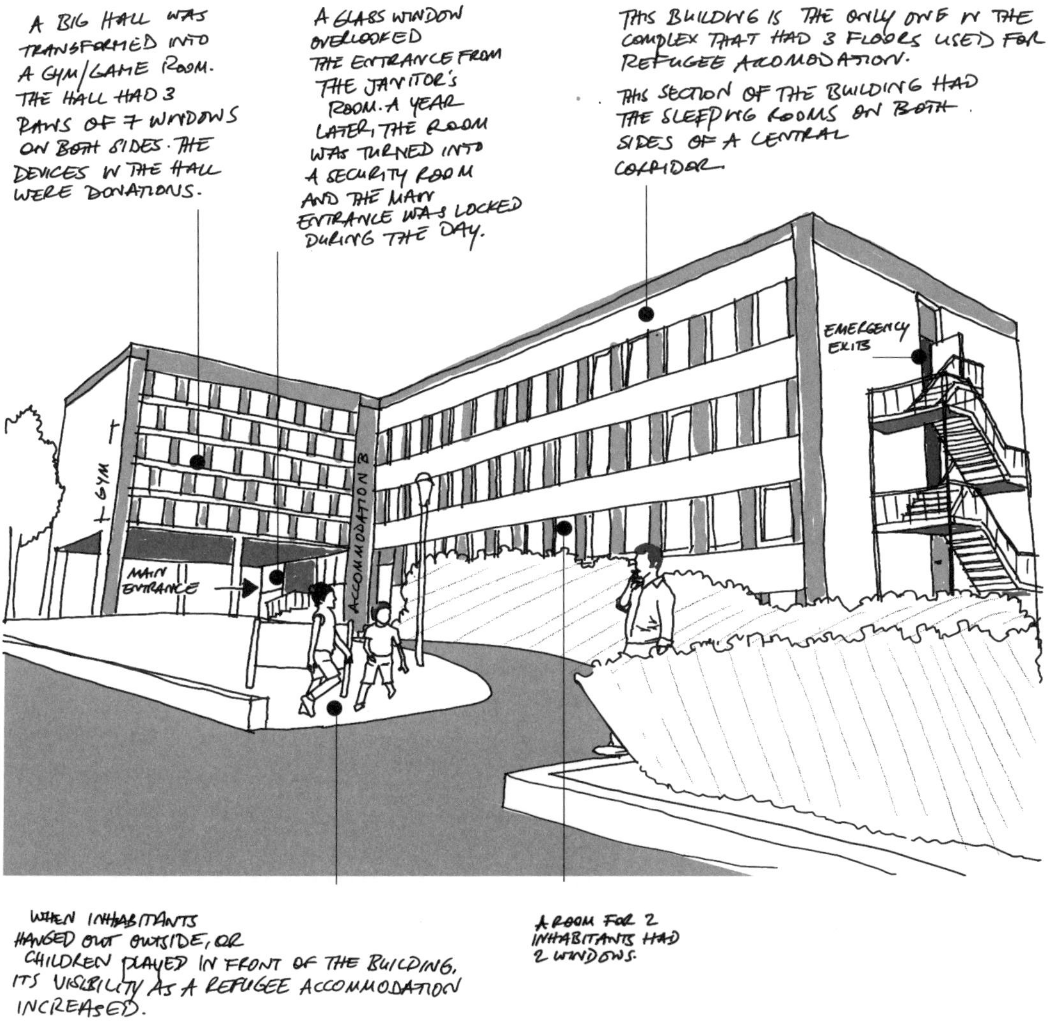

Figure 8. A perspective of the main building in the complex.

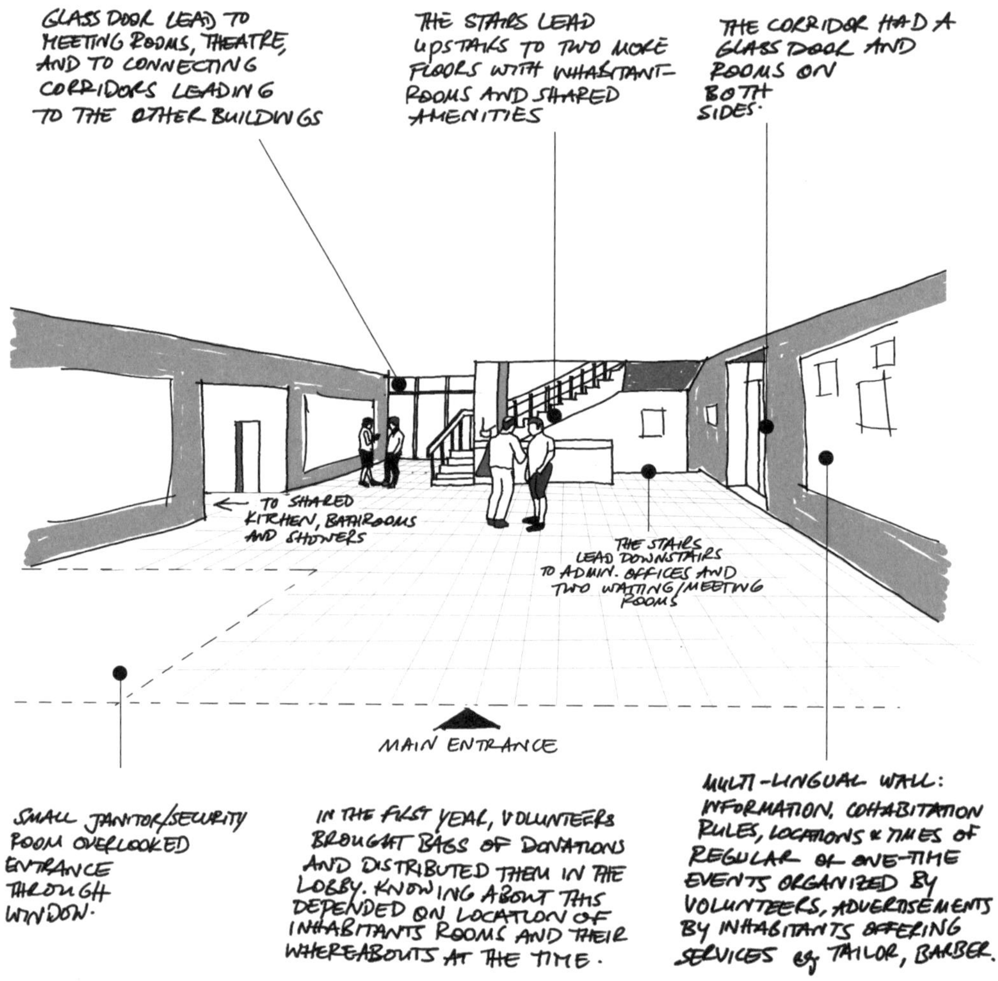

Figure 9. A perspective of the entrance lobby of the main building.

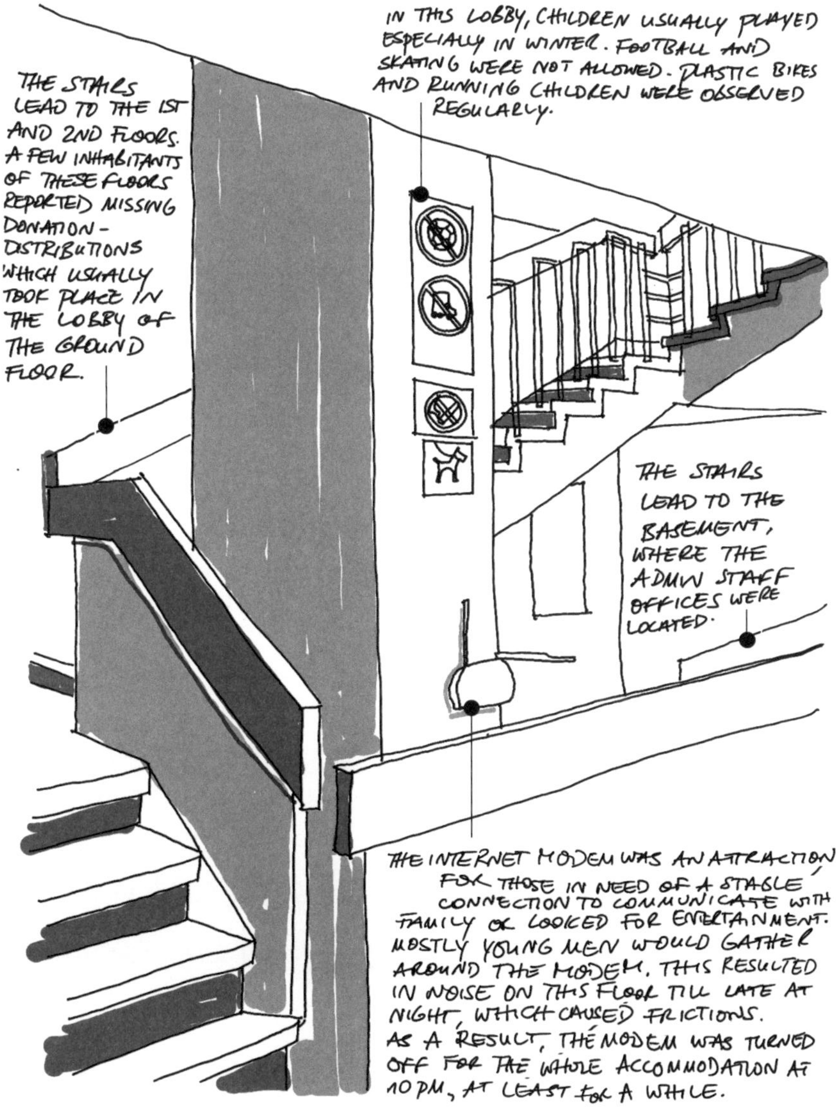

Figure 10. A perspective of the stairs and the location of the internet modem on the ground floor.

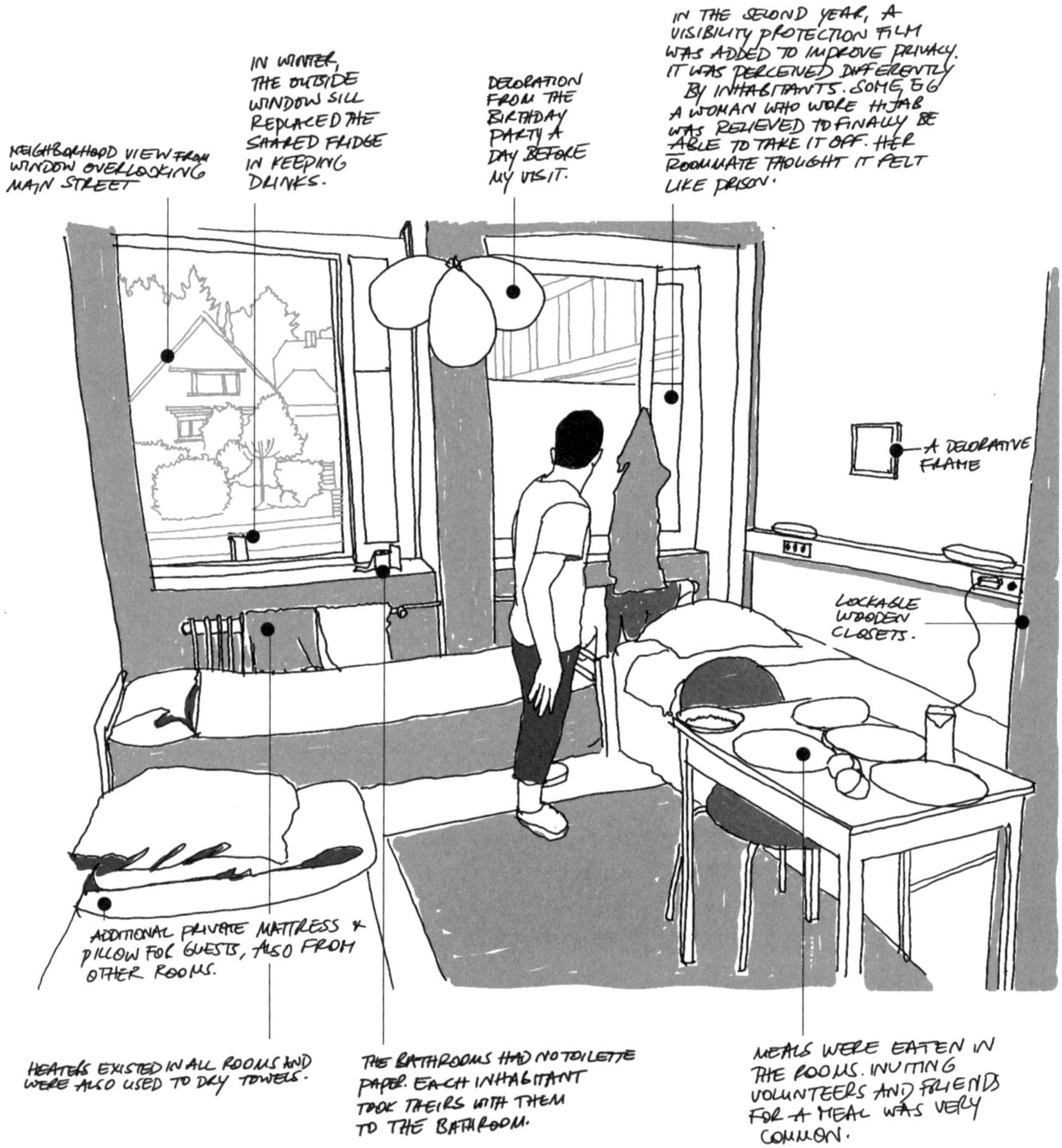

Figure 11. A two-man room; the young inhabitant had it to himself as his roommate was away.

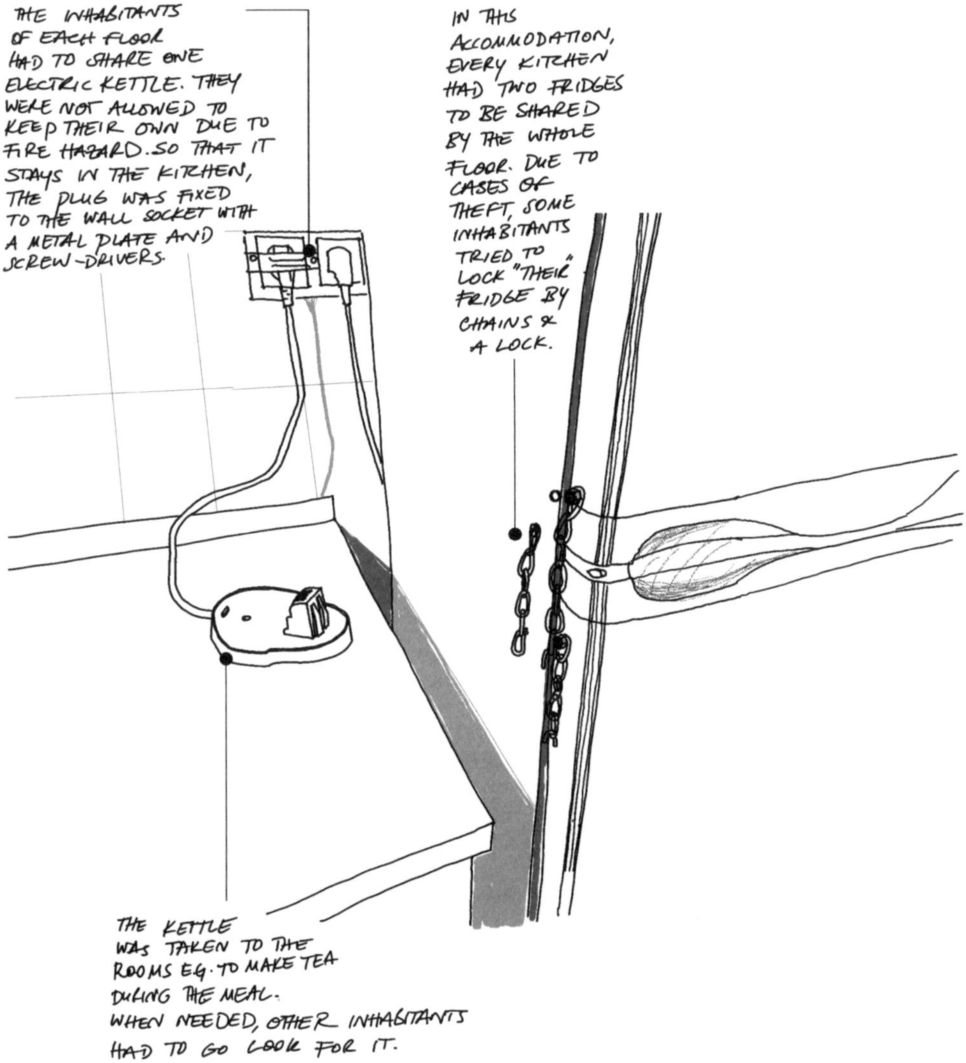

Figure 12. Details of the shared kitchen.

Figure 13. Game night (photovoice drawing).

Figure 14. Iftar in Ramadan, 2016 (photovoice drawing).

1. Relationships and interactions with the physical space

Regardless of the architecture and size of the accommodations, many Arab-speaking research participants referred to their accommodations as "*camm*," an Arabized version of "camp." Interestingly, the Arab-speaking informants did not use the Arabic word for camp – *Mukhayyam* – which has a very long history in the Middle East due to the existence of Palestinian refugee camps for more than 70 years. The Arabic word, I argue, is reserved for camps that started as tent-structures, containers, or barracks, as most Palestinian refugee camps started (Wari 2015, 116) before their urbanization led to their integration into the urban surroundings of their host cities. Despite this consolidation and integration, these camps are still referred to as *Mukhayyam*. Another frequent reference to these accommodations was the German word *Heim*. These references by the inhabitants show that it does not matter how new or permanent the building structure is, the availability and quality of infrastructure and services, or whether it is located in the Global North or South, for it to be considered a refugee camp by its inhabitants. What matters is the exceptionality of the accommodation situation, the stigmatization and otherness that its inhabitants feel. However, the physical spaces of the accommodations were perceived differently by their inhabitants, depending on personal characteristics (Carp 2008, 132), the diverse backgrounds, and the lifestyles of their users. This is in addition to the activities and movement patterns in these spaces, which were directly related to the spatial layouts of each accommodation.

In Accommodation A, most of the inhabitants left the accommodation during the day. Whether on their German courses, in vocational training, dealing with their asylum procedures, or hanging out in the city, the men spent, or tried to spend, their time outside the accommodation. Lack of volunteers and activities on-site gave the inhabitants even fewer reasons to spend their days at the accommodation. As a result, the city center was an extension of their lived space in the accommodation. The community spaces in the accommodation were not often used. In addition to the occasional use of a gym on the first floor, the TV in that floor's kitchen was only used by a small group of men at night, which was reported to exclude others from using the kitchen during that time.

In general, there was no feeling of "ownership" in the spaces of this accommodation. The high number of cohabitants per parcel and the height of the walls, which did not reach the ceiling, gave a strong impression of temporariness. Therefore, many belongings remained unpacked in suitcases on the floor or on top of the lockers, and personal expressions or decorations were hardly observed. An additional example of this lack of ownership is the disinterest in the collective garden habilitation project mentioned in Fig. 1. The project aimed to enlist asylum seekers to help increase seating in the garden while they waited for the resolution of their application, a process that resulted in putting many aspects of their lives on hold (Bjertrup et al. 2018).

Due to the more private nature of the rooms and the fewer number of people sharing them in Accommodation B, the rooms offered a better possibility of retreat and more inhabitants spent time inside the accommodation during the day compared with Accommodation A. This is partly because of the presence of women and children, and due to green open areas, the playground, and the abundance of communal spaces and organized activities.

Although the inhabitants were able to lock their rooms, many ended up not doing so during the day, especially since they moved through the floor to use the bathrooms, washing machines, kitchen, or to socialize with others. While this made the floor atmosphere more familial for the floor residents, it also violated the privacy of the inhabitants. In the first year, before the entrances were locked, volunteers opened the doors and barged into the rooms, while I was visiting, to offer their services or donations. Other inhabitants did that too; one floor spokesperson, a woman (50+) and mother of three adults who wanted to introduce me to other inhabitants, simply opened the doors of other rooms and entered.

The spatial layouts and size of this accommodation led to unequal access to resources like information and donations among the inhabitants. The location of an individual's room or the timing of their presence in the accommodation were important factors leading to this inequality. The inhabitants of the rooms close to the main entrance had a clear advantage over those living on other floors or in the other buildings, because information flyers were hung in the main building's lobby. Volunteers, who also came through the main entrance to pick up people for spontaneous activities or to distribute donations, usually kept the refugees present in the lobby informed. This excluded others who were in German class or in their rooms at that time. This randomness changed after the volunteer-coordinator position was established and with the introduction of the security room at the entrance, which led to more control of the entrance space.

Two months before the closure of this accommodation, and while the city was trying to decide whether to extend its rental contract, inhabitants of the accommodation spoke up to keep it open. Some showed off their decorated rooms, community spaces, children's and leisure activities, and "integration measures" to the visiting city officials from different political parties, in an attempt to convince them to extend its rental contract. On that day and during a chat with inhabitants from different rooms, two inhabitants (32 and 10 years old) explained that after two years, it had "strangely become home." They could not imagine taking a different bus line to go to another accommodation since they have gotten used to the space and life in it. The decision to close this accommodation was seen as absurd and unfair by both the staff and its inhabitants.[7] In general, the inhabitants of this accommodation had more sense of ownership of the space, which was apparent through the appropriation of spaces in the rooms, including decoration of visited rooms (more by women and families) or for parties (also by single men) and by displaying photos and personal items on the windowsills. Their ownership was also visible in their participation in different activities and projects, and in their territoriality (Storey 2017) on the different floors, as discussed later.

2. Relationships and interactions with cohabitants

The spatial layouts, demographic density of accommodations, shared amenities, and possibilities for privacy, and individual/personal differences, are all factors that play a role in the type of relationships among cohabitants. Higher density, less privacy, and higher competition for resources and use of spaces bring with them higher possibilities of conflict (Christ, Meininghaus, and Röing 2019).

A clerk in the city used five categories to accommodate people together in the same room – gender, age range, nationality, legal status, and health condition. These categories are meant to allow communication and reduce conflicts (Interview with city clerk 2016). Looking beyond the five categories, and according to the research's empirical findings, many people who ended up living together were found to have very different short- and long-term needs, preferences, and lifestyles. Things as small as times or ways to open or close the window for light, ventilation, or privacy could become a source of disagreement.

Although the inhabitants in Accommodation A were mostly divided in the rooms along national and linguistic lines, there was not enough time for people to get used to each other's lifestyles. The inhabitants were changing while people moved in and out, and a different set of nationalities was arriving after the borders were closed, changing the demographic and linguistic composition, and adding new groups to the accommodation system.

The interaction of asylum seekers with their cohabitants in this accommodation ranged from solidarity to conflict. Solidarity surfaced in times of deportations, in cases of perceived injustices towards a fellow inhabitant, or in the case of a cohabitant receiving guests (for example, a girlfriend, who was officially not allowed). In that case, the cohabitants would leave the room to give each other privacy. This solidarity was also in cooking for cohabitants who cannot cook or in sharing useful contacts and information (or, unknowingly, rumors) about asylum procedures, rights, possibilities, and daily life issues.

On the other hand, conflicts surfaced over the (mis)use of shared spaces, noise levels at night, different habits, and standards of cleanliness in the kitchens or bathrooms. Such conflicts were usually resolved by the staff, after several warnings, through collective punishment by closing the kitchens or bathrooms for several days, which only increased the pressure on the bathrooms and kitchens on other floors. Some inhabitants asked the staff for solutions like assigning the stoves/ovens to different rooms and locking them, or dividing the bathrooms along "cultural lines." Cases of theft in some rooms went unreported because it is almost impossible to prove who was responsible with the high number of cohabitants, and their different and changing timelines and lifestyles. One research participant reported that the cohabitants knew who stole things from their room, but the person was not reported to avoid conflict and further discomfort in the room by adding distrust to the high density and lack of privacy.

In Accommodation B, the floor inhabitants together created a spatial unit that would defend the communal and public spaces on the floor from being used by "strangers" from other floors. This appropriation changed the meaning and nature of the "private" and "public" divide. Examples of this include the internet modem (Fig. 10) and the TV located in the lobby of another floor and meant for public use. Friction would break out when people from other floors wanted to watch the TV because it was seen as an invasion of the "private" space of the inhabitants of that particular floor. While one reason for this type of friction would come from men who wished to defend their families from the gaze of strangers, a more prominent reason was the noise that such gatherings would bring.

On the other hand, the familial atmosphere on the floors led to other types of solidarity among the inhabitants of the floor and the accommodation. Some refugees inhabited different rooms at different times, thus becoming familiar to cohabitants of different floors and created close relationships with those living there. In one case, a family took in a young single man living on the same floor. They shared their food and provided a family atmosphere for the young man to socialize and feel less alone. Single men cooperated by offering or sharing their rooms with others to increase privacy if they left the accommodation for several days and their room was empty while other rooms were full.

3. Relationships and interactions with administrative staff and volunteers

In the context of refugee accommodation, there is a clear power imbalance between the refugees and the administrative staff. In addition to helping and supporting inhabitants in different matters, the staff make decisions on the scale of the accommodation and the rooms, which can affect the lives of asylum seekers and refugees. They control their abidance by the rules and sometimes punish them in case they do not comply. In most accommodations, the staff have the freedom to deal with different transgressions. Sanctions usually range from talking to the transgressor, collective punishment, transfer to different rooms or accommodations, and/or a ban on entering the building (*Hausverbot*).

Preferential treatment of certain nationalities by the staff was often a theme during my fieldwork, as it is in other literature (see Christ, Meininghau, and Röing 2019). This is especially due to the hierarchies that the asylum system creates with the inhabitants' different *Bleibeperspektive* or residency permits, and the different opportunities that they offer. It is also due to the cultural or linguistic background of some staff members who do, or are expected to, offer people from the same background more support than others. Additionally, fieldwork observations concluded that multilingual staff members, just like translators, exercise more power, not only compared with asylum seekers, but also compared with German colleagues.

Just like the staff, volunteers usually have a stable legal status, understand the system, and speak the host language, which most asylum seekers and refugees do not while living in collective accommodations. An additional factor in the power relations with volunteers is the dependence of inhabitants on their willingness or availability to offer support and help. These power relations are similar in centralized accommodations. However, there are differences in the power relations between different accommodations and in individual cases.

The welfare organization running Accommodation A offered a higher staffing ratio and worked on the weekends.[8] With two shifts, the inhabitants could receive support for longer hours of the day. Additionally, and due to the relatively limited number of volunteers, staff members organized some activities like a bike workshop, a cycling orientation to learn German traffic rules and habits, and the garden project. However, the male-only demographic of the accommodation with an almost female-only staff gave this accommodation a distinct atmosphere regarding gender and power relations. The staff also had more control in this accommodation, not only visually through their location at the entrance, but also on the private level of the parcel by controlling the shutters and windows (Fig. 4). Nevertheless, the relationships with the staff members ranged from close friendship to mutual avoidance and conflict.

The fact that the staff only spoke German and English reduced the potential advantage of some groups (such as Arabic- and Farsi-speaking) over others, which was observed in other accommodations. However, it also led some inhabitants to look for support from volunteers and translators elsewhere. Many relied on information – or rumors – from their cohabitants. Approaching "outsiders" for support caused occasional friction between the volunteers and the staff members, who perceived volunteers to be overstepping their limits or taking over their tasks, especially if they were already providing the same inhabitant with support on the same issue. However, the inhabitants insisted on outside help – sometimes asking several actors simultaneously to help with a certain task – either out of lack of trust in specific staff members due to communication barriers, or as a backup plan in case solicitations for help from one actor failed to satisfy their needs. This is one example of the agency that asylum seekers and refugees have. Other examples are their appropriation of space, their territoriality in defending their space, breaking or bending some rules, deciding how and where they chose to spend their time, or by moving away from the city or country (Seethaler-Wari 2018).

The staff of Accommodation B were available for one daytime shift (9 a.m. until 5 p.m.) on weekdays. The staff attempted to realize the rules and regulations and tried to be strict when rules were broken; however, their location in the basement, lack of visual control of the entrances, and the greater number of inhabitants all led to limited control compared with other accommodations. The staff still had an amount of power that was criticized by the inhabitants. For example, a staff member was once asked to call the ambulance for an ill resident but, upon visiting her room, decided that the case did not merit calling an ambulance. Being regarded as unqualified to decide on the severity of the medical case started the staff member off on the wrong foot with people who needed a long time thereafter to mend that broken trust.

Due to the multiple languages spoken by the staff members, this accommodation was better equipped than others to directly communicate with many inhabitants. The two staff members, one Arabic-speaking and one Farsi-speaking, received criticism from their own groups, at least during the first 18 months. Each was criticized for not helping "their own" like they should. Interestingly, they were both praised by the other linguistic/national groups for being friendly and helpful. This shows that the communication privilege that Arabic- and Farsi-speaking refugees had was accompanied by high expectations of preferential treatment and resulting disappointments.

The abundance of volunteers, sponsors, and initiatives around this accommodation removed a great amount of pressure from the administrative staff. The inhabitants were generally more informed about different refugee-related activities in the city, and many participated in German classes and sought support from volunteer services. Despite this abundance, a group of single Pakistani men complained that it was hard for them to find help or language support from volunteers. They claimed that the Syrian family next door had several volunteers helping them and that they had a helper present at all times during the day. The tremendous amount of help, support, and donations offered by volunteers was praised in every event I attended. However, issues were raised by research participants about the selectivity of their offers to specific accommodations, specific nationalities (*Bleibeperspektive*), genders or marital/social statuses of the refugees they chose to support.

Accommodations A and B: similarities and differences

In addition to the similarities that led to choosing these accommodations, the presented spatial layouts and inhabitation practices showed how both accommodations were also similar in the sense that neither could offer their inhabitants a sense of normality. They could offer limited, though varied, levels of privacy and comfort. Living in such largely visible collective accommodations stigmatizes their inhabitants and highlights their "otherness" to outsiders through the form of building they inhabit (Hauge, Støa, and Denizou 2017). Accommodations in industrial or commercial surroundings, like Accommodation A, added another layer of isolation felt by the refugees, that the different direct surroundings played a role in the time inhabitants spent in the neighborhood and how they spent their free time.

Another similarity was the presence of administrative staff on-site in both accommodations, regardless of the different staffing ratio and working times. This helped the inhabitants in their first phase of arrival to get oriented and communicate either in their own language or through access to translators until they could navigate their surroundings and live independently. Social workers helped the inhabitants by arranging for translators to accompany them on appointments, organizing leisure activities, and providing support in their asylum processes by helping fill out forms and explaining processes. Despite these similarities, both the spatial layouts and inhabitation practices showed how different daily life, social interactions, and opportunities can be for inhabitants, depending on the accommodation in which they end up.

The accommodations had different levels of control and strictness from the staff members. On one hand, the limited security in Accommodation B offered more "normality" in the first year, where leaving the accommodation for several days would go unnoticed, and where receiving guests, at least during the day, went mostly uncontrolled. This was not the case in Accommodation A. On the other hand, the lack of control also allowed outsiders to peep into their private spaces and lives, even with good intentions, violating their privacy, making assumptions about their needs, and patronizing them. This was not possible in Accommodation A.

Accommodation A had access to fewer volunteers, and accordingly had fewer opportunities to practice the German language, and less access to information and donations. However, the abundance of volunteers and donations in Accommodation B was accompanied by inequality in its distribution, which resulted in internal competition and friction/hard feelings among individuals, national and social groups who were excluded from donations, German classes, or from leisure activities for the benefit of "more privileged" cohabitants.

The difference in the demographic composition of both accommodations provided different overall atmospheres, different concerns, different gender and power relations with the staff, different patterns of conflicts among the inhabitants, and different intensities of competition over resources among individuals and groups. The difference in demographic composition and the diverse socioeconomic profiles of the inhabitants in Accommodation B also led some to socialize along class lines. An example is a university student who reported that her four-member family limited their interaction with others from the same country because they came from a different socioeconomic background, which I had not observed in Accommodation A.

The inhabitants of both accommodations experienced different levels of exclusion from the urban space, neighborhood space, and from resources and services. While Accommodation A was apparently more excluded from refugee-related activities in the city, and from access to volunteers and regular donations, specific national or social groups in Accommodation B were excluded from access to volunteers and donations based on their *Bleibeperspektive,* marital status, or room location. In that sense, there was more equality and less competition among the inhabitants of Accommodation A than B.

Another difference was the multilingual staff members in Accommodation B, who increased possibilities of communication for the inhabitants. However, it also gave an advantage to Arabic and Farsi speakers, and excluded other groups who had no available translators on-site. For Tigrinya, for example, translators were often requested without much success, and for more than a year, an inhabitant from Baluchistan, in Pakistan, was not able to communicate properly with others because he had no fellow countrymen, and translators could not be found for his mother tongue. The lack of multilingual staff in Accommodation A limited the potential advantage, and resulting competition, among linguistic groups and caused a lack of expectations of preferential treatment from the staff. However, this difference also limited the ability of inhabitants to communicate with the staff in their first months – especially with the lack of access to translators, causing the behavior of some staff members to be misattributed to discrimination rather than to correctness in applying the many regulations.

Conclusion

Through architectural ethnography, this article visualized the physical and social contexts of two accommodations in the city of Göttingen, allowing the exterior and interior spaces to speak for themselves. Methodologically, the drawings visualized the inhabitation practices that took place in the accommodations during the fieldwork. Drawing their details led me to think more about the multilayered and complex reality of accommodation. I had to engage with every piece of furniture and every action in the space, which raised additional questions for my research participants that photos would not have inspired. Drawing participants' photos also made me see every detail in these photos, thereby illustrating the space from the inhabitants' perspectives and adding their reported feelings and thoughts about it in text form. I, therefore, join the scholars and architects (see Kaijima, Stalder, and Iseki 2018, Tayob 2018, and Avermaete 2020) who use architecture ethnography, in encouraging drawing as an important complementary method or tool in the study of space. I believe that it is especially relevant when the research focus is the users of space and their socio-spatial practices.

The article brought together architectural drawings and ethnographic research methods, showcasing how diverse the social spaces of refugees can be. This is not only due to the different spatial layouts and privacy levels, but also the important roles that demographic constitution, power dynamics and relationships with the administrative staff, volunteers and with other cohabitants of the accommodation play in shaping the experiences of asylum seekers and refugees in their host environment, and the consequences of these spatial and institutional differences on the daily lives of their respective inhabitants.

The emerging similarities and differences between both accommodations were not meant to show which accommodation is better. Diverse asylum seekers with varying needs, lifestyles, and priorities had different feelings, perceptions, and perspectives about their lives in both accommodations.

Indeed, refugees and asylum seekers did negotiate the use and meaning in their spaces with the local actors – administrative staff and volunteers – or with their co-habitants. The blurred definitions and boundaries of "private" and "public" provided a margin for the inhabitants to redefine the boundaries and appropriate spaces to better meet their diverse needs as the article showed. Their activities were not limited to what the *camm* offered or allowed. Their inhabitation practices usually extended outside the room/parcel and the accommodation into the city, and further into other cities or countries if needed.

Finally, different actors in refugee reception and integration, whether local authorities, architects, or individuals working with the host cities, sometimes have to deal with certain circumstances, existing buildings, or spaces. Some existing buildings with their institutional arrangements can be more suitable for temporary accommodation and for facilitating better future trajectories than others. The accommodations described in the article show how different spatial and nonspatial institutional arrangements can result in decisions made elsewhere whose outcomes carry real consequences for inhabitation practices, levels of stigma and exclusion, number of volunteers, and first experiences and thereby for future trajectories of inhabitants. It also shows how all these actors influence the spaces through architectural design, administrative and political decisions, management, or inhabitation practices, illustrating how different actors are makers and authors of architectural space.

All illustrations in this contribution by the author.

1 In this paper, the term "asylum seekers" refers to people whose asylum application was still being processed. "Refugees" refers to asylum seekers whose asylum procedure was complete, resulting in a residency permit, regardless of the differences between the types of recognition (e.g, full protection according to the Geneva Convention, asylum entitlement, subsidiary protection, etc.) and duration of the granted residency. More on the process and possible outcomes of the asylum procedure in Germany can be found in Seethaler-Wari 2019, 12. **2** The term *Bleibeperspektive* is used in German to describe chances of recognition of an asylum application and prospects of remaining in Germany. It is a practitioners' term and does not have a legal standing (Seethaler-Wari 2019, 14). Having a good *Bleibeperspektive* means that the asylum seeker's nationality offers them a probability of higher than 50 percent of receiving full refugee protection or asylum. The categorization is revised every six months. In the second half of 2017, five nationalities had a good *Bleibeperspektive*: Syrian, Iraqi, Iranian, Eritrean, and Somalian. As of August 1, 2019, only Syrians and Eritreans had good chances of recognition (BAMF 2020). **3** Photovoice is a research method used in qualitative and participatory research to document and reflect the reality of research participants. Through photographs, drawing, or art works, research participants can bring new insights and perspectives by expressing their own point of view. **4** The German word for sponsor as used here is *Pate*. **5** Social workers are part of the administrative staff of every accommodation. However, most social workers I met in accommodations did not have a background in social work. Their individual qualifications and experiences were very diverse. Therefore, the article preferably uses the term "staff member." **6** I use "parcels" in the article to refer to compartments separated by partitions that do not reach the ceiling. **7** It is worth mentioning here that at the time of those chats, the number of inhabitants in the accommodation had decreased considerably, as many had found housing or moved elsewhere. **8** In this accommodation, translators were external part-time staff members. The staffing ratio here refers to administrative staff and social workers that are present on a daily basis.

References

Avermaete, T. 2020. "Die beschreibende Tradition. Eine kleine Geschichte der Architektur Ethnographie." *Arch+ Zeitschrift für Architektur und Urbanismus*, no. 238: 76–85.

Bjertrup, P. J., M. Bouhenia, P. Mayaud, C. Perrin, J. Ben Farhat, and K. Blanchet. 2018. "A Life in Waiting: Refugees' Mental Health and Narratives of Social Suffering after European Union Border Closures in March 2016." *Social Science & Medicine* 215: 53–60. https://doi.org/10.1016/j.socscimed.2018.08.040.

Bundesamt für Migration und Flüchtlinge BAMF. n.d. *Was heißt gute Bleibeperspektive?* [Website]. Accessed December 11, 2020. https://www.bamf.de/SharedDocs/FAQ/DE/IntegrationskurseAsylbewerber/001-bleibeperspektive.html?nn=282388.

Carp, J. 2008. "'Ground-Truthing' Representations of Social Space: Using Lefebvre's Conceptual Triad." *Journal of Planning Education and Research* 28: 129–42.

Christ, S., E. Meininghaus, and T. Röing. 2019. "'All Day Waiting' Causes of Conflict in Refugee Shelters in Germany." *BICC* Working Paper 3.

De Certeau, M. 1984. *The Practice of Everyday Life*. London: University of California Press.

Foucault, M. 1995. *Discipline and Punish: The Birth of the Prison*. Second edition. New York: Vintage Books.

Geertz, C. 1973. *The Interpretation of Cultures*. New York: Basic Books.

Hauge, Å., E. Støa, and K. Denizou. 2017. "Framing Outsidedness – Aspects of Housing Quality in Decentralized Reception Centres for Asylum Seekers in Norway." *Housing, Theory and Society* 34, no. 1: 1–20.

Hainmueller, J., D. Hangartner, and D. Lawrence. 2016. "When Lives Are Put on Hold: Lengthy Asylum Processes Decrease Employment Among Refugees." *Science Advances* 2, no. 8: 1–7. DOI: 10.1126/sciadv.1600432.

Kaijima, M., L. Stalder, and Y. Iseki. 2018. *Architectural Ethnography – Japanese Pavilion Venice Biennale*. Tokyo: TOTO.

Lefèbvre, H. 1991. *The Production of Space*. Oxford: Blackwell Publishing.

Massey, D. 2013. "Doreen Massey on Space." Social Science Space [Website]. https://www.socialscience-space.com/2013/02/podcastdoreen-massey-on-space.

Newman, O. 1972. *Defensible Space: Crime Prevention through Urban Design*. First edition. New York: MacMillan Publishing Company.

Newman, O. 1996. *Creating Defensible Space*. New York: US Department of Housing and Urban Development.

Ponterotto, J. G. 2006. "Brief Note on the Origins, Evolution, and Meaning of the Qualitative Research Concept Thick Description." *The Qualitative Report* 11, no. 3: 538–49.

Seethaler-Wari, S. 2018. "Urban Planning for the Integration of Refugees: The Importance of Local Factors." *Urban Planning* 3, no. 4: 141–55.

Seethaler-Wari, S. 2019. "Asylum Seekers of the Syrian Conflict: Procedures and Patterns of Settlement in Germany," *MPI-MMG* Working Paper, 19–04.

Stadt Göttingen. n.d. Demonstration auf der Siekhöhe. Göttingen–Stadt, die Wissen schafft [Website]. Accessed August 9, 2018. www.goettingen.de/aktuelles/2018-06-28/demonstrationauf-der-siekhoehe.html.

Storey, D. 2017. "Territory and Territoriality." In *Oxford Bibliographies in Geography*, edited by B. Warf. New York: Oxford University Press. DOI: 10.1093/obo/9780199874002-0076.

Tayob, H. 2018. "Subaltern Architectures: Can Drawing 'Tell' a Different Story?" *Architecture and Culture* 6, no. 1: 203–22. DOI: 10.1080/20507828.2017.1417071.

Vertovec, S., S. Becker, A. Fleischer, M. Schader, and S. Wari. 2017. "Addressing the Diversity of Asylum-Seekers' Needs and Aspirations: A Report to the Volkswagen Foundation." *MPI-MMG* Working Paper, 17-05.

Wari, S. 2017. *Palestinian Berlin: Perceptions and Use of Public Space*. Berlin: LIT Verlag.

Between Inhabitation and Dwelling: (Im)mobilities in Everyday Life

Maja Momić

This paper identifies and traces different inhabitation practices and trajectories of refugees in the city of Hamburg. By doing so, it showcases the many spheres of life – the legal, the material, the lived – that intertwine with these trajectories. The paper further shows how inhabitation operates as a ground for resisting oppressive mechanisms while simultaneously shaping the urban sphere. It conceptualizes inhabitation as a mode of relationality with others *and* the city through practices of mutual care, and by imagining – and performing – that which could be. Reflecting on the concepts of inhabitation and dwelling, the paper uses both to show their complementary nature while arguing their inseparability from other spheres of life. Finally, the paper explores the ambivalent relation between mobility and immobility based on the example of different dwelling patterns, thus demonstrating how movement and change can be examined only in relation to immobility and relative settledness.

Introduction

This paper proposes the notion of inhabitation as a *dispositif* for looking at the wider societal and urban processes. In particular, the paper uses refugees'[1] inhabitation practices in Hamburg as a lens for examining urban space production and inherent mobility-immobility relations. Foucault proposes *dispositif* as a web that connects various elements (discursive or not) along with their position shifts and changes of functions (Foucault 1978); a reading, an interpretation, a lens that aligns those elements. Although Foucault predominantly uses this term to describe various institutional or administrative mechanisms that use knowledge and power relations to exercise dominance and maintain certain social order – or precisely because of this – proposing inhabitation as a *dispositif* suggests a subversion of these power relations, as to be illustrated in the analytical part, later in this paper.

Agamben, furthermore, expands on Foucault's concept of *dispositif* or apparatus, by including "literally anything that has in some way the capacity to capture, orient, determine, intercept, model, control, or secure the gestures, behaviours, or discourses of living beings" (Agamben 2009, 14). I argue that the study of inhabitation practices not only provides insights into refugees' everyday lives and their surroundings, but also captures their relation to the wider urban space and the urban society. It further unveils oftentimes contradictory impacts of different regulations (asylum, migration, labor, and social policies) as well as their spatial translations (functional order, built spaces) on daily life and thus on inhabitation experiences and trajectories. Finally, the *dispositif* of inhabitation makes visible the spatial authorship and its potentiality. Through their practices of (urban) space appropriation and alteration, the inhabitants "develop the ability to manage the city for themselves, they give shape to the urban" (Purcell 2014, 151).

The paper begins by engaging with the notions of dwelling and inhabitation on a theoretical level.[2] Then, it situates these notions in the context of German laws and regulations regarding refugee accommodation – seemingly not suitable for (a Western idea of) dwelling, essentially uninhabitable. Next, the paper zooms into the accommodation system in the city of Hamburg and its sets of regulations that, at least at first sight, render refugees' inhabitation practices nearly impossible. By describing different dwelling situations of refugees in Hamburg, I will show that inhabitation, albeit sometimes provisional, is indeed inevitable, even in the most precarious conditions. This is visible on inhabitation practices both within the accommodations and across the city. In the section thereafter, on the example of the inhabitation trajectory of a woman with a so-called tolerance permit, I will illustrate how marginalization also has the potentiality to become a site of resistance – through inhabitation.

On dwelling and inhabitation

Despite his indisputably problematic political positions and the fair amount of criticism that followed (see Elden 2000, Young 2005, Harrison 2007, Holland et al. 2010, Brun 2016, Woods 2019), many scholars still refer to Heidegger's writing on dwelling as a starting point for theorizing this concept.[3] He defines dwelling as a basic human need and understands it as the way mortals *are* on the Earth (Heidegger 1994), illustrating thereby the close etymological and semiotic relation between the verbs "to build," "to dwell/to inhabit," and "to be" (Heidegger 1994, 141).[4] Thus, dwelling applies to all aspects of human life and cannot be restricted or reduced merely to a place of residence. In other words, we cannot not dwell – we dwell even when we are working, when we are traveling, in our free time, in different places of our sojourn. Building on Heidegger, Hasse also deals with thinking about dwelling as an existential area of human existence and expression (Hasse 2009). In his book *Unconcerned Dwelling: Dwelling Forms at Hidden Margins of Society,*[5] he examines dwelling situations of those who live away from bourgeois normality and thus do not necessarily correspond to the typical cultural understanding of dwelling, such as the homeless, inmates, seamen, monastery inhabitants, dwellers of circled wagons, etc. Hasse suggests that "as long as the day-to-day recurring matters of dwelling can be overcome, dwelling itself does not have to be of/a concern" (Hasse 2009, 14; translated by the author). In other words, extreme dwelling situations, marginal to the presumed center/normality, are most suitable for reflecting on – or rather dwelling upon – the notion of dwelling. Relating to Heidegger's notion of a crisis in dwelling where "qualified space is replaced by quantified space," Lefebvre notes that inhabiting (*habiter*) has been reduced to the notion of habitat (*habitat*) (Elden 2004, 190). While habitat is merely a container, a function, a brutal material reality, *habiter* expresses an activity, a situation, a practice, in relation to urban and social space (Elden 2004, 190). *Habitat*, or the quantified space, is what mostly preoccupies urban planners and architects, as they "give priority to functional arrangements of life: eating, sleeping, working, consuming" (Dadusc et al. 2019, 523). Further, it could be argued that the same logic of prioritizing habitat also lies behind the understanding of housing as a mere commodity, exchange value, a container-space defined a priori to dwelling (Lancione 2019). *Habiter*, on the other hand, "is that which will always overflow, and it is often translated as living" (Dadusc et al. 2019, 523).

Notably, Boano and Astolfo propose to expand the notion of dwelling by including "intersecting forms of caring, repairing and imagining the future" (2020, 569). Inhabitation is thus a relational practice, inseparable from everyday practices of care, repair, and reproduction. This framing of inhabitation engenders imagining – and living – cities, neighborhoods, and communities not solely "as sites of refuge, but as spaces where rights can be produced; spaces where the 'struggle' for inhabitation takes place" (Boano and Astolfo 2020, 567).

Situating dwelling in the legal framework

The notion of dwelling, as described above, fairly diverges from the current definition by the German Federal Administrative Law, which characterizes dwelling as a form of durable domesticity, individual housekeeping, and freely chosen residence (BVerwG 1996). Accordingly, refugee accommodation contradicts the very idea of dwelling; it is envisioned and laid out as temporary and does not involve individual decision-making over housekeeping or facilities. Moreover, it is not based on the self-determined choice of residence, as distribution mechanisms such as the Dublin Regulation at the EU level or the Königsteiner Schlüssel regulation at the federal level (reinforced by the *Residenzpflicht* – mandatory residence in the assigned city or district) have a clear priority over a refugee's autonomous decision.

Refugee accommodation is characterized by a clear separation of functions and a dry, pragmatic instrumental rationalism, therefore reminiscent of the ideal of early Modernist urban planning, and embodies "a trust in order and hygiene" (Herz 2008). Beyond doubt, the same reference (Charte d'Athènes and "The Functional City") was applied in the 1950s to conceive the Land Use Ordinance (*BauNVO*) and the Building Code (*BauGB*) – documents that imprint on urban and architectural planning in Germany down to the present day. In fact, the aforementioned legal definition of dwelling originates from the 1996 verdict of the Federal Administrative Court,[6] which excluded a children's home from a purely residential area on the grounds of not fulfilling the three main criteria of dwelling – permanent, self-reliantly managed, and freely chosen (residence). Henceforth, together with homeless shelters, student dormitories, and (senior citizens' or children's) nursing homes, refugee accommodation appertains to the "special dwelling types" (*Sonderwohnformen*) since it allegedly does not serve to the satisfaction of the housing needs, but rather to a custody with simultaneous supervision, care, and guidance (Fickert and Fieseler 2014).

Thus, in the construction of the legal concept, the focus is clearly on dwelling as a function dissociated and distinct from other functions. In reality, however, dwelling cannot be understood as a static notion – it rather varies through time, but also culturally and geographically – as every society brings forth the dwelling forms that are appropriate to it (Hasse 2009, 236). Paraphrasing Jürgen Hasse, a human being is considered to be dwelling in their culture as they settle down in the multifaceted city space with the means of this culture (Hasse 2012). In regard to the refugee accommodation, the aspect of settling down is quite challenging, not only due to the uncertainties related to chances and duration of staying, but also because of its spatial setting, that is, the (in)ability of spatial appropriation, arrangement, and organization of personal space according to dwelling habits, rituals, routines, and material cultures.

Inhabitation as a site of resistance

Drawing upon his decades-long research on cities in Africa and South Asia, AbdouMaliq Simone (2016) engages with the apparent uninhabitability of certain environments and the ways in which the inhabitants negotiate it. According to Simone, it is the Western, colonial perspectives that label and normalize "as uninhabitable the places where many people attempt to make a life" (2016, 138). He further argues that "if we only pay attention to the rollout of contemporary spatial products as exemplars of urban neoliberalism, we might miss opportunities to see something else taking place, vulnerable and provisional though it may be" (2016, 151).

Building on bell hook's distinction between "that marginality which is imposed by oppressive structures and that marginality one chooses as site of resistance – as location of radical openness and possibility" (hooks 1989, 23), Michele Lancione invites us to engage with *dwelling as difference* that "emerges from uncanny places, uninhabitable 'homes' and multiple violent histories" (Lancione 2019, 275). Similarly, Boano and Astolfo characterize inhabitation as "a relational practice occurring in marginal and fragile environments and constituted by multiple incremental and transformative acts with the ultimate purpose to hold and resist marginalisation" (2020, 569).

Hannah Arendt argues that the only way for us to become aware of the "right to have rights" was "only when there suddenly emerged millions of people who had lost and could not regain these rights because of the new global political situation" (1968, 177). Since (civil) rights are very closely related to (national) citizenship, the question arises about the rights of all people who inhabit the city, regardless of their (im)mobility status. Here, Lefebvre brings the "right to the city" into play, which he uses to interrogate the rights of urban citizens (1996): Do inhabitants, in the same way as citizens, have the right to the city? He argues that it is not a (national) citizenship, but "the everyday experience of inhabiting the city that entitles one to a right to the city" (Purcell 2014, 142). The right to the city is "set in motion when inhabitants decide to rise up and reclaim space in the city, when they assert use value over exchange value, encounter over consumption, interaction over segregation, free activity and play over work" (Purcell 2014, 151). Migration, among other forms of marginality, has the capacity to reshape and redefine the social map of the city (Lentin 2002), thus "unsettling, at least temporarily, established norms, structures and relations of urban life" (Hatziprokopiou et al. 2016, 53).

Furthermore, as Colin McFarlane points out, housing "is a doing – if it is *dwelt* or *inhabited* as much as it is built – this dwelling is a form of urban assembly" and "the city itself a gathering process" (2011, 250, original emphasis). Yet, migrants' and refugees' everyday lives often remain hidden and made invisible, especially with respect to inhabitation as material and materializing practices (relational arrangements of actors, manifestation of everyday practices, reproduction, care, rituals, habits, appropriation, items, built environment, policies, etc.).

Case study Hamburg: contextualizing inhabitation practices

In order to portray different patterns and trajectories of *inhabiting displacement* in Hamburg, I have tried to engage with as diverse inhabitants as possible and have traced their inhabitation practices.[7] While most data were collected between 2015 and 2018, I also stayed in contact with several individuals thereafter. I used a mix of

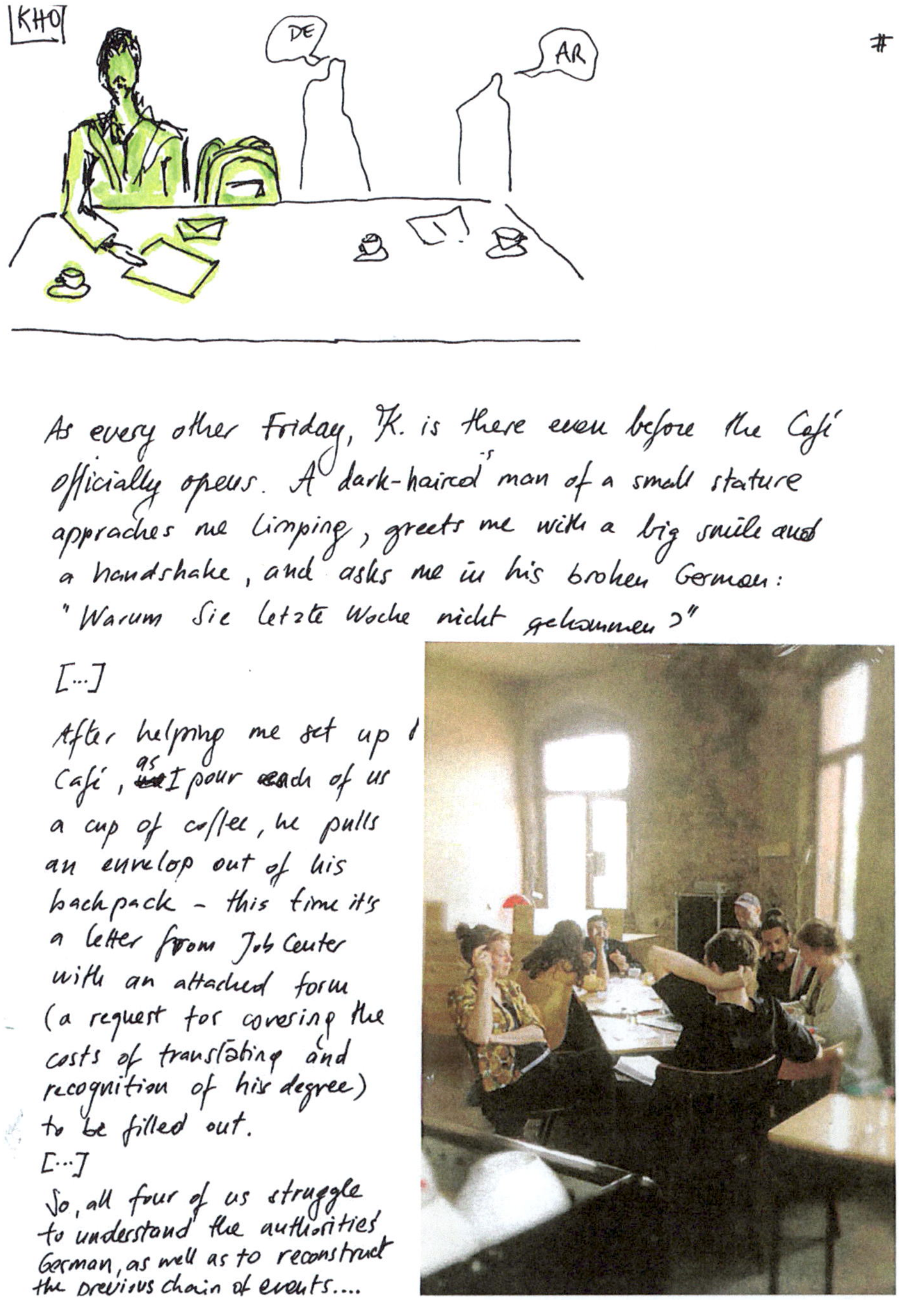

Figure 1. Café routines, journal entry, June 2017. Source: Author

architectural and ethnographic methods: mapping, typological analysis, diagrammatics, observation and participatory observation, dense descriptions, go-alongs, narrative and semi-structured interviews. In order to unfold structural linkages and discover emerging patterns from rather heterogeneous collected data, I analyzed and correlated them with the aid of grounded theory (Glaser and Strauss 1967, Glaser 1978).

Architecture of Hamburg's refugee accommodation system

Refugee accommodations in Hamburg are distributed over the entire city. They vary in sites, architectural typologies, and forms of (co-)habitation. From a legal perspective, there is the distinction between initial reception centers and follow-up accommodations.

Initial reception centers are usually collective accommodations. This means that several people share a room or a sleeping hall. Shared sanitary facilities are sometimes inside the building, in other cases they are in separate containers outside the dormitories. Since cooking on one's own is not allowed, there are no kitchens for the residents. Instead, the food is delivered by private catering companies and served in a canteen. The washroom is accessible to residents only at scheduled times. To use it, washing coins are needed, which in turn can be purchased only at certain times.

The premises, surrounded by a fence, are usually accessible through a main entrance, which is controlled by security officers. In addition, some first reception facilities have so-called common rooms, which refugees cannot necessarily use at any time – sometimes they may stay there only under the supervision of the employees. At other times, they are locked and inaccessible to the residents. The building typologies of the Hamburg initial reception facilities vary greatly: from container modules and pavilion buildings, houseboats, to converted office or school buildings, construction market halls, to tents and modular wooden huts. The latter two typologies were used for accommodation starting from the late summer of 2015, when sometimes up to 600 people seeking asylum and in need of shelter would arrive in Hamburg in a day and there was little scope for planning. Later, when the number of arrivals started to decrease drastically due to the closing of the borders, they were gradually shut down.

The initial reception center is intended for registration, application for asylum, and collecting information about asylum seekers' rights and duties.[8] Prior to winter 2015, they would stay here between six weeks and three months. Then, with an amendment of the Asylum Seekers Benefits Act,[9] this duration was prolonged to six months, *de jure*. De facto, however, many people linger in these facilities for a much longer time.

Having applied for asylum, refugees are redirected, if available, to a follow-up accommodation – either another shared accommodation or a flat, depending at least partly on the specific situation (for example, families, individuals).[10] Architectural typologies vary similarly: converted office and military buildings, pavilions, container modules, rented residential buildings, and, in exceptional cases, new buildings. The latter was made possible only by temporarily suspending some procedures of the National Building Code,[11] allowing the city to construct premises in the standard of social housing, using them as refugee accommodation with the double occupancy for the first 15 years, then 15 years as social housing. After expiry of the rent control period, these flats will probably be available to the free housing market, that is, rented for a higher price or sold. On the positive side, this illustrates that it is possible to change strict regulations, if there is a will. On the downside, those who were finally assigned a "proper" flat would not have any guarantee that they could stay there in the long term.

Although laid out as temporary, refugee accommodations often become a durable solution due to shortages of sequent housing provision. Like in other major cities, affordable housing is a scarce commodity in Hamburg, and in order to access it, refugees have to compete with other disadvantaged groups, thus causing additional social division and stronger rejection of refugees within the local society. Furthermore, the access to housing is thwarted by "profoundly unequal relations of power, resource, and knowledge" (McFarlane 2011, 655) – such as language, the type of residence permit (depending in most cases on the country of origin), familiarity with current procedures and requirements, and support by the locals; in short by economic, social, and cultural capital (Bourdieu 1986). Subsequently, many refugees perennially linger in the follow-up accommodations, thus creating a non-porous system where those accommodated in the initial reception centers are denied a transfer to a follow-up accommodation despite having spent over six months in Germany and, in some cases, being already in possession of a temporary residence permit. These people, stuck in the system due to its non-functioning, constitute a new category coined by the local authorities – *Überresident*, the "over-resident," which means they have overstayed their mandatory residence in the initial reception centers. According to the Central Coordination Staff for Refugees, the number of over-residents in Hamburg was 2,559 in November 2017. By comparison, in June 2016 there were about 10,000 people still housed in an initial reception facility due to missing spots in follow-up accommodations (FHH 2017).

This illustrates how the question of accommodating refugees shouldn't be considered as an isolated "problem" to be quickly solved (for example, by providing ready-made "container-spaces") but should rather be thought in relation to the dynamics of the city, which is perpetually "on the move" (Knowles 2011), or in constant change. If situated in this dynamic, the refugee accommodation (question) has the potentiality to unveil the already existing cracks and missing correlations in urban and housing policies and management (Momić 2018).

In the accommodations, fire protection and escape routes are the most common arguments against the appropriation of space by its residents. Following this logic, the

plan →	**initial reception camp** →	**follow-up accommodation** →	**housing market**
function	registration, application for asylum and collecting information about their rights and duties	integration courses, job center, etc.	...
status	asylum seeker	permit to remain until deported (*Duldung*); temporary permit (*Aufenthaltsgestattung*); residence permit	min. residence permit
building typology	containers, pavilions, houseboats, gyms and market halls, converted office buildings, tents, etc.	converted office and military buildings, pavilions, container modules, rented residential buildings, new construction, etc.	...
accommodation form	shared accommodation	shared accommodation or a complete flat	...
duration	officially: 6–12 weeks update winter '15: up to 6 months ←	officially: until obtaining a residence permit ←	...
reality	the emergence of the figure of the *Überresident*	access to the housing market: for many an impermeable filter	

Figure 2. The institutional accommodation system in Hamburg: between plan and reality, overview, 2016. Source: Author

inhabitants are not allowed to place carpets, curtains, and in most cases any furniture other than that provided by the accommodation in their rooms. Similarly, there should be no furniture, shoes, or baby carriages in the hallways. However, there are some exceptions: inhabitants of particularly provisional reception centers, such as halls that sheltered hundreds of people at times, were allowed to use fence elements, screened by bedsheets, to create provisional private rooms. At the same time, for fire safety reasons, a fire station was installed to monitor people from an elevated observation point day and night, which in turn contradicts the notion of privacy. The lack of standards of minimal privacy is compounded by the urge to quickly accommodate people. In some cases, for example, in a tent shared by 16 people, the individual retreat area is confined to the surface of a double camp bed (less than 2 m^2), where they sleep, read, drink tea, and store their personal belongings. There is also little or no room for rest, study, prayer, or mourning. For example, those who attend a German language course complain that they have to study on the bed, in the rooms where other people may want to sleep, talk, or listen to music.

In the follow-up accommodations, on the other hand, conflicts often arise through the use of shared kitchens and sanitary facilities. Some are culturally/religiously conditioned; for example, a dispute over whether pork may be roasted in a shared oven or whether the kitchen could be used for personal hygiene. Other conflicts, such as non-functioning cleaning plans, are familiar to every flat share. Some conflicts merely arise from the fact that many people live together in a small space. Even on a larger scale, such as a neighborhood or city, "diversity only sometimes means idyll, often enough, it also means conflict" (Terkessidis 2010, 14). Lebuhn criticizes the use of the term "communal accommodation" in reference to the refugee shelters by denouncing it as "a euphemism beyond comparison" – since neither room occupancy nor the use of common spaces is based on the principle of voluntariness, he argues that it is *a forced community* at best (2016).

Furthermore, the daily routine is structured by the recurrent activities of the camp: common sleeping times, mealtimes, laundry times, etc. In between, there is plenty of time to sleep and think, a lot of uncertainty, and a lot of waiting – for the asylum process decision, for a transfer to a (better) accommodation, for the German course, for the appointment at the employment office, an internship, training or a workplace, an apartment, family reunification, etc. The inevitably long waiting often leads to resentment or disillusionment and thus to a state of continuous physical and social immobility: "a permanent state of emergency" (Agamben 2005).

In summary, the architecture of the initial and follow-up accommodation corresponds with and translates into respective policies and regulations that determine refugees' *de jure* possibilities and restrictions. It could be argued that these facilities fulfill their purpose, if the purpose is preventing homelessness and managing emergency, thus promoting a culture of surveillance and control (Agier 2011), by accommodating or even *storing* people, that is, providing them with shelter, storage space, a sheer *habitat* – a priori to inhabitation. Moreover, the separation of functions reaches here into the very production of space; architects build refugee accommodation, policymakers regulate refugees' everyday lives, private security firms secure accommodations' premises, catering contractors deliver the food, cleaning contractors clean the accommodations, thus condemning refugees to complete idleness.

Many of the inhabitants' complaints about life in an accommodation concern precisely the fact that they are condemned to doing nothing. Hannah Arendt describes and analyzes the *conditio humana* (human condition) on the basis of the three basic human activities: work, labor, and (political) action (Arendt 1958). Accordingly, refugees would become people without activity – conditioned by the asylum and labor regulations, controlled by security measures, restricted to institutionalized boredom; their accommodation is planned and built for them, spaces (in a purely Euclidean sense) are assigned to them, without possibility for spatial appropriation. Moreover, their access to housing and work, and eventually active participation in the (urban) society – Arendt's action – is thwarted by bureaucracy. Even those who have obtained residency and a work permit face discrimination on the housing and labor market and end up competing with other disadvantaged groups. With Arendt, it could be argued that they are condemned to *vita [in]activa*.

Inhabiting *the uninhabitable*?

"Building uninhabitable places," Boano and Astolfo argue, "is the negation of the historical a priori of architecture: to inhabit" (2020, 563). As illustrated above, architecture of refugee accommodations substantially materializes and reinforces policies and regulations and thus emerges as a force disabling its *historical a priori*, that is, rendering inhabitation practices nearly impossible.[12] However, building upon the notion of inhabitation discussed above, the following section illustrates how inhabitants negotiate the apparent uninhabitability (Simone 2016) of the accommodations through a variety of subversive dwelling practices.

Sometimes it is enough to roll out a carpet (in spite of the rules, such as those governing fire protection) in order to create a living room atmosphere in the bedroom during the day. Often, the resumption of familiar daily routines and rituals – for example, communal eating, drinking tea, or smoking shisha – is an illustration of a partial reconstitution of everyday life. During my research, I was often invited into private rooms (those serving simultaneously as bedrooms, living rooms, dining rooms, etc.) for a meal (prepared in shared kitchens) as a thank-you for translating, helping to fill out some forms or applications. Although in the beginning I was slightly uncomfortable (or even guilted) and humbled due to asymmetrical power relations – albeit a migrant myself, I carry the privilege of being a researcher, speaking German, living in a flat, and thus having more favorable conditions for receiving guests – the inhabitants made me realize that the act of being a host (in the country and the building that is hosting them) engenders forms of agency and empowerment and subverts, at least transiently, these power relations. It is important to acknowledge and make visible these inhabitation practices, yet not to overly romanticize them or assume that they replace the fundamental right to housing. Many of these encounters would end with me thanking my hosts for the food and hospitality and them apologetically saying that they would host me even better when they – *Insha'Allah* – move to an apartment of their own.

Despite manifold inventive practices of spatial appropriation, some *matters* of dwelling, such as learning, praying, cooking, or receiving guests, cannot always be fulfilled within a refugee accommodation (especially in the case of initial reception centers). As a result, some of these dwelling practices fall out, while others are outsourced in the

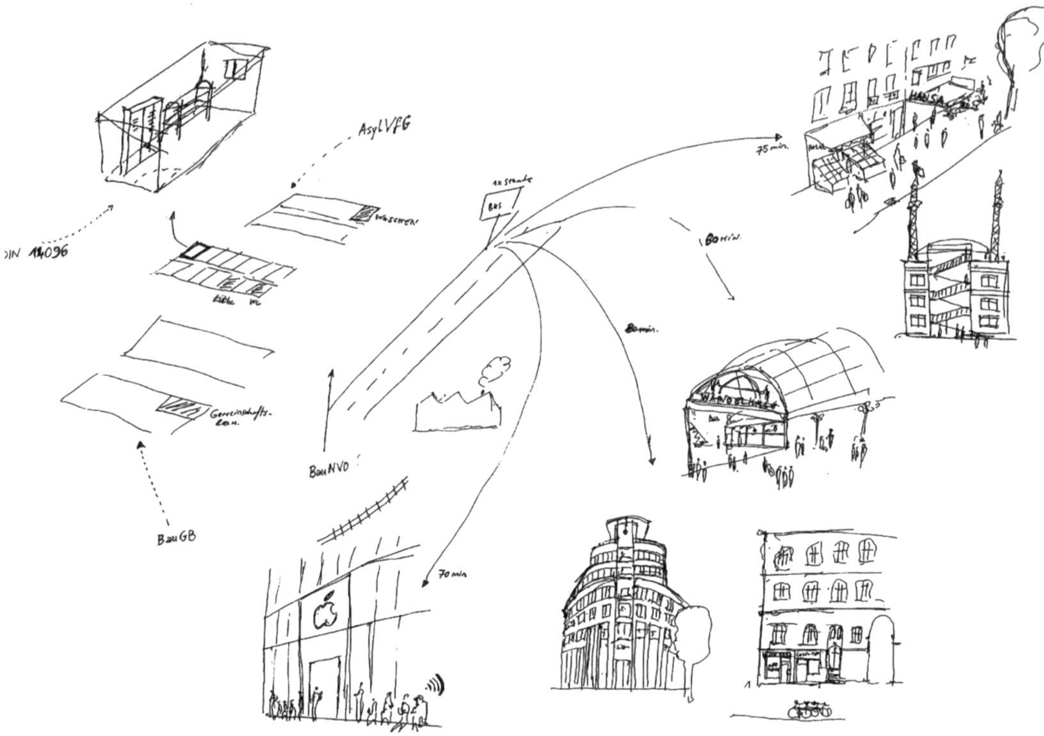

Figure 3. Inhabiting the city. Source: Author

urban space. For example, places such as the main train station, churches, mosques, streets with ethnic shops, cafés, premises of NGOs, etc. take over the function of the living room, the kitchen, the study, or the dining room. Here emerge various spaces of encounter. Sometimes, as little infrastructure as internet access and seating possibilities are sufficient to qualify a place as a living room in a broader sense.

Some places offer a more or less successful replacement and fulfill the familiar functions of dwelling, while others get newly defined through the encounters and interactions with the city and its other inhabitants. Through practices of inhabitation and appropriation of space, both within accommodations and across the city, inhabitants subvert the rules and limitations imposed on them and thus challenge entrenched "norms, structures and relations of urban life" (Hatziprokopiou et al. 2016). In so doing, they "de-alienate" urban space and "reintegrate it into the web of social connections" (Lefebvre 1996).

Temporalities of inhabitation trajectories: Zora's story[13]

If refugees are, in the first place, arguably creating an absence (place of origin) rather than establishing a new presence (arriving and settling down), the question arises: How long does the arrival actually take and has one even arrived at all at some point? In the previous sections I touched upon the temporal dimension of inhabitation trajectories, for example, perennial lingering in the accommodations even for those legally permitted to rent apartments but unable to do so due to the shortage of affordable housing. In this section, I will expand on the temporality of arrival and inhabitation by using the example of an inhabitant who does not fit in the textbook category of refugee and thus has had a different trajectory. In particular, I will shed light on inhabitation practices of a woman with the so-called tolerance permit (*Duldung*). In so doing, I will illustrate even further marginalization among the already marginalized, and simultaneously, how that marginality has a potentiality to become a site of resistance (hooks 1989) – through inhabitation.

Through my role as a translator and a volunteer, I engaged with many Roma from the Western Balkans in possession of a tolerance permit (*Duldung*), a particular legal status that is not a residence permit, but a temporary suspension of deportation. Asylum applications of people who come from the so-called safe countries of origin (*sichere Herkunftsländer*) are usually sweepingly denied and dismissed.[14] If the authorities cannot deport them at the time,[15] they are granted a *Duldung*. Sometimes this becomes a protracted situation. In this time period they are not allowed to work, attend a regular German course, or rent a flat. In substance, they are *stored* in the accommodations, ready to be *shipped away* any time.

Zora, for example, together with her whole family, lived with this status from 2009 to 2018. Furthermore, her *Duldung* was never issued for a period longer than six months; for nine years, she showed up at the foreigners office in rhythms of a couple of weeks, a month, three months, six months, anxious about their next decision. In between, she waited. But she didn't live a *vita* [*in*]*activa*. She didn't let her inhabitation be restricted solely to the accommodation, instead she inhabited the neighborhood and forged bonds both within her community and with the locals/neighbors. She was not able to rent a flat, but through her networking skills, she managed to get a transfer and move to an accommodation in a multiethnic, open neighborhood, close to her children's school (as opposed to 7 kilometers away from her previous accommodation in a non-residential periphery). This became her home and over the years, she became an indispensable figure in the local community. She was cooking and helping in a neighborhood café that operated on donations. For several years in a row, she co-organized cultural events on International Roma Day in the neighborhood center, participated in theatre projects, and spoke about the situation of Roma in the Balkans and in Germany at different events. Furthermore, she joined local activists and lawyers in counseling newly arrived migrants. Her own protracted inhabitation of the threshold (Stavrides 2010, Muzzonigro and Boano 2013) enabled her to relate to their experiences of displacement, disorientation, not knowing the language or the rules.

In fall 2018, thanks to the support of her network,[16] she finally obtained a residence permit, which also enabled her to start *officially* working at the counseling center, which she had already been doing. In so doing, she was performing rights that she did not yet have, thus illustrating the understanding of rights not as an essential/absolute category but rather as a potentiality (Isin 2017). Therefore, she first became an urban inhabitant, and only later achieved an official, albeit limited, form of recognition.[17] Zora's story indicates that inhabitation *is* being in relation with others and the city, through practices of mutual care and repair and by imagining – and performing – that which could be.

Conclusions: from refugees to inhabitants

By showing snippets of personal realities and dwelling trajectories, this paper has outlined the *dispositif* of inhabitation as a web, intercepting and connecting various spheres of life (the legal, the material, the lived) along with their position shifts and changes. One substantial position shift was that of the main subject: the inhabitant. Refugee, the initial category of practice, turned out to be a limited framing for various subject positions of displacement in the field and illustrated further marginalization among the already marginalized. Unveiling different dimensions, including temporal and spatial, of inhabitation practices throughout the paper let the figure of inhabitant emerge and indicate how, through inhabitation, that marginality has a potentiality to become a site of resistance. The inhabitant, thus, has the agency and capacity to appropriate space, to care and repair, to imagine, and to resist.

The paper has illustrated how different factors such as unequal access and mobilities, distribution of rights, etc., shape the possibilities, restrictions, and experiences of inhabitation. Inhabitation, in its turn, is a ground for resisting oppressive mechanisms and shaping the urban (space) and (im-)mobilities within it.

It has further stressed the importance of letting the perspective of the inhabitants themselves emerge in their daily lives as not only being affected by the regulations, but also finding ways to deal with them and challenge them. Thereby, the focus is not solely on subverting the rules, but also on creating new possibilities through the inhabitation, thus acknowledging their contribution and engendering their potential in the urban space production. However, giving voice to these subjects and their inhabitation practices "is not about romanticizing their traumatic becoming, but about challenging the silencing of their uncanny politics" (Lancione 2019, 283).

Finally, the paper explored the ambivalent relation between mobility and immobility based on the example of different dwelling patterns (for example, subjects on the move constrained by detention, outsourcing dwelling functions across the city, etc.), and thus demonstrated how movement and change can be examined only in relation to immobility and relative settledness (Manderscheid 2012).

---

1 Finding the right term that conveys and includes different subject positions of displacement has been a challenge for this paper. Specifically in the study here, different groups were involved: asylum seekers, recognized refugees (which prompts the question "when does one stop being a refugee?"), and "the tolerated" (those whose asylum application was denied, but are not deported, yet). This shows the absurdity of these (one could argue arbitrary) categories. The category of "refugee" is the one I encountered to be the most frequently used in the field by authorities, the legal system, and even their state-appointed accommodations are labeled as "refugee accommodations." I do not want to reinforce it, nor do I believe that these subjects are limited to such framing. Henceforth, I use the term "refugee" with precaution, with the intention to deconstruct it throughout the paper. Therefore, while the first part of the article uses "refugee" as a category of practice (Brubaker and Cooper 2000), in the second part, I move towards the notion of inhabitant to show their agency and capacity to appropriate space through care, repair, and imagination, in sum, by resisting. **2** In this paper, I use both concepts of dwelling and inhabitation. Rather than seeing them as contrasting, I argue that they are complementary. While dwelling means being-in- and becoming-into-the-world and is thus inseparable from other spheres of life, inhabitation expands on it by including feminist (care and reproduction) and decolonial perspectives (as a site of resistance). See section "On dwelling and inhabitation." **3** Criticism of Heidegger includes implicit nationalistic and patriarchal supremacy. **4** The old high German word for building *buan* means to dwell, to reside *(wohnen)* and is similar to the modern word to be – *(ich) bin*, or (I) am. **5** Original title is *Unbedachtes Wohnen: Lebensformen an verdeckten Rändern* *der Gesellschaft*; translation by the author. **6** Bundesverwaltungsgericht, Wohnnutzung; Begriff des Wohnens; Wohngruppe eines Kinderheims; Reines Wohngebiet (BVerwG Beschl. v. 25.03.1996, Az.: 4 B 302/95). **7** Diverse origins, gender, family situation, legal status, different types and locations of accommodations, etc. **8** Asylverfahrensgesetz (AsylVfG) § 44–§ 54. **9** Asylbewerberleistungsgesetz (AsylbLG). **10** AsylVfG § 53. **11** §246 BauGB (National Building Code) – There is an exception in some federal states that allows them to build social housing projects and use them to accommodate refugees for a limited time period. This exception furthermore permits quicker construction by skipping some steps in the permit process. **12** The accent here is on perceiving architecture not only in its sheltering (habitat-providing) function/role, but also as a force that disrupts and hinders inhabitation (Weizman 2019). **13** Name changed. **14** According to the European Commission, "a country of origin of asylum applicants is considered safe if it does not, or not generally, produce refugees. Receiving countries may use the concept of safe country of origin as a basis for rejecting summarily (without examination of the merits) particular groups or categories of asylum applicants." Countries of the Western Balkans are considered "safe" by the German authorities. Based on their own experiences, the people I have engaged with have repeatedly claimed that for Roma, these countries are anything but safe. As a minority, they face many forms of discrimination there, including but not limited to, racial and institutional discrimination (lack access to education, employment, housing, etc.). **15** There could be various reasons for this, e.g. medical reasons, missing passport, statelessness, etc. **16** A lawyer friend filed a lawsuit on her behalf, which dragged on in the court for years. **17** I am not making the argument that a residency permit engenders a genuine recognition in terms of rights, because even full citizenship sometimes does not. However, for Zora, after many years of inhabiting the threshold to deportation, this was a big achievement.

References

Agamben, G. 2005. *State of Exception.* Chicago: The University of Chicago Press. Original edition: 2003. *Stato di eccezione.* Turin: Bollati Boringhieri.

Agamben, G. 2009. *What is an Apparatus? And Other Essays.* Stanford, CA: Stanford University Press.

Agier, M. 2011. *Managing the Undesirables. Refugee Camps and Humanitarian Government.* Cambridge: Polity.

Arendt, H. 1958. *The Human Condition.* Chicago: University of Chicago Press.

Arendt, H. 1968. *Imperialism: Part Two of the Origins of Totalitarianism.* San Diego: Houghton Mifflin Harcourt.

Boano, C. and G. Astolfo. 2020. "Inhabitation as More-Than-Dwelling. Notes for a Renewed Grammar." *International Journal of Housing Policy* 20, no. 4: 555–77.

Bourdieu, P. 1986. "The Forms of Capital." In *Handbook of Theory and Research for the Sociology of Education*, edited by J. Richardson, 241–58. New York, NY: Greenwood.

Brubaker R., and F. Cooper. 2000. "Beyond 'Identity'." *Theory and Society* 29, no. 1: 1–47.

Brun, C. 2016. "Dwelling in the Temporary: The Involuntary Mobility of Displaced Georgians in Rented Accommodation." *Cultural Studies* 30, no. 3: 421–40.

Dadusc, D., M. Grazioli, and M. Martınez. 2019. "Introduction: Citizenship as Inhabitance? Migrant Housing Squats Versus Institutional Accommodation." *Citizenship Studies* 23, no. 6: 521–39.

Elden, S. 2000. "Rethinking the Polis: Implications of Heidegger's Questioning Political." *Political Geography* 19, no. 4: 407–22.

Elden, S. 2004. *Understanding Henri Lefebvre.* London: A&C Black.

European Commission (EC), Migration and Home Affairs. n.d. Safe Country of Origin [Website]. Accessed February 28, 2021. https://ec.europa.eu/home-affairs/e-library/glossary/safe-country-origin_en.

Fieseler, H., and H. C. Fickert. 2014. *Baunutzungsverordnung: Kommentar unter besonderer Berücksichtigung des deutschen und gemeinschaftlichen Umweltschutzes.* Cologne: Kohlhammer.

Foucault, M. 1978. *Dispositive der Macht. Über Sexualität, Wissen und Wahrheit.* Berlin: Merve.

Freie und Hansestadt Hamburg (FHH). 2017. "November: 500 Plätze in Wandsbek eröffnet und letzte 'prekäre Unterkunft' geschlossen" [Website]. Accessed December 21, 2017. http://www.hamburg.de/zkf-pressemeldungen/10028058/2017-11-06-zkf-bilanz-november.

Glaser, B. G., and A. L. Strauss. 1967. *The Discovery of Grounded Theory: Strategies for Qualitative Research.* New York: Aldine de Gruyter.

Glaser, B. G. 1978. *Theoretical Sensitivity.* California: The Sociology Press.

Harrison, P. 2007. "The Space Between Us: Opening Remarks on the Concept of Dwelling." *Environment and Planning D: Society and Space* 25, no. 4: 625–47.

Hasse, J. 2009. *Unbedachtes Wohnen: Lebensformen an verdeckten Rändern der Gesellschaft.* Bielefeld: Transcript Verlag.

Hasse, J. 2012. "Wohnen." In *Handbuch Stadtsoziologie*, edited by F. Eckardt, 475–502. Wiesbaden: Springer VS.

Hatziprokopiou, P., Y. Frangopoulos, N. Montagna. 2016. "Migration and the City." *City* 20, no. 1: 52–60.

Heidegger, M. 1954. "Bauen Wohnen Denken." In *Vorträge und Aufsätze*, 139–56. Stuttgart: Klett-Cotta.

Herz, M. 2008. "Refugee Camps or Ideal Cities in Dust and Dirt." In *Urban Transformation*, edited by I. Ruby and A. Ruby, 276–89. Berlin: Ruby Press.

Holland, N. J., and P. Huntington, eds. 2010. *Feminist Interpretations of Martin Heidegger.* University Park, PA: Penn State University Press.

hooks, b. 1989. "Choosing the Margin as a Space of Radical Openness." *Framework: The Journal of Cinema and Media*, no. 36: 15–23.

Isin, Engin F. 2017. "Enacting International Citizenship." In *International Political Sociology: Transversal Lines*, edited by T. Basaran, D. Bigo, E. P. Guittet, and R. B. J. Walker, 185–204. London: Routledge.

Knowles, C. 2011. "Cities on the Move: Navigating Urban Life." *City* 15, no. 2: 135–53.

Lancione, M. 2019. "Radical Housing: On the Politics of Dwelling as Difference." *International Journal of Housing Policy* 20 no. 2: 273–89.

Lebuhn, H. 2016. "Gemeinschaftsunterbringung Geflüchteter? Eine falsch gestellte Frage." *LuXemburg Online* [Website], April 2016. http://www.zeitschrift-luxemburg.de/gemeinschaftsunterbringung-gefluechteter-eine-falsch-gestellte-frage.

Lefebvre, H. 1996. *Writings on Cities*, edited by E. Kofman and E. Lebas. Oxford: Blackwell.

Lentin, R. 2002. "At the Heart of the Hibernian Post-Metropolis: Spatial Narratives of Ethnic Minorities and Diasporic Communities in a Changing City." *City* 6, no. 2: 229–49.

Manderscheid, K. 2012. "Mobilität." In *Handbuch Stadtsoziologie*, edited by F. Eckardt, 551–70. Wiesbaden: Springer-Verlag.

McFarlane, C. 2011. "The City as Assemblage: Dwelling and Urban Space." *Environment and Planning – Part D* 29, no. 4: 649–71.

Momić, M. 2018. "Das flüchtige Wohnen? (Wohn-)Alltag von Geflüchteten in Hamburg im Spannungsfeld zwischen Regelwerk und Wohnpraktiken." In *Fluchtpunkt Hamburg. Zur Geschichte von Flucht und Migration in Hamburg von der Frühen Neuzeit bis zur Gegenwart*, edited by N. M. Fahnenbruck and J. Meyer-Lenz, 229–44. Bielefeld: Transcript.

Muzzonigro, A., and C. Boano. 2013. "Dwell the Threshold: Encountering Otherness." *Planum* 27, no. 2: 9–15.

Purcell, M. 2014. "Possible Worlds: Henri Lefebvre and the Right to the City." *Journal of Urban Affairs* 36, no. 1: 141–54.

Simone, A. 2016. "The Uninhabitable?" *Cultural Politics* 12, no. 2: 135–54.

Stavrides, S. 2010. *Towards the City of Thresholds*. Trento: Professionaldreamers.

Terkessidis, M. 2010. *Interkultur*. Berlin: Suhrkamp.

Weizman, E. 2017. *Forensic Architecture: Violence at the Threshold of Detectability*. Brooklyn, NY: Zone Books.

Woods, M. 2019. "Hospitality; or, a Critique of Un/inhabitability." *Cultural Politics* 15, no. 2: 202–22.

Young, I. M. 2005. "House and Home: Feminist Variations on a Theme." In *Motherhood and Space*, edited by S. Hardy and C. Wiedmer, 115–47. New York, NY: Palgrave Macmillan.

Architecture and Beyond: In/formal Spaces of Urban Refuge – Berlin

Nassim Mehran

This paper sheds light on the spatiality of refugee accommodations and the distinctive local approaches in Berlin between 2015 and 2018. Considering resettlement as a multidimensional process, the article argues that these structures should not be regarded as abstract standardized architectural entities that can be implemented through predesigned guidelines. Instead, it accentuates refugees' impromptu performances outside of the state-appointed spatialities to reclaim their agency and autonomy. It elucidates how these accommodations are actively made and remade by their inhabitants, merging formal and informal resettlement modalities. By emphasizing the interconnection between different architectural and urban scales, the paper pleads for planners and policymakers to approach these spaces beyond formal architectural paradigms and integrate them into the broader urban perspectives.

Architectures of refuge; spatialized temporalities

For those who flee violence and armed conflicts, safe and secure accommodations are among the most significant emergency needs. On a global level, millions of refugees are currently housed in different kinds of shelter. Varying from self-made to thoroughly planned and securitized typologies, the spaces of these accommodations are initially formed around the complex interplay between state and non-state actors, international institutions (for example, UNHCR), NGOs, and other local humanitarian agencies (Clouette and Wise 2017, 42; Turner 2016, 139). The urgency of (mass) displacement and the number and pace of refugee arrivals, together with the particularities of legal, spatial, and administrative practices that constitute each host-context, result in the emerging hybrid architectural structures of settlement. Thus, differentiation between these structures and conceptualizing a systematic definition seems to be extremely complicated (McConnachie 2016, 397; Migreurop 2005; Witteborn 2011, 1142). They are diverse based on their socio-demographic characteristics, spatial organization, location, size, density, dependence on external aid, level of control exercised over their inhabitants by national or international authorities, and the relation between their inhabitants and the host society. The different existing terminologies (such as camp, reception centers, home, shelter, accommodation, etc.) partially capture the complexity of displacement and reveal some aspects of displaced populations' resettlement, including the objectives of governing actors from above, in relation to the agency and autonomy of displaced populations from below (Kreichauf 2018, 7).

One of the primary attributes that defines the spatiality of these accommodations, ranging from emergency responses to durable solutions, is the question of time and duration of stay. The decision to either stay (be allowed to remain) or to eventually (be forced to) leave, results in the formation of different typologies and strategies of sheltering. The duration of these options also directly affects both state policies together

Figure 1. Refugees protesting against the difficult living conditions in "segregated" accommodations in Berlin, 2016. Source: Imago/Christian Mang

with displaced populations' struggles from below to appropriate space, to dwell, to inhabit, to be (Sanyal 2014a, 135; 2014b, 558). However, in either case, the duration of stay in transitory spaces usually exceeds initial estimations. While these accommodations are not designed for long-term residency, their deplorable and substandard living conditions jeopardize refugees' well-being (Starvaggi 2018). In this framework, the architecture of these spaces is usually reduced to international and standardized humanitarian guidelines for distributing the displaced populations within these structures as well as separating them from the host environment. As abstract spatial devices, organized by a repertoire of architectural techniques, these settings are physically and virtually isolated from their larger surroundings and, thus, lose their relation and connection to the broader regional, national, and, in sum, urban scale (Clouette and Wise 2017, 166). On the contrary, when states put long-term resettlement policies, though conditioned, into practice, the landscape of accommodations and living conditions to which displaced populations get exposed throughout their various stages of stay differs significantly. As such, the displacement-resettlement nexus is a multidimensional process, taking into consideration various temporal dimensions and spatial scales of displacement. From this perspective, refugee accommodations can be considered as the spatialized temporalities of aid operation, demarcating the political and economic dimensions of the humanitarian apparatus. The coupling of the temporalities and spatialities of urban refuge is manifested in two modalities of resettlements, formal and informal, each operating within different geographical stretches and spans of time.

The formal modes of resettlements include those spaces that are initially created and run by state or non-state actors, within the state-appointed spaces, inside or outside of city peripheries. In these spaces, in addition to sheltering refugees (for example, "accommodation centers," prevalent in the Global North, and "camps," found both in the Global North and South), a series of rules and regulations from above are enforced to direct their inhabitants' everyday lives.

Although urban refuge is a pervasive global phenomenon, its informal dimensions have not been well-documented compared with the corpus of work published on formal spaces of refuge. Nonetheless, in various instances, forcibly displaced populations make an active decision to avoid state-appointed spaces of settlement and, thus, choose to remain on the precarious side of informality. Many examples can be found of spaces created by and for displaced populations, outside of formal settings, in various geographies and locations, inside and outside of cities. Although some refugee accommodations are designed formally, displaced populations improvise and create informal spaces of settlement, or alter the use of their designated spaces. These spatial appropriation processes from below, together with the formal basis of resettlement, merge and constitute spaces of urban refuge. The level of so-called informality present in these conditions offers refugees a sense of autonomy for self-care and self-sustainment, which formal spaces of resettlement can never provide by themselves. Nevertheless, the amalgamation of formal and informal resettlement modalities engenders an intricate urban pattern that cannot be easily assessed. Therefore, revisiting and understanding these spaces in a broader empirical and theoretical context, as suggested in what follows, helps rectify the existing policies in order to develop more effective ones and can have immense benefits for planners, city officials, governments, and policymakers, who typically practice through formal planning paradigms.

The urbanization of refuge

After World War II, refugee camps emerged as temporary housing solutions provided by the United Nations Refugee Agency during the 1950s for the displaced European refugees.[1] At this point, "being a refugee" became recognized as a standardized figure and practice within different scientific and administrative disciplines and communities. Subsequently, as a generalizable standardized technology of power for managing and containing the mass displaced population, refugee camps were put into practice (Malkki 1995, 495; Sanyal 2014b, 558). In the literature, the term "camp" is usually attributed to large-scale sites of refugee accommodations and transitional settlements in border regions, which house masses of people with an insecure and exceptional legal status and provide minimum living standards (Migreurop 2005; Turner 2016, 139). Ranging from small tent settlements to larger, crowded spatial entities, camps are multilayered, complex, and ordered by diverse objects and programs (Hailey 2009, 5; Lewis 2008). Over the course of years, with the changing realities of refuge, from a temporary situation into a protracted state of indetermination, camps, most commonly, evolve into permanent urban spaces of settlement. This has raised discussions about the essence of camps. Inspired by Agier (2008, 102), Turner (2016, 139) portrays camps as the spatial embodiment of the state of quarantine, thus materializing the state of extraterritoriality, exception, and social exclusion. Although the formation of camps is generally deemed inevitable on the political level, it is wrong to consider it as a place that provides easier circumstances for its inhabitants. A prolonged stay in a camp brings about a range of different psychosocial pressures, from human right violations to conflicts over limited resources. In addition to evidence indicating the negative health impact of camps on refugees, studies show that encampment does not necessarily enhance the intended state's

Figure 2. The Azraq refugee camp, located 100 kilometers outside Amman, Jordan, 2015. Source: AFP/Khalil Mazraawi

security measures. Furthermore, these sites isolate their inhabitants from normal social existence, exacerbate marginalization, and separate refugees from the local population (Agier 2008, 102; Dualeh 1995, 1369; Sanyal 2014b, 558; Toole and Waldman 1990, 3296).

As recent patterns indicate, prolonged conditions of displacement have resulted in extended moves towards cities, where "camp" residents can blend into the local environment and access better living conditions, urban facilities, and possible job opportunities. However, the humanitarian aid system is mainly designed to serve people in camps outside cities. Referring to this issue, UNHCR has acknowledged the ongoing challenge for effective protection and aid delivery (Loescher, Steiner and Gibney 2003; UNHCR 2001). The urbanization of refuge is formed on the interface between the urban and the humanitarian space and has brought about a complex context and different challenges for governments, practitioners, and scholars alike in addressing the needs of various groups of refugees, migrants, and non-migrants with different legal and social status.

Figure 3. Sports halls being prepared to accommodate refugees in Berlin, 2015. Source: Thorsten A. Buhl

Figure 4. Tempohome, the container villages in Tempelhofer Feld, 2019. Source: Liudmila Radyk

Given that each city plays a distinct role in both implementing national refugee policies and developing urban strategies in response to the instant and long-term needs of both its refugee and local populations, this paper illustrates Berlin's specific agenda, and limitations, in providing accommodations to its recently arrived refugee populations. In further detail, this paper discusses the complexities of the so-called formal urban accommodation in Berlin to showcase the various levels of informalities and improvisations from below, which constitute the formation and experience of these spaces by both its inhabitants and the broader urban community.

Berlin, spaces of urban refuge (2015–18)

Since the "long summer of migration" in 2015, Germany has become the main host country of refugees in the EU, receiving more than 1.2 million asylum seekers. During the same year, Berlin alone hosted 33,281 refugees. This led to an obvious challenge and dysfunction in the established political and administrative systems for facilitating different services (BAMF 2016; Eurocities 2016; Kreichauf 2018, 7). The emergency situation and the multiscaled spatial-management strategies of the newly arrived refugees brought forth different approaches towards providing accommodations. Hence, former emergency shelters were expanded. Several preexisting buildings (such as office buildings, warehouses, commercial and industrial buildings, hotels, sports halls, the airport, etc.) were repurposed. These types of accommodations usually functioned as mass accommodation and the initial reception centers. They often only delivered basic non-monetary social benefits such as daily meals (Dahdah and Dippel 2018, 74; Mehran 2020, 15).

From these centers, depending on availability, refugees were rehoused into two other types of accommodation, which were expected to provide better living conditions to their residents. Some were Tempohomes, light and mobile structures, such as tents and containers, usually installed in the form of container villages in vast abandoned areas, mostly outside the city center. The other were MUFs,[2] which are modular prefabricated five-story buildings that typically provide smaller private living units, with rooms for one to three persons, or family rooms and shared kitchens (LAF 2016 a and 2016 b).

In/formalities of architectures of refuge

The architectural apparatuses mentioned above were chosen and designated formally to bind refugees within a concrete top-down legal and administrative framework. However, in practice, they functioned differently. This diversity resulted from the superimposition of national legislation, the internal organizational system and enforced rules, the exclusivity of their residents' demographics and legal status, and the buildings' physical and environmental dimensions. Drawing on the practical application and performance characteristics of these settings, in this section, the study elucidates why the refugee accommodation should not be considered as abstract standardized spatial entities that can be implemented through predesigned architectural guidelines.

Home or a disciplinary space? On the one hand, these accommodations have performed as structures to facilitate housing for the newly arrived refugees. On the other hand, they are the material realization of administrative exercise of power on refugees to control and deter incoming migrants and protect the EU's order and security. Similar to camps discussed earlier, here, the politics of spatial production are closely tied with the politics of producing refugee subjects (Sanyal 2014a, 135; 2014b, 558). It is widely stated in the literature how disciplinary regimes and imposed laws of asylum make these spaces immediately different from those in their surroundings, which primarily belong to the citizens of the state. Besides poor living conditions and minimal welfare support, control over refugees' mobility is one of the most tangible features of governing the refugee population. In Germany, the "obligation of residence" and the "obligation of home" are two binding laws that limit refugees' mobility within the federal state during their asylum procedure (Frings and Steffen 2016, 9). As a result, even if the refugees are free to move outside of their accommodation, they must report their movements regularly. The implementation of various surveillance strategies through the security guard and the installation of fences maintains a clear visual distinction from their surroundings. These mechanisms restrict refugees from moving beyond these barriers and, thus, prevent them from building a worthwhile relationship with the host society.

Social care or neoliberal experimentation? – The dysfunction of the governmental system in managing the aforementioned emergency situation and its arising political complexities opened the door for the engagement of private investors and for-profit businesses (Parsloe 2017, 35). Privatization of both the provision and management of accommodation through the involvement of non-state and profit-seeking actors, along with the transfer of tasks from public authorities to private companies (such as catering companies, security firms, container and construction companies) has resulted in the cutting of social benefits and the decline of living standards in these accommodations (Stiftung SPI 2016). The operation of accommodation by businessmen, property speculators, and non-professionals in social services and humanitarian crises has resulted in more lucrative strategies than the provision of security and a safe living environment for the inhabitants (Chazan 2016).

Loss of domesticity – Living in initial reception centers could adversely affect the well-being of refugees, particularly refugee women. Therein refugees are in a constant state of struggle either for understanding and adapting themselves to the living conditions inside these spaces, or for appropriating their environment according to their needs. Inside the accommodation, homely and domestic activities take place in the immediate presence of a large number of unknown people. This leads to disruption in privacy, which means having no autonomy over everyday life (Mehran 2020, 15). Being forced to share essential daily facilities with a large number of residents with different backgrounds, together with challenges in re/defining interpersonal distances, strict rules, experiences of violence, social isolation, discrimination (based on religion, gender, or ethnicity), and intra/inter-community conflicts were reported as major consequences of the spatial dysfunctions of the refugee accommodation (Mehran 2020, 15).

Dependency or agency? – Assistance systems' neglect of refugee agency has serious repercussions on the incorporation of refugees into the host society. The general attitude that many problems will be identified or solved by those in control fostered "dependency on assistance" of the state and NGOs (Hyndman 2000, 25–8; Szczepanikova 2013, 130). In Berlin, long-term dependency on local accommodation and limited access to the housing market made the process of resettlement particularly challenging. Therefore, despite passing the asylum procedure, most of the refugees, while having work permits and being able to afford private housing, remain dependent on public accommodation, which neither provides proper living conditions nor helps refugees in self-orientation (El-Kayed and Hamann 2018, 135). At the same time, however, some refugees stay active participants within their local communities and seek to remain active agents of their living situation. They generate individual strategies, actions, and decisions within their spaces of arrival, which influence the process of their urban incorporation and resettlement. Residents of these accommodations try to reshape and transform these supposed temporary spaces to make them more homelike and livable. They rearrange the furniture, including beds and benches, and hang blankets or sheets around beds to provide a sense of privacy or belonging. Drawing graffiti is another way of expressing their frustration, hope, and enduring identities. These attempts aim

Figure 5. Difficult living conditions in the former Tempelhof Airport, particularly for women, 2015. Source: Imago/Jochen Eckel

to develop a sense of home and domesticity within the spaces of accommodations (Dahdah and Dippel, 2018; Mehran 2020, 15; Parsloe 2017, 35). The struggle of refugees in appropriating these places through these everyday forms of resistance cannot be overlooked. However, as Sanyal (2014a) has discussed in the case of refugee camps, it is critical to consider the limits of such actions and the complexity of resistance on the ground due to various imposed legal restrictions of management and control. In this context, refugees, in addition to lacking a home, a nation, and citizenship, lack "proper agency, proper voice, proper face," which they try to reclaim even through the smallest measures (Soguk 1999, 243).

Not a single act of architectural design – The prolonged stay in refugee accommodation and refugees' evolving needs to build a new normal and a meaningful future contradicts the initial concept of these structures as transitional spaces. Their ever-changing accommodated population does not allow a balance between the needs of residents and the available facilities. Although there are various planning guidelines in handbooks for putting in place and developing refugee accommodations (Sphere 2018; UNHCR 2017), these guidelines usually have a technocratic approach towards the design of space and only respond to refugees' basic physiological needs. They generally have a limited approach to facilitating psychological, cultural, and self-fulfillment needs.

However, it is necessary to consider refugee accommodations as a part of dynamic processes of resettlement that are not static. They are formed through the constantly alternating relation between aid agencies, states, donors, and recipients of aid. As such, they are under continual transformation, particularly by the practices of refugees who reside in, use, and alter them. Consequently, refugee policies and spatial interventions and management of these spaces cannot be seen as a single act of design, based on guidelines.

Architectural embodiment of prolonged temporality – The embodied "prolonged temporality" shapes refugees' very intimate spatial experiences. The co-opted buildings continue displaying their non-residential elements and traces of their previous usage, such as billboards, furniture, windows, and signs, which are difficult to remove or change (Safouane 2017, 1922). Besides continuous rehousing, frequent changes within a particular accommodation negatively influence the daily activities, social connections, and personal ties. They hamper the formation of any sense of normalcy. Pending asylum applications, the uncertainty and insecurity about the future, and the long-term undetermined stay in these places where human resources such as social, cultural, material, and personal ties are negatively affected can adversely hinder (re)gaining the resources one needs for interacting with or incorporating into the host society and amplify dependencies on staff, social workers, and accommodation facilities.

In/formalities of urban refuge

The performance of refugee accommodations within the city of Berlin, as architectural units, is not reduced to their physical boundaries. They are, on the one hand, components of a complex spatial urban system and, on the other, fundamental spaces of refugees' urban trajectory of resettlement. In this section, the article addresses the informal modalities of resettlement through which the spatiality of the refugee accommodations constantly entangles with the broader urban scale and merges into different dimensions of urban life, thus becoming part of everyday urbanism.

Politicized and contentious – The question of the sites and locations of refugee accommodations in Berlin has been a controversial matter and placed refugees at the heart of an impassioned public debate about the right to housing and public space and the prohibition of profit-focused development. Overturning some protective legislation and choosing politicized and contentious sites of non-residential, iconic buildings and historic monuments (such as Tempelhof), which were mostly considered as common goods and had public value, put refugees on a high level of objectification (Parsloe 2017, 35).

Disruption in urban continuity – The inherent spatial characteristics and public value of the structures that were co-opted as refugee accommodations in Berlin have brought about different challenges for the authorities, designers, and stakeholders, as well as for those who have to reside in them (Parsloe 2017, 35). Similar to camps, urban refugee accommodations are often morphologically visible. They are clearly demarcated within their immediate urban environment. The clear visual and spatial outlining due to striking scales and unusual physical features such as a housing project, poor access to public transportation, presence of security guards, and their location (at the edge of the city, on vast abandoned pieces of land, or industrial areas, etc.) play a crucial role in isolating these places and their residents. Moreover, the dense and crowded accommodations inhabited by refugees who are considered non-citizen result in the stigmatization of the refugees and social rupture between these accommodations and their adjacencies. Consequently, the residents of these structures become socially recognizable and classified as part of the "refugee" group, as a mass of strangers or "others" under the control of national and governmental laws. Therefore, these sites' social disintegration within their wider urban fabric can adversely affect the interaction between the receiving society and the refugee population.

Process of democracy – The spatiality of each refugee accommodation is determined by the specificity of the social relations that are formed within and in relation to it. These spaces are constituted out of relations between refugees, staff, and the local community. The frameless dynamic between refugees and the local population, especially with neighbors in the immediate surrounding of accommodations, and the possible conflict between these groups over urban resources, make these structures complicated sites to manage. The design of these places not only performs a leading role in refugees' daily, and future, lives, but also brings about a sudden change in the local population's everyday realities. Therefore, in addition to refugees, the host society is directly involved in the transitional period of resettlement. Considering resettlement as a bilateral process, both refugees and civil society should be engaged in the process of designing, managing, and implementing necessary policies and facilities. Therefore, it is critical to introduce forms of accountability and a cooperative culture for involving different social groups and policymakers to become stakeholders in making decisions which create or reform urban structures they inhabit.

Refugee, not as an abstract person, but as a member of an urban social network – In parallel to the concepts that represent refugee accommodations as spaces of exclusion and exception, some scholars consider them as sites of emergence and the formation of new identities, practices of new social norms, a materialization of distinct political lives, resistance strategies, acts of agency, and reclaiming autonomy (Corbet 2012, 38; Malkki 1995, 495; Redclift 2013, 308). Despite the closed nature of the refugee accom-

Figure 6. Sonnenallee, the so-called Arab Street in Neukölln-Berlin, historically evolved to host and serve diverse local and migrant communities from different ethnic backgrounds, particularly Arabs, 2018. Source: Mohamed Badarne

modations, some refugees could engage in outside activities, establish social relations and friendship networks, work in informal economies, and develop collectives to protest or represent their communities' interests. In their efforts to build connections or establish a normal social life, either as individuals or as communities, refugees operate outside the formal, state-defined boundaries of refugee accommodation. They extend their presence beyond those immediate, defined circles of their accommodation. Moreover, refugees' interpersonal ties based on kinship and community membership with preexisting migrants and non-migrant communities help them in learning about opportunities of employment, accommodation, jobs, etc. Additionally, different local individuals, groups, institutions, and organizations mediate between refugees, local communities, and political and economic institutions; a network of different services and assistance consisting of the healthcare system, travel agents, lawyers, bankers, labor recruiters, brokers, interpreters, and housing agents has emerged to help refugees in encountering different informational, financial, and documentary barriers. Moreover, refugees' social networks and their connections to non-profit or political organizations are a crucial component of the individual's urban trajectory as they help refugees to receive support and information to find housing, understand one's rights and demands, and involve different actors such as volunteers, preexisting ethnic and religious communities, universities and NGOs, who help to overcome the spatial, legal, and mental boundaries.

Figure 7. An Arabic tailor shop in Sonnenallee, 2018. Source: Mohamed Badarne

However, one should not fail to consider that not having equal access to social resources can develop a feeling of discrimination, isolation, or in some cases, result in conflict.

Figure 8. A women's dress shop in Sonnenallee, 2018. Source: Mohamed Badarne

A contextualized process – Refugee resettlement should be considered as a contextualized process. Each city's spatial features bring about specific imprints on its social struggles, introduce different urban realities and agencies on the ground, and provoke a particular kind of politics. Therefore, in Berlin, the city's particularities should be taken into consideration as a base for resettlement trajectories. "Everyday cosmopolitanism" in Berlin may act as a spatial catalyst for refugees of diverse ethnic and religious backgrounds to mix, mingle, and engage with each other on a daily basis, or it might amplify the formation of sectarianism. The city historically hosted and was re-formed by the frequent movements and settlements of international migratory entries, and, thus, is an emblematic place of migration (Bergmann 2011, 45). The existing social networks of migrants such as the Turkish and Arab migrant communities which, historically, have established an urban bedrock in central areas (in Neukölln, Wedding, and Kreuzberg) play a crucial role in the everyday urban practices of the newly arrived refugees. These communities in Berlin gradually disband, extend or blend into new emerging communities. As such, relations between refugees and the host society evolve into complex and overlapping geographies beyond the legal boundaries of the accommodation spaces, beyond the refugee-host society dichotomy.

Figure 9. A traditional Arabic teahouse in Sonnenallee, a stamping ground for young men, 2018. Source: Mohamed Badarne

Figure 10. Syrians protesting against the war and violence in Idlib, in front of the Russian embassy, 2019. Source: Fadi Elias

Moreover, cities do not only serve as a physical space where conflicts are shaped; they are also the ground through which collectives and solidarities are formed. In Berlin, voluntarism and local civil-society engagement brought about a new level of urban activism. Civil society initiatives played a critical role in softening the process of urban resettlement, fostering a more open host society, creating shared neutral spaces and developing a sense of a "society of migration" (Hamann and Karakayali 2016, 69; Karakayali and Kleist 2016, 65). The common urban practices of everyday living carried out by a large number of migrants and refugees have virtually transformed this large city. Their active and visible presence and cultural influences, on the streets and in public spaces, are a way of claiming their right to the city; part of a struggle for citizenship and self-development within the larger urban landscape. They announce their physical, social, and cultural presence in the host society by leaving an imprint on different modes of urban life by building self-made urban communities; cultural, religious, and political collectives; and new urban economies. These practices, which Asef Bayat (2010, 43) termed as "non-movements," have a significant transformative impact on the city through entangling their logic into the social and administrative urban fabric.

Figure 11. Refugees and supporters protesting against plans to house them in the Tempelhof refugee shelter, 2016. Source: dpa/Wolfram Kastl

Conclusion

As a metropolitan city, Berlin is being constantly regenerated through everyday practices of individuals, collectives, and institutions. In this framework, the instant emergence of the abstract architectures of refugee accommodations - which were initially organized to separate refugee sites from civic life, control the movement and resources of refugees, and embody the national political system - gradually went beyond their initial bureaucratic physical layout and became interconnected to their immediate surroundings and, finally, to the city as a whole. Consequently, the space of urban refuge constituted a wide network of urban relations in both formal and informal sectors. Although formal and informal modalities of resettlement seem to be separated processes, they work in concert. While the concrete architectural framework of these structures - through which geopolitics, humanitarian action, and national policies collide - did not allow them to easily enmesh into the existing fabric of the city, each refugee accommodation, depending on its local particularities, developed a distinct configuration to its urban vicinity. This specific urban relation is unique and bilateral. As a result, it deconstructs the generalized image of these structures. Therefore, these spaces should not simply be considered as temporary housing or as a break in normality to assist refugees. On the contrary, they introduce opportunities, challenges, and orientation towards the future. The quality of these spaces should be seen as a course in refugees' and the local community's urban lives that has long-term consequences. For this reason, designing and implementing these ever-changing, dynamic spaces exceeds a one-time architectural task based on a predefined physical guideline. Given that the process of resettlement is a complex, reciprocal, multidimensional, multi-actor task, urban refugee accommodation should be assessed considering perspectives of different involved individuals, groups, and institutions. From this perspective, the task of architects and other actors is not limited to implementing predefined orders and guidelines, but to monitor and reflect on the situation continuously. In addition, refugee accommodation, both as a lived space or a political concept, offers a lens for understanding wider urban processes and approaches towards citizens' social care and rights to the city. Despite the strict top-down regulation, one cannot neglect the imprint of refugees' everyday practices and resistances, both inside and outside the accommodations, on transforming urban politics and the urban society. This indicates their positioning outside of the state-appointed spaces by reclaiming their spatial agency and autonomy through an alternate definition of what it means to settle and to inhabit. In doing so, these complex, dynamic settings should be integrated into general urban development discourse. Their material existence should not be seen as an exceptional spatial device for controlling refugees, but they should be considered as urban segments, whose performances are dynamic and complementary to the wider urban environment. In this context, the notion of refuge and refugee accommodation should be regarded as an urban reality and not as an extraordinary situation. From this standpoint, the process of resettlement is a collective, democratic ongoing urban process, and every temporary measure should be framed as a proactive step within the comprehensive urban development framework. Otherwise, there is a risk of simplifying an inherently complex and multifaceted urban reality.

1 The United Nations Refugee Agency comes under the aegis of the United Nations High Commissioner for Refugees (UNHCR). **2** In German: *Modulare Unterkünfte für Flüchtlinge.*

References

Agier, M. 2008. *On the Margins of the World: The Refugee Experience Today*. Cambridge: Polity.

BAMF. 2016. *Das Bundesamt in Zahlen 2015, Asyl, Migration und Integration*. Bundesamt für Migration und Flüchtlinge [Website]. https://www.bamf.de/SharedDocs/Anlagen/DE/Publikationen/Broschueren/bundesamt-in-zahlen-2015.pdf?__blob=publicationFile.

Bayat, A. 2010. *Life as Politics: How Ordinary People Change the Middle East*. Cairo: American University in Cairo Press.

Bergmann, M. 2011. "Die Sonnenallee in Berlin als Raum grenzüberschreitender Ökonomien." In *Eigensinnige Geographien: Städtische Raumaneignungen als Ausdruck gesellschaftlicher Teilhabe*, edited by M. Bergmann and B. Lange, 45–70. Wiesbaden: VS Verlag für Sozialwissenschaften.

BMJV. 2016. Asylum Act [Website]. https://www.gesetze-im-internet.de/englisch_asylvfg /englisch_asylvfg.html #p0425.

Chazan, G. 2016. "Migrants Bring a Profitable New Era for Shelter Providers." *Financial Times*. https://www.ft.com/content/8f8722a0-20d2-11e6-9d4d-c11776a5124d.

Clouette, B., and M. Wise. 2017. *Forms of Aid: Architectures of Humanitarian Space*. Basel: Birkhäuser.

Corbet, A. 2012. *The Community-Based Approach in Haiti: Clarification of the Notion of "Communities"* and *Recommendations*, ALNAP. Port-au-Prince: Groupe URD.

Council Directive 2003/9/EC. 2003. "Laying Down Minimum Standards for the Reception of Asylum Seekers." https://eur-lex.europa.eu/legal content/EN/ALL/?uri=celex%3A32003L0009.

Dahdah, A., and A. Dippel. 2018. "German and French 'Spatial Management' of Refugees Illustrated by Syrians' Urban Experiences in Berlin and Marseilles." In "Cities: Identities, Appropriation of Space and Resistance Practices," special edition of *Alternatif Politika* (May 2018): 74–98.

Directive 2013/33/EU. 2013. "Laying Down Standards for the Reception of Applicants for International Protection." https://eur-lex.europa.eu/legal-content/EN/ALL/?uri=CELEX%3A32013L0033.

Dualeh, M. W. 1995. "Do Refugees Belong in Camps?" *The Lancet* 346: 1369–70.

El-Kayed, N., and U. Hamann. 2018. "Refugees' Access to Housing and Residency in German Cities: Internal Border Regimes and Their Local Variations." *Social Inclusion* 6, no. 1: 135–46.

Eurocities. 2016. "Refugee Reception and Integration in Cities." http://nws.eurocities.eu/MediaShell/media/RefugeeReport_final.pdf.

Frings, D., and E. Steffen. 2016. *Die neuen Wohnsitzauflagen und die sozialrechtlichen Auswirkungen*, Flüchtlingsrat NRW.

Hailey, C. 2009. *Camps: A Guide to 21st-Century Space*. Cambridge, MA: MIT Press.

Hamann, U., and S. Karakayali. 2016. "Practicing Willkommenskultur: Migration and Solidarity in Germany." *Intersections* 2, no. 4: 69–86.

Hyndman, J. 2000. *Managing Displacement: Refugees and the Politics of Humanitarianism*. Minneapolis, MN: University of Minnesota Press.

Karakayali, S., and J. O. Kleist. 2016. "Volunteers and Asylum Seekers." *Forced Migration Review*, no. 51: 65–68.

Kreichauf, R. 2018. "From Forced Migration to Forced Arrival: The Campization of Refugee Accommodation in European Cities." *Comparative Migration Studies* 6, no. 7: 1–22.

LAF. 2016a. "MUF 2.0." https://www.berlin.de/laf/wohnen/allgemeine-informationen/muf-2-0/.

LAF. 2016b. "Tempohomes FAQ." https://www.berlin.de/laf/wohnen/allgemeine-informationen/tempohomes-faq/.

Lewis, J. 2008. "Phenomenon: The Exigent City." *The New York Times*, June 8, 2008, https://www.nytimes.com/2008/06/08/magazine/08wwln-urbanism-t.html.

Loescher, G., N. Steiner, and M. Gibney. 2003. "Problems of Protection: The UNHCR, Refugees and Human Rights." Refugee Studies Centre. https://www.rsc.ox.ac.uk/publications/problems-of-protection-the-unhcr-refugees-and-human-rights.

Malkki, L. H. 1995. "Refugees and Exile: From 'Refugee Studies' to the National Order of Things." *Annual Review of Anthropology* 24: 495–523.

McConnachie, K. 2016. "Camps of Containment: A Genealogy of the Refugee Camp." *Humanity: An International Journal of Human Rights, Humanitarianism and Development* 7, no. 3: 397–412.

Mehran, N. 2020. "Spaces of Urban Refuge and Social Stress." PhD dissertation. Humboldt University of Berlin.

Migreurop. 2005. "Definition of Camps." http://www.migreurop.org/article972.html?lang=fr.

Parsloe, T. 2017. "Appropriating Buildings to House Refugees: Berlin Tempelhof. Shelter in Displacement." *Forced Migration Review*, no. 55: 35–6.

Redclift, V. 2013. "Abjects or Agents? Camps, Contests and the Creation of 'Political Space'." *Citizenship Studies* 17, no. 3–4: 308–21.

Safouane, H. 2017. "Manufacturing Striated Space for Migrants: An Ethnography of Initial Reception Centers for Asylum Seekers in Germany." *International Journal of Voluntary and Nonprofit Organizations* 28, no. 5: 1922–39.

Sanyal, R. 2014a. "The Work of Exile: Protracted Refugee Crises and the New Palestinian Normal." In *The Post-Conflict Environment: Investigation and Critique*, edited by D. B. Monk and J. Mundy, 135–57. Ann Arbor, MI: The University of Michigan Press.

Sanyal, R. 2014b. "Urbanizing Refuge: Interrogating Spaces of Displacement." *International Journal of Urban and Regional Research* 38, no. 2: 558–72.

Soguk, N. 1999. *States and Strangers: Refugees and Displacements of Statecraft*. Minneapolis, MN: University of Minnesota Press.

Sphere. 2018. *The Sphere Handbook*. https://spherestandards.org/handbook-2018/.

Starvaggi, M. 2018. "Refugee Camps: How a Temporary Approach is Harmful to Health." Archive: Architecture for Health [Website]. https://archiveglobal.org/refugee-camps-temporary-approach-harmful-health/.

Stiftung SPI. 2016. "Häufig gestellte Fragen: Unterkünfte für Flüchtlinge und Asylsuchende in Berlin." https://www.mbt-berlin.de/mbt/publikationen/Broschueren/7-FAQs-Berlin.pdf

Szczepanikova, A. 2013. "Between Control and Assistance: The Problem of European Accommodation Centres for Asylum Seekers." *International Migration* 51, no. 4: 130–43.

Toole, M. J., and R. J. Waldman. 1990. "Prevention of Excess Mortality in Refugee and Displaced Populations in Developing Countries." *JAMA* 263, no. 24: 3296–302.

Turner, S. 2016. "What Is a Refugee Camp? Explorations of the Limits and Effects of the Camp." *Journal of Refugee Studies* 29, no. 2: 139–48.

UNHCR. 2008. "Building a Europe of Asylum: UNHCR's Recommendations to France for its European Union Presidency (July – December 2008)." United Nations High Commissioner for Refugees [Website]. https://www.refworld.org/docid/484e71812.htm.

UNHCR. 2001. "Urban Refugees." United Nations High Commissioner for Refugees [Website]. https://www.unhcr.org/urban-refugees.html.

UNHCR. 2017. "UNHCR Global Trends – Forced Displacement in 2017." United Nations High Commissioner for Refugees [Website]. https://www.unhcr.org/globaltrends2017/.

Witteborn, S. 2011. "Constructing the Forced Migrant and the Politics of Space and Place-making." *Journal of Communication* 61, no. 6: 1142–60.

Displacement, Arrival, and Housing: The Case of Leipzig (Germany) and Mocoa (Colombia)

Lina Sánchez Steiner

According to the UNHCR, at the end of 2019 79.5 million people worldwide fled from war, conflict, and persecution. Displaced people mainly arrive in cities in search of protection and shelter. This paper describes different arrival and long-term accommodation processes in host cities of the Global North and South. Two different cities are analyzed: Leipzig, in Germany, the country with the third-highest number of refugees and asylum seekers; and Mocoa, in Colombia, the country with the largest population of internally displaced persons. Both cities vary considerably concerning their size, political contexts, and social and geographical conditions; however, both cities share the challenge of finding housing solutions for displaced populations. The aim of this paper is to give insights on how governments and other local actors in different institutional contexts act concerning the provision of long-term housing. Likewise, the article shows how displaced persons, beyond being passive aid-receivers alone, assume an active role to solve their housing problem.

Introduction

There are currently 79.5 million displaced people in the world, including refugees (26 million),[1] internally displaced persons (IDPs) (45.7 million),[2] asylum seekers (4.2 million),[3] and Venezuelans displaced abroad (3.6 million) (UNHCR 2020, 2). Regardless of the differences in legal status, all groups have in common that they had to flee and leave their place of origin and seek protection and another place of residence outside or inside of their country of origin.[4] Another characteristic of refugees, IDPs, and asylum seekers is that these people generally arrive at a location that they formerly did not know. Furthermore, there exists uncertainty about the length of stay (short-, medium-, or long-term) and the possibility to return to their country of origin. Arrival therefore implies seeking temporary shelter and, in most cases, subsequently finding a longer-term housing solution. This article describes the arrival and accommodation processes of displaced people in host countries and cities of the Global North and South. This analysis, however, does not focus on temporary shelters or refugee camps, but instead on long-term housing.

Two different processes are analyzed, one in Germany and one in Colombia. Germany is currently the country (after Turkey and Colombia) with the third-highest number of refugees and asylum seekers; Colombia is the country with the largest population of IDPs (UNHCR 2020, 2). As such, both countries have faced a high degree of forced displacement. This paper presents the case of the city of Leipzig (Germany), where the arrival processes and accommodation provisions are regulated by the state, together with the case of the city of Mocoa (Colombia), where both those processes are predominantly self-organized. Both cities vary considerably concerning their size, political contexts, average income of the population, and geographical and climatic conditions. However, both cities share big challenges to find housing solutions for displaced populations, while facing high population growth. As the two case studies have been investigated separately at different time periods and with different objectives, the article will not provide a systematic comparison of the two cases and will not test existing hypotheses.[5] In contrast, the aim is to follow a more narrative approach and to explore general patterns on how governments and other local actors in different institutional contexts act in terms of the provision of long-term housing. Likewise, the article will show how displaced persons, beyond being passive aid-receivers alone, assume an active role in solving their housing needs. According to their needs, and according to the country and system in which they are located, they develop diverse solutions and practices (more in Colombia, less in Germany) that complement or replace the actions of the state and, thus, influence urban development.

Leipzig: a regulated arrival process and the struggle for affordable housing

After decades of population decline, Leipzig – a city located in the federal state of Saxony in eastern Germany with 587,857 inhabitants in 2018 (City of Leipzig 2020) – is now one of the fastest-growing cities in Germany. After the German reunification in 1990, Leipzig lost population, housing rents lowered, and a high percentage of buildings became unoccupied. For approximately 10 years now, Leipzig has turned into an attractive city for artists and young families. Between 2011 and 2018 the population grew an average of 11,116 inhabitants per year, which resulted in a growing demand for housing and rising housing prices.[6]

The displaced population in Germany has been influenced by the so-called refugee crisis in Europe in 2015 and 2016, "when more than one million people applied for asylum, many of who were recognized as refugees or granted complementary forms of protection" (UNHCR 2020, 22). More than half were from Syria while other countries of origin included Iraq, Afghanistan, Eritrea, Iran, and many others. According to the German refugee regulations and laws, the distribution of asylum seekers has to take place by a specific distribution mechanism called "Königsteiner Schlüssel," which stipulates that, depending on their population numbers and tax revenues, each of Germany's 16 federal states has to take a certain percentage of the total of asylum seekers coming to Germany. The federal states then distribute "their" refugees to the municipalities. In 2016 the federal state of Saxony received 5.08 percent of all asylum seekers coming to Germany and Leipzig received 13.52 percent of all asylum seekers coming to Saxony.

In 2018, around 13,000 displaced persons lived in Leipzig: 3,000 persons received benefits under the asylum seekers' legislation – AsylbLG (Asylbewerberleistungsgesetz) – and 9,849 persons received benefits under the regular social legislation (Sozialgesetzbuch SGB II) (City of Leipzig 2019).[7]

Arrival process and first regulated accommodation in Leipzig

Like other German cities, arrival and provision of first accommodation in Leipzig is a strictly regulated and planned process and it is organized by both the national and the federal state government. The process contains three phases:

a. The first transition phase – initial reception centers. When asylum seekers arrive in Germany they report to the authorities and are transferred to initial reception centers (*Erstaufnahmeeinrichtungen* – EAE) for from six weeks to six months. The state of Saxony is responsible for administering these EAEs. In general, NGOs or charity organizations are commissioned to run them. During this time, official registration, application of asylum and, if needed, first medical care provisions take place. The EAEs host in general a large number of asylum seekers and have a capacity for up to 700 people. The accommodations are rather precarious as many people have to share bedrooms, toilets, dining rooms, and social areas, which is indicative of the temporal character of the EAEs. Social workers and security personnel are permanently present in the centers. Until 2019 there were two EAEs in Leipzig. One of them is an old military barrack complemented with temporary pavilions. The other is a set of new buildings built in 2016.

b. The second transition phase – community centers (central accommodation). After a maximum of six months in the EAE, the respective municipality assumes the responsibility and organizes for the refugees accommodation in so-called community centers (*Gemeinschaftsunterkünfte* – GU). The GUs are in general smaller than EAEs although substantial differences between the GUs do exist. Some GUs can only accommodate up to 50 people while others have a capacity of up to 350. In some of the bigger GUs, the asylum seekers have shared bedrooms, toilets, and social areas. Small GUs are often made up of smaller apartments for families. Social workers provide permanent support to the inhabitants of the GUs. Until 2019, there were 30 GUs in Leipzig. The different GUs in Leipzig vary considerably regarding their size and building type. Some GUs are located in large old, prefabricated buildings, others in smaller residential buildings, and a few in container villages. In 2015, school buildings together with sports- and exhibition halls were also used as GUs.

c. The permanent phase – apartments (decentralized accommodation). If the asylum application is approved, or if the municipality decides that refugees are ready to live without constant social care (this can take months or even years), they will be accommodated in decentralized accommodations such as apartments. The municipality pays the rent but the responsibility of finding an adequate apartment in the city belongs to the displaced persons themselves. There is no officially designated public assistance in this process. However, several volunteer organizations and NGOs assist refugees in finding apartments.

During the first two phases, displaced people live with great uncertainty regarding their stay in Germany. Even though the GU accommodations should be only temporary, many people, generally big families, stay there for years because access to adequate apartments is limited and the competition for low-cost housing in Leipzig is high. Therefore, some inhabitants of the GUs live there for a longer period of time than officially intended.

Long-term housing: the challenge of finding a flat in Leipzig

According to the German asylum law *(Asylgesetz)*, as a rule, accommodation of asylum seekers should take place in the GUs. Therefore, municipalities have to focus primarily on providing these accommodations. The Leipzig City Council approved a municipal accommodation policy for asylum seekers in 2012 and 2013. The policy states that the municipality has very limited GU capacity. Therefore, decentralized accommodation in apartments needs to be improved. These apartments can be rented by asylum seekers themselves or directly by the municipality (so-called warranty apartments) (Leipzig City Council 2013, 16). Before 2017 there were not that many warranty apartments, and these were rented only to refugee families in case of hardship such as serious, long-term illness.

The official accommodation policy of the City of Leipzig states that "asylum seekers have no restriction in the choice of a separate apartment, as long as the apartment is cheaper than that in a community center or as long as it is within the framework of the KdU [cost of the accommodation] guideline" (Leipzig City Council 2013, 16). The municipal KdU guideline sets the maximum rental prices and maximum living space (square meters). However, the maximum values allowed are rather low.

The author investigated in 2016–17 the housing situation of displaced people who had already found an apartment in Leipzig. The aim was to determine the challenges in finding apartments, the housing preferences, and the location and characteristics of their apartments. An online survey was carried out. Due to language barriers, the survey was not conducted directly with displaced persons but with *Wohnungspaten* (volunteers who helped refugees find accommodation).[8] The database of the NGO Kontaktstelle Wohnen (an NGO that supports refugees to find flats) formed the basis for the selection of the respondents. The total of 200 registered *Wohnungspaten* (until August 2016) received an email asking them to fill out a survey. Sixty-five volunteers agreed to cooperate and replied. However, only 33 volunteers had success in finding apartments for refugees and were able to answer the questions in the survey. The volunteers found a total of 34 apartments and six WGs (shared apartments) and provided housing opportunities for 143 displaced persons (40 households). Of course, these data are not representative of the entire city. However, the survey did cover 7 percent of the 2,028 asylum seekers who lived in apartments in Leipzig (until December 2016).

The results show that the displaced persons covered by the survey prefer apartments in central districts of Leipzig. Popular districts are Zentrum, Zentrum-Ost, Zentrum-Süd, Südvorstadt and Plagwitz (Fig. 1). The good accessibility of public transportation and proximity to schools, daycare centers, and other educational institutions that children and adults already attend plays a crucial role. In contrast, proximity to friends, family, and people of the same nationality or good accessibility to previous community centers, social workers, or current jobs are not a decisive factor (Sánchez Steiner 2017, 10). However, apartments in central districts are expensive and the rental prices almost always exceed the maximum rents determined in the KdU guideline. Under these conditions asylum seekers are not really free to choose their place of residence (contrary to the goal of the official accommodation concept of Leipzig) and it is very difficult for them to find an adequate apartment. One alternative is to find an apartment rented through the municipal housing company of Leipzig (LWB) or through publicly oriented housing cooperatives. Those apartments are cheaper, but very few

Figure 1. Residential districts of displaced people in Leipzig. Source: Sánchez Steiner (2017, 13)

apartments are available in the central districts of Leipzig.

Cheap and available apartments for refugees often only exist on the outskirts of the city (such as districts with many prefabricated buildings from GDR times) (Fig. 2) and in districts where right-wing ideologies are more prevalent.[9] Hence, the survey participants often refuse to live in districts such as Grünau-Mitte, Grünau-Nord, and Grünau-Ost as well as Grünau-Siedlung and Lausen-Grünau (Fig. 3). Moreover, they also avoided eastern districts such as Neustadt-Neuschönefeld and Volkmarsdorf.

The investigation shows that only 22 percent of the households live in their preferred district while 43 percent live in the same or in a neighboring district of their previous community center. With a few exceptions, these populations often live in districts with a high proportion of people with a migratory background and of unemployed people, in the east and west (Fig. 4). The concentration in these districts of different social groups receiving state aid (such as refugees or the unemployed) is explained by the availability of low-rent apartments.

In addition to the district within the city, displaced persons looking for their own apartments also expressed preferences with regards to the apartment itself. Half of the households prefer a particular apartment size; of those, 42 percent are living in the size apartment they wanted. The situation is similar when it comes to the number of rooms: 65 percent of the households request a certain number of rooms; 46 percent then obtain the corresponding apartment. Thirty-three percent of the households wanted their apartment to be located on a specific floor. Half of them have managed to live on their preferred floor. Some participants of the survey prefer their apartments on the ground floor (53 percent) or the first and second floors (47 percent). No household wanted apartments located on the third floor or higher. However, 18 percent of the apartments and shared flats in which displaced persons now live are located on the ground floor, 40 percent on the first

Figure 2. Prefabricated high-rise building in Grünau, 2016. Source: Sánchez Steiner

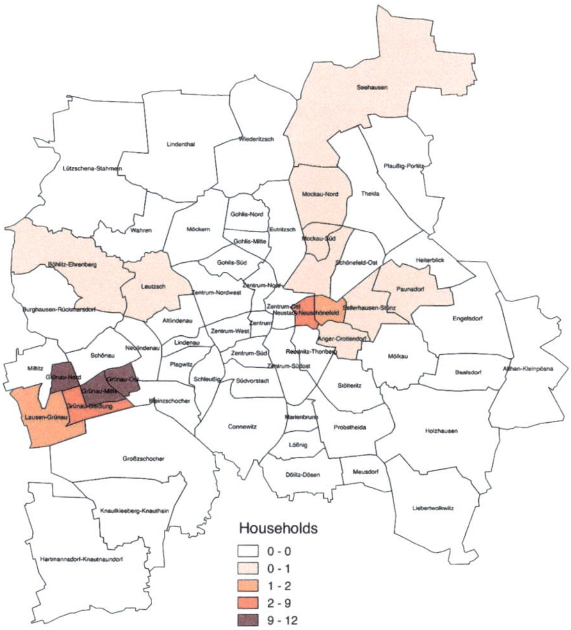

Figure 3. Location preferences: districts in which displaced people prefer not to live. Source: Sánchez Steiner (2017, 10)

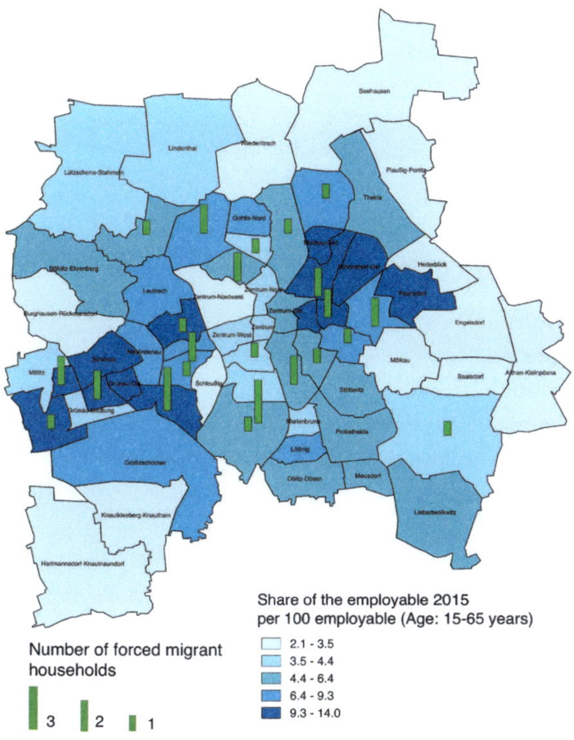

Figure 4. Location of unemployed people and of displaced people in Leipzig. Source: Sánchez Steiner (2017, 15)

and second floors, while 27 percent are located on higher floors.

Regarding the living space of the apartments (shared flats excluded), the survey found that most apartments (83 percent) are smaller than the “appropriate area,” according to the KdU guideline. However, there are differences between household groups (Fig. 5). The KdU guideline stipulates that, for example, an area of 85 m² is “appropriate” for a family of four; according to the survey, this household group actually has an average of 18 percent less space. Looking at families with six members, the same pattern is visible: six people live, on average, in 86 m², and not in the 105 m² recommended in the KdU. This shows that displaced people live in rather cramped living conditions. However, this is not just a problem for them. The housing market in Leipzig generally has very few apartments available for big families with five and more persons or for single households (both typical household sizes of displaced people). The housing options do not always correspond to the household size.

Two other aspects can also play a role in finding suitable living space: the living habits and the household structure. In an interview, a social worker explained that some Arabic-speaking persons (probably from rural areas in their home countries) prefer apartments on lower floors because they are not used to living in high-rise buildings and are afraid of heights. On the other hand, refugee household structures often differ from the average household structure in Leipzig. There are refugee families with seven children or with grandparents in the same apart-

Household size	Living space of the forced migrants (average in m²)	"Appropriate area" according to the KdU guideline (m²)	Difference
One Person	39	45	13 %
Two Persons	54	60	10 %
Three Persons	71	75	5 %
Four Persons	70	85	18 %
Five Persons	88	95	7 %
Six Persons	86	105	18 %

Figure 5. Comparison between actual living space of displaced people and KdU guidelines. Source: Sánchez Steiner (2017, 17)

ment or a husband with two wives and children. For some people it is often more important to have a very large living room (also used at night as a bedroom for parents) than several smaller rooms.[10] The floor plans of most existing housing in Leipzig do not reflect those household structures and housing preferences.[11]

Another considerable challenge in finding an apartment is social discrimination in the housing market. The survey shows that foreigners, displaced people without residence permits, and social welfare receivers (including Hartz IV) are often rejected by landlords. Asylum status also plays a role: recognized refugees with residential status get apartments more often than asylum seekers. The chances for displaced persons are generally limited if they have to compete with German tenants. This result of the survey is backed by an experiment (testing) of the Anti-Discrimination Office of Saxony, which found out that 60 percent of refugees confront racist discrimination in the Saxony housing market (ADB 2017).

Mocoa: a self-organized process and the building of new settlements

Mocoa is a little Andean-Amazonian city with about 36,000 inhabitants, located in southeastern Colombia, in the Putumayo Department. As a result of the historical population development in Colombia, political and administrative institutions are located particularly in the center of the country, while the peripheral Amazonas region is segregated from the country's social development and has traditionally been affected by an uncontrolled extractive economy. The weakness of the state institutions and the lack of institutional presence in this region has facilitated the establishment of armed groups like guerrilla, paramilitary units, and drug cartels.

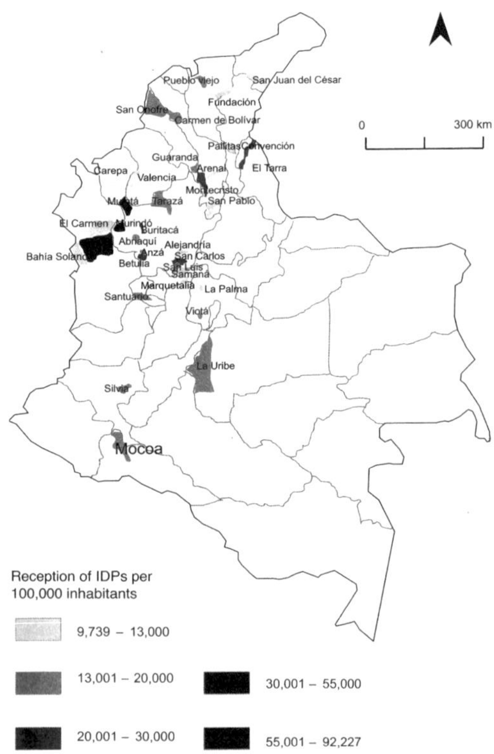

Figure 6. The 50 municipalities most affected by IDPs 1995–2005. Source: CODHES and CEC (2006, 42)

Disputes over access to land, use of agricultural land, and extraction of natural resources along with the production of cocaine have resulted in a highly violent environment, displacing thousands internally and forcing them to move from rural areas to the urban centers. Mocoa, as the provincial capital of the Putumayo Department, is one of the cities

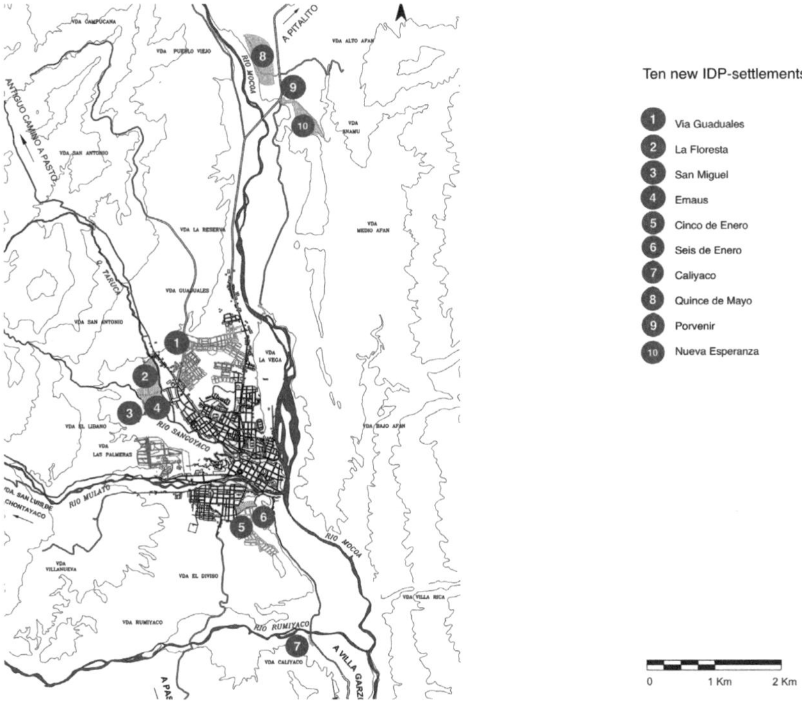

Figure 7. Ten new informal IDP settlements on the outskirts of Mocoa. Source: Sánchez Steiner (2012)

where people are relatively safe from violence, while the surrounding region is an area afflicted by violent conflict.

According to the government's Victims Registry of Colombia, eight million IDPs were registered from 1985 to 2019 (UNHCR 2020, 30), equal to 20 percent of the total population of Colombia, which has 40 million people. Mocoa is among the 50 municipalities with the highest proportion of IDPs in Colombia (Fig. 6). About 40 percent of the population in the city are IDPs. According to the Colombian Law 387 on Internal Displacement of 1997, IDPs have the right to be protected and to receive humanitarian assistance.

The author investigated between 1998 and 2008 the arrival and settlement process of displaced persons in Mocoa.[12] More recent reliable data are not available, but it can be assumed that the situation has not changed significantly.[13] Qualitative methods were used for the research. Interviews were conducted with representatives of organizations of displaced people, public officials, and social workers from NGOs. Additionally, cartography and aerial photos were analyzed. IDPs in Mocoa were (and are still) mainly small farmers and indigenous people who flew from poor rural areas of Putumayo and other nearby departments. The national and local government and the international organizations gave the IDPs humanitarian assistance like food or medical care, but they did not provide them with any accommodation. The IDPs themselves created short- and long-term accommodation possibilities using their own resources. Ten years after arriving in the city, many of the IDPs lived in the old poor neighborhoods of the city, while many others had built themselves new settlements on the outskirts of Mocoa (Fig. 7).

Arrival and self-accommodation process: Mocoa, the refuge-city

Based on the process in Mocoa, the author developed the model of *ciudad-refugio* (refuge-city) (see Sánchez 2012, 198). The model shows how the self-organized settlement process of IDPs works and which urban transformations take place (Fig. 8).
The self-organized settlement process consists of two phases:

a. Transition phase, individual process (rented rooms or apartments). This phase takes place as an individual process. IDPs, mainly as single-family households, arrive in the city and live temporarily with relatives and friends or rent rooms or apartments in poor neighborhoods of the city that lack appropriate infrastructure. Due to their difficult financial situation, unemployment, and the associated difficulties in paying rent, IDPs are forced to move several times. During this time, which can last months or years, IDPs get the opportunity to know other IDPs and, thus, try to find alternative solutions for their housing situation. Often, they decide to finally leave the inner city and their precarious housing conditions.

b. Permanent phase, collective process (self-built settlements in the outskirts). This step is a collective, self-organized process. Groups of IDP-families, who got to know each other at their previous place of residence in the inner city (transition phase), plan to occupy plots on the outskirts of the city. They also make elaborate plans for their new neighborhoods as part of their long-term solutions for housing and income generation through the occupation of public or private disused or underused areas. This process did not happen without conflicts in Mocoa. The police intervened to stop the occupation of the plots, without success. After days of confrontations, displaced persons managed to stay. As the municipality had no other solution to provide accommodation, the police suspended their actions. Subsequent negotiations with the municipality focused on improving settlement conditions or the possibility of relocation. In this phase, two different new settlement types were built:

— Urban settlements: These settlements have the typical characteristics of many "slums" around the world. They are located on the immediate periphery of the city and have predominantly residential use. The settlements are structured in small lots, with dense buildings with poor infrastructure. Wood and bricks are mainly used as building materials.

— Agro-urban settlements: These settlements are located further away from the city on the expanded periphery and consist of a mix of residential and agricultural use. This hybrid use contributes to the employment or income increase of displaced populations. These settlements are structured through large lots, they are low in density, and also have a poor infrastructural supply. The building materials also mainly consist of wood and bricks.

Role of social actors in the settlement development in Mocoa

Clearly, all these settlements are the result of self-organization. They do not comply with building norms and urban planning regulations and face many problems regarding the (lack of) infrastructure. However, the establishment of the settlements is a participatory planning process with self-conception, self-design, and self-construction, all taking place without institutional control. In the whole planning and construction process, no architects, engineers, or urban planners are involved. However, IDPs do not develop these settlements alone. There are complex actor constellations that indirectly support this development and provide "humanitarian assistance" in the form of building materials for the "temporary" construction of shelters, roads, schools, agricultural facilities, and churches. This way, the settlements transform into permanent neighborhoods and their construction takes place through the shared responsibility of various actors. Although the municipal planning authorities know about these processes, they do not intervene. Their institutional capacities are very limited.

The following two case studies, looking at an urban settlement (Cinco de Enero) and an agro-urban settlement (Quince de Mayo), show how the intervention of social actors is carried out and how different actors intervene. On the one hand, there are national public institutions such as the Department of Social Development (ACCIÓN SOCIAL), the Colombian Institute for Family Welfare (ICBF), the Institute for the Planning and Promotion of Energy Solutions (IPSE), the Ombudsman's Office, and the National Police; as well as regional public institutions such as the Corporation for the Sustainable Development of the Southern Amazon (CORPOAMAZONIA); and local institutions such as the Putumayo government and the municipality of Mocoa.

On the other hand, there are international agencies such as the International Organization for Migration (IOM), the United Nations High Commissioner for Refugees (UNHCR), and the Red Cross. Private service companies such as the Putumayo Energy Company and local social organizations such as the Neighborhood Community Action Boards (JAC), the Putumayo Indigenous Zonal Organization (OZIP), and the Indigenous Councils also intervene. Furthermore, local political leaders and religious institutions like the Catholic Church have taken part in the process.

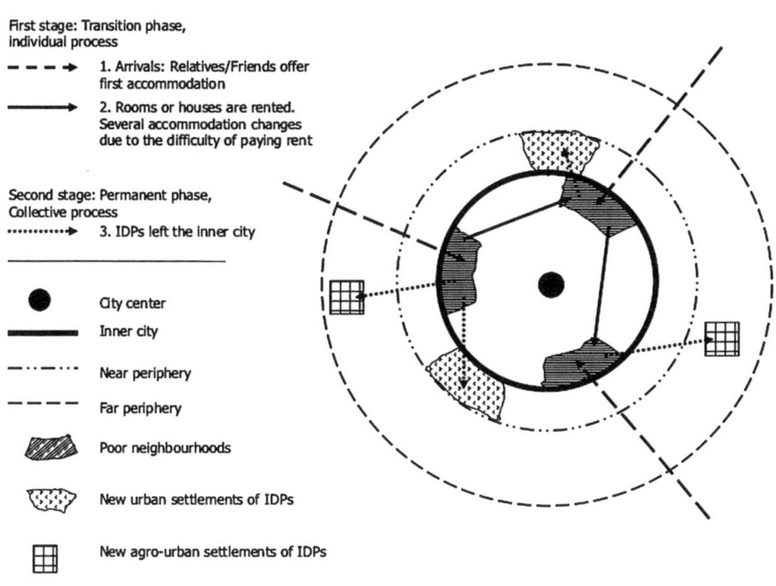

Figure 8. Model of *ciudad-refugio* (refuge-city). Source: Sánchez Steiner (2012, 198)

Cinco de Enero: an indigenous urban neighborhood

As its name indicates, this neighborhood originated on January 5, 2003, on land near the municipal cemetery located southeast of the city.[14] The occupation, carried out clandestinely at night, was planned for more than a year by a group of indigenous IDPs. The occupied land is of historical importance for the indigenous people: It is a piece of land that was part of an old indigenous territory that became the property of the Capuchin Mission and then of the JAC of the José Homero neighborhood. With the occupation, the indigenous people announced the legitimate recovery of the lands of their ancestors. Although the JAC came to defend the occupied territory and the police intervened using repressive and violent strategies, the occupants remained, supported by OZIP and the Ombudsman's Office.[15]

The IDPs distributed the spaces imitating the layout of the adjacent urban mesh, taking full advantage of the reduced space to accommodate 75 families. It is steep terrain, and the area covers around one hectare and consists of eight blocks and just over 70 plots. The area of each plot ranges from 65 to 120 m^2. The use is essentially residential and only two of the plots were intended for communal use (Fig. 9). The connection to public services is quite precarious.

The various actions of construction and connection of infrastructure were supported by different actors. The Red Cross donated rainwater collection tanks and latrines. The Putumayo government and the municipality of Mocoa managed access to a natural well to carry drinking water. A political leader, during a political campaign for congress, donated cables and managed with the Putumayo Energy Company the connection to electricity.[16] ACCIÓN SOCIAL (responsible for the implementation of the national IDP policy), UNHCR, and the local governments showed a weak position with the absence of strategies to guide the settlement processes of displaced people.

Quince de Mayo: an agro-urban village in Mocoa

As in the previous case study, the date of occupation of the land gave the name to the village. On May 15, 2002, a group of displaced persons occupied land located 4 km north of the center of Mocoa. The knowledge and experiences of community leaders in agricultural work and social organization in their hometown were useful in carrying out the planning and development of a village of 86 families. The occupied land was part of a large 98-hectare public property owned by IPSE. Because the land had no intended use, the IPSE did not take action against the occupation and, on the contrary, offered to cede the land to the municipality in the long term.

The first occupants created a social organization. The group opened roads and began measuring and marking plots. Over time, new occupants arrived, who settled in the already demarcated plots and built precarious shelters. At that time, institutions intervened and influenced a subsequent consolidation; the Red Cross and ACCIÓN SOCIAL donated materials to cover the shelters and protect them from the weather. Intending to use the land for agricultural production, the occupants traced plots much larger than those usually found in urban areas but smaller than the average in nearby rural areas. Its intention was not to annex the city as an urban neighborhood but to create an agro-urban village, close to the services and security that the city offers.[17]

The occupied area covers around 20 hectares and has 85 to 100 plots. The approximate area of each plot is 2,400 m^2 (30 × 80 meters). In this area, housing occupies the

Figure 9. Urban settlement Cinco de Enero, Mocoa, 2007. Source: Sánchez Steiner (2012)

smallest part of the land and the remaining space is used for agricultural production. Poultry and fish-farming for commercial purposes stands out, complemented by vegetable gardens for family consumption (Fig. 10). The organized group obtained formal permission from CORPOAMAZONIA for the use of water and dumping of waste. IOM and ACCIÓN SOCIAL provided money for the construction of fishponds and poultry houses, animal feed, and micro-business development loans.

The planners of the village (first occupants) allocated specific areas for communal use. Generous plots were arranged for the construction of a school, a communal hall, a church, and a playground. The ICBF contributed money for a nursery, the Catholic Church promoted fundraising events to build a chapel, ACCIÓN SOCIAL and IOM

Figure 10. Agro-urban settlement Quince de Mayo, Mocoa, 2007. Source: Sánchez Steiner (2012)

contributed money for the "temporary" construction of the school. The Putumayo government and the municipality invested money to connect the village to the local water supply system. Political leaders in election times "donated" material to improve the vehicular road and managed to install electricity. The construction of septic tanks was supported by the Red Cross through investment in latrines. The neighborhood was also connected with the official urban public transport service. As in the case of Cinco de Enero, the weakness of institutions such as ACCIÓN SOCIAL, UNHCR, and the municipality of Mocoa with respect to the absence of strategies to guide the settlement process, was also evident.

Conclusion: the active role of displaced persons

Major differences between the arrival and accommodation processes of displaced people in both cities do exist. In Germany, a politically and economically stable country of the Global North, many resources and strong institutions exist that steer the management of the short- and long-term accommodation of refugees. In contrast, Colombia has an unstable economy and a political system with weak institutions – a situation which is comparable to other countries of the Global South. This results in the disability of public authorities to oversee and manage the settlement processes of displaced people. Furthermore, the percentage of these populations is far higher in Mocoa than in Leipzig, which makes the situation in Mocoa far more challenging.

Another difference is that long-term accommodation in Leipzig takes place in formal housing, but refugees do not really have the possibility to choose where to live. The prices of the housing market as well as the lack of adequate floor plans dominate the process and limit the possibility for refugees to find adequate housing. In Mocoa, accommodation takes place in self-made housing. While the location of housing depends on the availability of free plots that can be occupied, IDPs have the opportunity to choose and the chance to design and build their housing according to their needs. Furthermore, they create income opportunities through the construction of new settlements. Possibilities of food production are taken into consideration in the planning of the settlements.

However, the processes in the two cities share some similarities: In both cities displaced people frequently live on the outskirts or in neighborhoods that often lack important social provisions. This exposes the difficulties of integrating these people into the housing market. Another similarity is the weak role of urban planning programs and especially public participation methods. Despite the fact that both countries adopted a planning law in which participation was a requirement, no participatory processes with displaced persons for improving their housing situation took place, in either Leipzig or in Mocoa.

Likewise, the role of architects and planners in both contexts has been weak. In Leipzig, some architects have been commissioned to build temporary refugee community centers. At the same time, groups of German architects have published books with ideas and proposals to design and build better refugee shelters.[18] However, attention and action regarding long-term housing for refugees is scarce. Probably one of the reasons why architects are hardly involved is the fact that only a few new residential projects are planned. Housing for refugees in Germany takes place predominantly in existing unoccupied housing stock. However, the Leipzig case shows that the vacant apartments that are accessible to refugees are those which nobody else wants because of their low construction quality and their location in neighborhoods with social problems. This experience shows that architects and urban planners can offer much more than the planning, design, and construction of new buildings. The adaptation of the existing housing stock to the needs of the new residents, both in public spaces and within the buildings and the apartments themselves, is a future challenge. In Mocoa, a small city in the middle of the Colombian conflict where architects and planners are scarce, the responsibility of planning and housing development often remains in the hands of the inhabitants and construction workers, as the case study shows.

Displaced persons are frequently perceived only as humanitarian aid receivers and their active role as providers of housing solutions is disregarded. The presented case studies, on the contrary, demonstrated the agency and creativity of these people. In Mocoa, IDPs assumed the most important role in solving their long-term housing problem and fulfilled the role of architects and planners, with enormous financial and technical limitations, but with creativity, participatory planning, and community organization. All this happened outside of formal regulations of urban planning but with the informal support of politicians, international and religious organizations, and public institutions. This is a contradictory formal/informal procedure that works not only in Mocoa, but also in many other Colombian cities. In Leipzig, refugees are appropriating space and adapting their apartment layouts according to their cultural habits and household size. This is an issue that requires further investigation.

The recognition of the active role of displaced people is very important for the conception of participatory processes in both Germany and Colombia and seems to be key for the improvement of housing programs. Architects, planners, and new residents need to cooperate to develop sustainable and future-oriented housing opportunities.

---

1 "Refugee," according to the 1951 Refugee Convention, is a person who is "owing to well-founded fear of being persecuted for reasons of race, religion, nationality, membership of a particular social group or political opinion, is outside the country of his nationality and is unable or, owing to such fear, is unwilling to avail himself of the protection of that country; or who, not having a nationality and being outside the country of his former habitual residence, is unable or, owing to such fear, is unwilling to return to it." **2** "Internally displaced persons" (IDPs), according to the United Nations Guiding Principles on Internal Displacement, are persons forced or obliged to flee from their homes, "in particular as a result of or in order to avoid the effects of armed conflicts, situations of generalised violence, violations of human rights or natural or human-made disasters, and who have not crossed an internationally recognised State border" (UNHCR 2006, 12). **3** "Asylum seeker" is an individual "who is seeking international protection. In countries with individualised procedures, an asylum seeker is someone whose claim has not yet been finally decided on by the country in which he or she has submitted it. Not every asylum seeker will ultimately be recognised as a refugee, but every refugee is initially an asylum seeker" (UNHCR 2006, 4). **4** In this article, the general term "displaced," to describe people, a person, or a population, will be used to refer to this whole group of people, regardless of their legal status. **5** The investigation of the Mocoa case was published in Sánchez Steiner (2012). It aimed to study the urban transformations that emerged with the arrival of displaced persons between 1998 and 2008. The Leipzig case study was published in Sánchez Steiner (2017) and aimed to understand the housing situation of displaced persons between 2016 and 2017. **6** The author calculated the average based on population data of the City of Leipzig (2020). **7** Displaced persons who are still in the asylum process or whose asylum application has been rejected have an *Aufenthaltsgestattung* (permission to remain) or a *Duldung* (permission to remain until deported). This group receives subsistence benefits under the AsylbLG. After staying for 15 months, these people receive benefits under the regular social assistance (Sozialgesetzbuch II). These correspond to the level of the "Hartz IV" rate. The benefits (money) under this legislation are higher than the benefits under the AsylbLG. **8** The author conducted talks and accompanied some displaced persons during their apartment searches in Leipzig. However, due to the project's low budget and the lack of financial resources to pay translators' fees, the author decided to obtain secondary data from volunteers and social workers, rather than directly from displaced persons. Hence, most of the data regarding the search for apartments are based on volunteers' estimations. The author recommends conducting complementary studies directly with displaced persons that would provide more detailed information. **9** An example of this is the district of Grünau, one of Leipzig's largest prefabricated housing estates on the city's outskirts, where right-wing extremism takes place. In the 2017 German parliamentary election, the district (with 29.5 percent in the Lausen-Grünau quarter and 29.4 percent in Grünau-Nord) was one of the most successful urban voting districts for the AfD party in Germany (Zschocke 2019, 68). The AfD (Alternative for Germany) is a German nationalist and right-wing populist political party. **10** Conversation with a social worker of a community center in Plagwitz (west of Leipzig). **11** Further research is therefore recommended to investigate refugees' appropriation of space and adaptation of apartment layouts. **12** The investigation was developed in two phases. The results of the first phase were published in 2007. The second phase, the author's doctoral thesis, was published in 2012. **13** The only significant change to the research results can be attributed to a heavy rainfall-landslide disaster that took place in 2017 and partially destroyed three settlements that were located in areas of high natural risk. **14** Cinco de enero means January 5. **15** Interview with an indigenous leader from Cinco de Enero, Mocoa, November 10, 2007. **16** Interview with a leader from Cinco de Enero, Mocoa, November 10, 2007. **17** Interview with the wife of a leader from Quince de Mayo. Mocoa, November 12, 2007. **18** See, for example, Jörg Friedrich et al. (2015).

References

ADB. 2017. *Rassistische Diskriminierung auf dem sächsischen Wohnungsmarkt. Situationsbeschreibung & Handlungsempfehlungen.* Antidiskriminierungsbüro Sachsen, Leipzig: ADB.

City of Leipzig. n.d. *Bevölkerungsbestand.* Amt für Statistik und Wahlen [Website]. Accessed December 20, 2020. https://statistik.leipzig.de/statcity/table.aspx?cat=2&rub=1&obj=0.

City of Leipzig. *Flüchtlinge in Leipzig* [Website]. Accessed August 9, 2019. https://www.leipzig.de/jugend-familie-und-soziales/auslaender-und-migranten/fluechtlinge-in-leipzig/.

Friedrich, J., S. Takasaki, P. Haslinger, O. Thiedmann, and C. Borchers. 2015. *Refugees Welcome. Konzepte für eine menschenwürdige Architektur.* Berlin: JOVIS Verlag.

Leipzig City Council. 2013. *Fortschreibung des Konzeptes Wohnen für Berechtigte nach dem Asylbewerberleistungsgesetz in Leipzig*, Beschluss-Nr.: BS/RBV-1826/13, Leipzig, 2013.

Sánchez Steiner, L. 2007. *Impacto urbano del desplazamiento forzado en Mocoa- Putumayo. Elementos de diagnóstico y planteamientos para un reordenamiento espacial.* Bogotá: CINEP.

Sánchez Steiner, L. 2012. *La ciudad-refugio. Migración forzada y reconfiguración territorial urbana en Colombia.* Barranquilla: Editorial Universidad del Norte, Consejo Profesional de Arquitectura y sus Profesiones Auxiliares.

Sánchez Steiner, L. 2017. *Ergebnisbericht. Umfrage über die Wohnsituation von dezentral untergebrachten Geflüchteten in Leipzig.* Leipzig: Bundesverband NeMO e.V.

UNHCR. 2020. *Global Trends – Forced Displacement in 2019.* Geneva: United Nations High Commissioner for Refugees.

UNHCR. 2006. *UNHCR Master Glossary of Terms.* United Nations High Commissioner for Refugees, Rev.1. https://www.refworld.org/docid/42ce7d444.html.

Zschocke, P. 2019. "Im Schatten der Stadt. Ist Leipzig-Grünau ein Modellwahlbezirk der AfD?." *Leipziger Zustände*, chronik.LE (January 2019): 68–71.

Architectures of Displacement: On the Aesthetics and Politics of Humanitarian Shelter

Romola Sanyal

The idea of refuge tends to rely predominantly on the model of the camp and the tent as spaces and forms which house displaced populations. In this paper, I interrogate this focus on these specific sites and spaces of displacement and suffering. I examine the ways in which camps have come to take their current form and how they are aestheticized through different technologies. Specifically, I ask: what work does the camp do for different stakeholders, from aid workers, to academics, artists, architects, and popular writers? I argue that the aestheticization of displacement serves to elicit sympathy and support for specific forms of suffering while ignoring other spaces and populations who are equally marginalized. In doing so, I critically question what it means to talk about architectures of displacement.

Introduction

Mainstream depictions of refugees rely on a relatively narrow and standardized set of images and narratives about displaced people. They are represented as racialized bodies either migrating, navigating treacherous and hostile lands and seas, or confined to tightly controlled and hopeless camps and detention centers. The camps themselves have become symbolic of refuge, particularly in the Global South.[1] Here, in some images, refugee camps, replete with their blue-and-white UNHCR tents, stand in row after orderly row. In others, the tents have been replaced with makeshift structures and shacks. The camps are teeming with people – often tens of thousands of men, women, elderly, and children – but beyond the boundaries of this space, the landscape appears to be in rural and often barren areas, emptied of people or life. Scholarly and popular works highlight not only the prolonged periods for which these supposedly temporary camps stand, but how that extension of time shapes social and economic lives, enabling commercial and other activities to take place in these spaces (Agier 2002; Montclos and Kagwanja 2000).

These refugee camps, produced out of geopolitical impasses and a collapse of upholding refugee rights, have become shorthand for refuges, particularly for those thousands fleeing violence in countries in the Global South.[2] Academic and popular narratives have also lent themselves to the production of such normalized images of refuge. Considerable scholarship across different disciplines has engaged with understanding and debating the camp, its spatiality, politics, and subject formations. Popular articles have referred to them as "exigent cities" or "emergency urbanism," highlighting both the vast numbers of people that come to inhabit these spaces and the lengths of time they spend in them (Lewis 2008). In this piece, I examine the different ways in which images of camps have come to symbolize displacement and refuge. I do this by tracing a history of producing camps, and the ways in which different stakeholders – artists, scholars, and humanitarians – manufacture an essentialized version of a camp.

In doing this, I query why the camp as an icon of displacement continues to persist in a time when over half the world's refugees live in urban areas, and increasingly large numbers of displaced people are moving to urban areas rather than camps. Why are other emerging spaces of refuge unable to do the same kind of "work" that camps do to capture the image of forced displacement? Here, I argue that the aestheticization of the camp, as a specified, demarcated space of a particular kind of suffering, acts as a form of social responsibility for these specific stakeholders, who either study or are invested in narrating a unique kind of suffering and displacement that is different from others. While I recognize that various kinds of refugee shelters and camp-like spaces have re-emerged within the Global North, I restrict my discussions to the so-called Global South, where I have conducted most of my research, because this is the part of the world where the vast majority of refugees are warehoused in different ways and where the urbanization of mass displacement has profound impacts on cities. In the first section I discuss how the space and design of refugee camps have evolved over time to not only enable the care but also the control of displaced populations. In the second section I show how different media are complicit in creating particular images and narratives about displaced populations and camps. In the final section, I draw on contemporary humanitarian practices in urban areas and discuss how the convergence of forced migrants and the urban poor complicates the process of aestheticizing displacement.

Exigent cities – refugee camps as symbolic spaces

In June 2008, the *New York Times Magazine* ran an article titled "The Exigent City," by Jim Lewis. In it, the author raised myriad issues with the design and production of camps. These ranged from the impossible temporality of refugee camps and their large number of inhabitants, to the politics of temporality associated with the built environment of the camp, to the lack of architectural and design engagements with these spaces of refuge. While much has changed in the years since the article was published, much has remained the same. Refugee camps continue to proliferate across the globe, despite the fact that more and more refugees are moving into urban areas. Camps continue to be seen as temporary spaces with makeshift structures even though we know that protracted displacement has now become a norm rather than an exception. Camps continue to dominate popular, academic, and artistic imaginations as the designated space for displaced people. This should be in some ways unsurprising as the temporary logic of the camp that underpinned its creation has continued to influence its form. Here, a cursory glance at the history of refugee camps is useful.

Experimentation with camps draws on different histories of separating and managing people. As Herscher (2017) notes, the genealogy of the camp is linked to the history of relief in Victorian England, particularly the creation of workhouses that eventually metamorphosed into colonial camps in India and later South Africa during the Anglo-Boer war. In these iterations, the camp simultaneously acts as a space of relief, of containment, and of removal. The German uptake of this model, particularly in their deployment of it for the extermination of Namibians on Shark Island, ultimately provides the basis for its use as concentration camps in the Holocaust. Ironically, as both Herscher (2017) and Malkki (1995a) note, the concentration camp not only acts as a space of managing displacement in the post-World War II period but also provides the model for contemporary designs for refugee camps. As such, they were, according to

Malkki (1995a, 498), "emplaced as a standardized generalizable technology of power" at the end of World War II. These "Displaced Persons camps," as they were historically known, allowed for the orderly repatriation of people, their screening and quarantine, and the creation of an entire bureaucracy of administrators, functionaries, doctors, and the like. Malkki (1995a, 498) shows how, in World War II camps, spatial isolation, the management of refugees and displaced persons, and the practices related to them were often ad hoc in nature and in a constant state of improvisation. She further argues that not only were former concentration camps sometimes used as "Assembly Centers" for refugees when the war ended, but the architecture of the concentration camp made it particularly suitable for the control of masses of people and for the prevention of epidemics and the administration of quarantines.

The camp model that emerged from the ashes of World War II has evolved and circulated through the world. As processes of decolonization, civil conflicts, and other forms of violence have grown and spread, so too has the global humanitarian system that supports those displaced from them and the camp model itself. The UNHCR, which is responsible for refugee protection, together with a range of NGOs, manages these spaces and ensures that inhabitants are cared for in line with certain minimum humanitarian standards and provided with basic supplies and necessary spaces. The UN and allied organizations register refugees and conduct health screenings, provide documentation, and calculate the approximate population in order to ensure that correct and cost-effective amounts of aid and services can be delivered (Sanyal 2014b). Camps themselves continue to be laid out in a manner that enables efficient delivery of goods and services and the disciplining and control of inhabitants, and in doing so, become "almost cities." As far back as the 1970s, after working with refugees displaced from the Bangladesh War of Independence, Frederick Cuny commented on how to design and plan refugee camps. He observed that:

> This was the realization that when large numbers of people are concentrated in a small geographic area, in effect a camp ceases to be a camp; in actuality it becomes a town or a small city with all the accompanying problems. A refugee camp must have housing, water, sewers, roads, clinics, fire protection, garbage disposal, parks, schools – everything found in a town. Thus, development plans for refugee camps should be considered with the same detail as a master plan for a town (Cuny, 1977, 127).

Contemporary handbooks such as the *UNHCR Handbook for Emergencies* seem to support this view. They suggest that camps be designed in cooperation with communities living there and that minimum standards are to be upheld that determine the size and preferred layout of camps. For example, the handbook notes that "[i]deally, the recommended surface area is 45 m^2 per person when planning a refugee camp (including kitchen/vegetable gardening space). However, the actual surface area per person (excluding gardening space) should not be less than 30 m^2 per person" (UNHCR 2007, 210). Likewise, *The Sphere Handbook* (Sphere Association 2018, 251), which provides a global standard for developing shelter in humanitarian crises, notes that temporary settlements or planned or self-settlements should be based on urban design and town planning principles. The handbook advises that camp planners organize families and groups together and more generally support existing and future social networks, contribute to safety and security, enable self-management, and maintain the privacy and dignity of separate households. Furthermore, in relation to prescribing a minimum land area for displaced people in a planned settlement, the handbook advises that the minimum usable surface area be 45 m^2 per person in camp-type settlements, including household plots. This area is intended to encompass a range of services and activities such as roads, cooking areas, education and recreation areas, healthcare and religious facilities, sanitation, markets, and so forth. Sphere also suggests that settlement planning considers changes in the population (Sphere Association, 2018, 250–51).

The *UNHCR Handbook for Emergencies* also offers a sketch of what a sub-block of a camp may look like in what might appear to be a balance between temporariness and permanence. The language of the guidelines, which pays attention to security needs of families while being sensitive to social and cultural norms of displaced communities, appears to signal an acknowledgement of the possibility of protraction in the case of displacement. These ideal camp layouts are meant to offer "dignity" and "security" for those who are displaced but primarily to ensure that camp inhabitants are cared for in specific, prescriptive ways that often restrict their movement outside these spaces. In other words, plans reveal the ways in which inhabitants are beneficiaries with limited agency rather than political beings able to exercise autonomy. It is unsurprising, then, that camps continue to be viewed as total institutions of containment and discipline, and inhabitation within these spaces is seen to be devoid of politics and therefore of a full life. Many scholars have pushed back against these dehumanizing narratives. While acknowledging the difficult living conditions wrought by permanent temporariness, scholars have highlighted the capacity of camps to evolve and for inhabitants to exercise political agency in myriad ways (Feldman 2015; Ramadan 2013; Sanyal 2011).

Representations of the camp

I move here from analyzing how a particular form has come to be standardized and institutionalized to considering how it is aestheticized by different media and stakeholders creating a particular iconography of displacement. The camp offers not only a standardized model for managing displaced populations, but also the possibility of "finding" and visually capturing displacement in very specific ways. Different media including journalism, art, and academia have contributed to the imagining of refuge as a distinct geography. These have tended to cast the refugee as an essentialized figure - either as a victim or as a hero (Kihato and Landau 2020). Likewise, camps have come to be cast as spaces both of incarceration and rebellion. Narratives and visual representations, particularly of camps in the Global South, focus on both suffering and resilience of such spaces to signal ultimately the impossible permanence of humanitarian space. There is an interesting parallel here with how "slums" have become the shorthand for urbanization in the Global South (Rao 2006; Roy 2011) and as sites for the aestheticization of poverty (Roy 2003). They too have come to be seen as sites of entrepreneurial misery. It appears then that the Global South becomes a sum total of its disparate and dystopian parts. I discuss this later in this section.

If the Third World city is worlded through the slum, the Third World refuge is worlded through the camp. The camp becomes the site of the aestheticization of displacement. This process unravels in a number of ways. Firstly, it emerges through the production of a particular and institutionalized "architecture of displacement," especially through its tents and grid layouts in seemingly remote, rural landscapes. UNHCR blue-and-white tents that are part of a larger humanitarian apparatus of control and care can also be seen as ushering in a new architectural aesthetic of refuge. Here, aid is provided over increasingly protracted periods of time to keep people alive, but it does not facilitate a future. As a result, humanitarianism produces spaces of the present; in other words, they are sites that symbolize inhabitance only of the now, not one with a meaningful future. This then operates as an architecture of deprivation, one where people are not only denied more or better aid, but also are deprived of aspirations. Secondly, as a space of containment, it offers ready access to images of populations who are sequestered and of their living conditions. Popular discussions around refugees, particularly in news outlets, focus on refugee camps as sites of misery and limbo, creating what Lille Chouliaraki (2006) has elsewhere described as "the spectatorship of suffering." Focusing on the terrible living conditions, security situation, remoteness, and misery in different refugee camps around the world allows journalists to evoke – through words and images – life and inhabitation of camps as uniquely miserable with particularly dire living circumstances.

Artistic attempts at trying to capture the essence of exile, dispossession, and the permanent temporality of refugees continue to predominantly focus on their fragility, their enduring makeshiftness, offering opportunities to not only allow the re-creation of such spaces, but renderings of how to intervene in them. Examples of various exhibits displaying camp conditions or illustrating their spatial specificities abound. Médecins San Frontières famously ran *A Refugee Camp in the Heart of a City* installation in different cities around the world. Through it, the organization tried to develop an understanding in the average population about the main struggles of the millions of people who are displaced and to showcase the work of MSF itself. At a smaller scale, various exhibitions have also taken place probing the specificities of camps and their spatialities. One in London in 2017 attempted to showcase and share spatial knowledge about refuge. Another in Vienna in 2019 exhibited the work of a group of architects building specific structures in displaced persons camps. These are just two examples of undoubtedly larger numbers of exhibits that take place around these issues. Each one attempts to use artistic means to demonstrate specific concerns about camps to larger audiences. The aim is often to share with the public and other experts knowledge and ideas about the camps. In some cases, it is unclear what this sharing of knowledge ultimately achieves and who is involved in the conversations, beyond the experts and the (often already familiar) public. The exhibits themselves, as I have noted elsewhere in my work on exhibiting poverty, are devoid of the people themselves, of sensory, or other affective elements that make up the experience of such spaces (Sanyal 2004). Consequently, it creates a sanitized and safe environment through which to consume displacement.

No less problematically, academic work has also lent itself to the development of the camp as the site of refugee inhabitation. In fact, there is limited discussion of the ways in which academic work also enables the aestheticization of displacement or indeed of poverty or marginalization. From anthropologists to geographers, sociologists and indeed architects, there has been for several decades a disproportionate focus on refugee camps and detention centers as key sites in which to study refugees, their politics, humanitarian aid, and so forth. Work on architecture and architectural history on displacement and forced migration, limited as that may be, focuses on the camp and the tent as the key sites and objects of analyses and how they have constituted spaces of architectural experimentation and education (Herscher 2017; Siddiqi 2018; Sanyal 2011). As noted earlier, those working on more contemporary and critical scholarship on camps have troubled our conceptions of them by challenging the standard, reductive, and dehumanizing narratives. They have critically examined spaces of camps themselves as sites of hope and despair, of agency despite constraint. They blurred the boundaries between camps and their foils – cities – and helped us develop new spatial vocabularies (Feldman, 2015; Martin 2015; Montclos and Kagwanja 2000; Pasquetti and Picker 2017; Ramadan 2013; Sanyal 2014b). Others have also noted the emergence of the camp in a variety of forms within the Global North, not necessarily as formal, institutionalized spaces, but often as spontaneous, self-built sites, created by migrants on their messy journeys towards their destinations (Katz et al. 2018). Such scholarship that moves beyond the reductive, formal refugee camp narrative is necessary, but much of it continues to focus on specific identifiable, iconic sites where groups of migrants/refugees can be found and cared for. The question here is how do we imagine other geographies of displacement? The migration away from camps is gathering speed, but conceptual work, particularly from the Global South where most of the displacement is located, is desperately needed.

Finally, refugee camps remain the focus of much humanitarian and policy work. Although humanitarians themselves are engaging in other sites of displacement, this shift has been slow and reluctant. On a field trip to Lebanon, some years ago, I asked a UN agency worker why they continued to focus on informal tented settlements located predominantly in rural/semi-rural areas when most displaced Syrians in Lebanon were living in informal urban areas. This elicited a defensive response, but also one which neatly skirted the urban question. While I do not wish to replace one geography of displacement with another, the insistence in focusing on distinct informal tented settlements located mainly on agricultural land piqued my interest. In this instance, the reasons were manifold including the various politics swirling around about supporting refugees. But after further research on humanitarian interventions, it became evident that the urban work itself was difficult. Often the reluctance to work with urban refugees is because urban interventions are more complex than those in camps, especially as NGOs have to grapple with complex governance structures, systems, and politics in cities that they do not encounter in a camp. A recent discussion paper by the Active Learning Network for Accountability and Performance (ALNAP),[3] for example, highlighted a few examples of how humanitarian organizations can intervene in urban areas, but the work remains limited and piecemeal (Campbell 2018). On the other hand, continued policy and practice work takes place in camp settings addressing everything from toilet design to gender-based violence.[4] Camps then function as tabula rasa for the humanitarian sector as well as laboratories of experimentation with and management of populations. Finally, as a distinct site dedicated to the management of relief operations for refugees, camps are easier to "sell" to donors in exchange for funding. As Krause (2014) notes in her work, donors buy visibility through the funding of manageable and attractive projects. To produce a project that is practicable, visible and attractive on the humanitarian-urban interface is far more difficult to achieve. I elaborate on this further on.

In sum, as a distinct, bounded space of difference, camps function as spaces of care and control. Camps offer sites that can be easily aestheticized as those of displacement, deprivation, difference, relief, and exception. Here refugees appear as a literally captive group to be represented to the world. Work on the aestheticization of poverty has long grappled with what it does and how it does it. Ananya Roy (2003) views it as a romanticization of an organic form. Others working on art and image have studied how the painting and photographing (often of mothers with children) in particular ways aims to elicit sympathy. However, in doing so, artists and photographers need to produce and capture their subjects in relatable ways. Thus, they cannot be too poor, or alien, but similar enough to be deserving of our sympathies and charity. They note that the attention to poverty is not merely to capture social suffering but is also a form of performing social responsibility (Fluck 2010; Ventura 2017). This can be extended to the reproduction of particular forms of social suffering, also occupying the margins of the world – in this case displaced people. Thus, although exhibits engage in problematic representations of suffering, they also perform a role as a site of learning, enabling forms of empathy and solidarity to emerge despite (or perhaps because of) the distance. This ultimately enables the production of particular visions of suffering and marginalization eliciting specific forms of charitable, institutional, and other support and interest.

Missing spaces, hidden populations

While an architectural history of displacement is underway through the efforts of several critical scholars in this field, as the sections above note, this history focuses on spaces, namely camps, in which particular typologies of buildings constructed for and by displaced persons are made visible. In other words, as suggested earlier, the camp has become the shorthand for refuge, the implications of which, particularly in the Global South, are manifold. However, settlements for displaced people span a wide spectrum, from camps to informal settlements, including self-settlements that refugees themselves create. As Oliver Bakewell (2014) among others have noted, such spaces lie outside of official camps and, thus, do not benefit from their support (although their inhabitants, if registered, can do so). Those who choose to self-settle forgo the aid safety net of the camp, but self-settlement may provide livelihood and other opportunities that may not be available in camp spaces. There is a need then to recognize the flexibility between camp spaces and spaces outside as people move between the two and to rethink spaces that emerge in between. Many such self-settlements can be seen to occupy gray spaces (Yiftachel 2009) as they are neither formal nor informal, and benefit from support neither by humanitarians nor by local governments.

Amongst self-settled populations, urban populations are the largest. Urban refugees constitute more than half the world's refugee population (and growing) and there is a need to address them more robustly. It should be noted here that urban refugees are not a new issue. Rather, refugees have been moving to urban areas for a long time. In fact, one could argue that some aspects of asylum are fundamentally urban in character. In the Judeo-Christian tradition, for example, cities of refuge provided safety for those who were escaping from blood libel. In this ancient tradition, one could only acquire safety in the space of the city of refuge (Bau 1985). It is, thus, interesting that in this strand of asylum, not only was refuge urban, but it was also exceptional as one could only be free from persecution within this specific urban space. Even beyond this history, refugees have been coming to and been hosted in urban areas through generations. Whether looking at the Huguenots who escaped to London from France in the 17th century, or Partition refugees moving to Delhi, Karachi, Kolkata, or Lahore, or refugees moving to find asylum in Beirut, Nairobi, Johannesburg, or Bogotá, cities have been key sites for displaced persons to find homes. This scholarship has mostly been rooted in regional histories and has stood outside of policy work. Only recently has there been a concerted move among scholars to more critically engage with urban refugees. This has occurred for various reasons, not least because UNHCR, the organization responsible for protecting refugees' rights, has only recently formally acknowledged and supported urban refugee work. The reticence of UNHCR to engage with urban refugees, despite it being a significant policy issue for some time, has been down to several reasons, including political motivations of host and donor nations.

The scholarship on urban refugees continues to grow, and this has encompassed a range of different issues that have been urban in nature. These have included studies of livelihood opportunities for refugees, as well as their exploitation in the urban economy, society, and housing (Coddington 2018; Fábos 2015; Jacobsen 2006). Research has also studied social networks, urban informality, mobilities across urban space, the policing and controlling of refugees, and politics of hospitality including around ideas of the city as sanctuary (Bagelman 2016; Brun 2010; Darling 2009; Pasquetti 2015; Pasquetti and Picker 2017; Sanyal 2014b). As is evident, the issues faced by refugees in non-camp settings are manifold and complex, particularly as refugees are living in informal, unsanctioned spaces and therefore subject to various kinds of harassment and exploitation. Tensions between refugees and non-refugees also ignite around access to services and goods that may be limited outside the camp setting. In other words, inhabiting spaces outside of camps on the one hand offers certain freedoms and opportunities. On the other hand, it ushers in new forms of precarity and exploitation.

Architectures of urban refuge

Spatial analyses of refugees in cities continue to be extremely limited. There is little attention paid to the kinds of experiments that are taking place around shelter for urban refugees, especially those who do not live in camp-like conditions. Within the European context, there is work emerging analyzing the kinds of buildings and spaces that are being constructed to host refugees. René Kreichauf (2018) has, for example, discussed different forms of housing for refugees in Europe. He writes that in Berlin, for example, housing for refugees included the division of hangars and large halls into smaller segments using walls and tent structures to house up to 2,500 people. They do not meet Berlin's minimum reception standards. Further accommodation options also include the creation of Tempohomes and modular accommodation (MUF). He notes that there are 20 Tempohome villages consisting of eight residential container complexes, one administrative building, one central supply building, and a gatehouse. The MUF, he observes, are five-storied prefabricated buildings housing up to 500 refugees. He also points to the use of centers in former military bases or hospitals in countries such as Greece, Germany, and Denmark as accommodation sites (Kreichauf 2018). In other cases, migrants are creating their own makeshift solutions as they move through

European cities in search of asylum (Katz 2016). Yet, as these scholars note, this signals more than anything else, the re-emergence of camp infrastructures in Europe. Other kinds of accommodation interventions by humanitarian agencies include the creation and rental of private accommodation in countries such as Greece, the United Kingdom, as well as non-European countries such as Lebanon. Scholars have analyzed the processes by which these accommodation systems operate, studying how their humanitarian and "dispersal" strategies have taken on neoliberal logics and have been deeply problematic (Darling 2016), but the spatial and design analysis of this kind of accommodation is emerging. In their work Brun and Thorshaug (2020) look at the ways in which internally displaced people (IDP) accommodation in a private building in Georgia has limited space for multiple uses and occupants and how this compels residents to modify them into flexible, personalized spaces.

NGOs and private actors are also playing a role in the production of urban refuge. In Lebanon, for example, NGOs involved in the provision of private accommodation have attempted to incentivize landlords by offering to upgrade their houses. This is done through improving the structural conditions of the houses themselves and bringing them up to minimum standards acceptable by humanitarian organizations. Examples of this include guidelines by the Shelter Sector which note, for instance, the different kinds of upgrades that can be done to substandard buildings. These include weatherproofing; bringing spaces up to Sphere standards with minimum requirements of space per square foot per person; minimum water, sanitation, electrical and other infrastructure that is to be included in the shelter unit; and the considerations that need to be taken into account with regard to people that may have physical and other disabilities. Several NGOs have publicized upgrading projects that they have concluded through social media as well. This is done in exchange for hosting a refugee family, either rent-free or for reduced rent for a fixed period of time, usually a year or 18 months. This architecture of upgrading is a new and emerging form of refuge that lies at the intersection between understanding the future of humanitarianism and that of urbanization, especially as we move towards more privatized, informal modes of accommodating people.

Beyond the bureaucratic and official provision of housing are the various forms of dwellings and homes created by refugees themselves. It is crucial to acknowledge here that refugees have not always been provided with housing but have often made it themselves or found ways to house themselves within urban environments. The discussions of self-built settlement or self-accommodated refugees remain largely hidden in the literature. Troublingly, an understanding that refugees can be city-makers themselves, not just through the production of their own spaces, but through constructing the city as well, is overlooked. For example, while historical analyses of refugees from the Partition of India, and along the eastern border between India and present-day Bangladesh are ubiquitous, these mostly remain mired in larger political and social questions, taking space as a neutral backdrop against which social relations unravel or focusing on refugees alone rather than thinking about them in the larger developmental context and alongside other subaltern groups of that time (Bose 2000; Chatterjee 1992; Chatterji 2011). This is deeply problematic as subjects and spaces co-constitute each other and understanding how identities of refugees evolve requires one to be attentive to the kinds of spaces they occupy and remake over time. In my own work on Partition refugees in Kolkata, I attempted to craft an urban history of refuge through interviews and analyses of documents and texts. What became evident through this work were the forms of auto-construction that refugees undertook to develop their homes and spaces in the city. Interviewees talked about occupying land forcibly as they apparently had no other options for dignified accommodation. Sudeshna Banerjee (2003) astutely notes that refugees who occupied land and created these colonies came from higher caste, but lower-middle class backgrounds and had previously anchored their caste and masculine identities and authority in their landed status in East Bengal. In the aftermath of Partition, when this land was permanently lost to them, they attempted to recover it through the taking and shaping of colony settlements. The lands that were squatted upon and brought into the urban fringes belonged to either the state or private landowners. The occupation of land became a legally and politically contentious issue causing the displacement of others such as Muslim residents of the area, and affected practices of welcome even in the charged atmosphere of post-Partition India (Chakrabarti 1990; Ray 2002; Sanyal 2014a). Occupation was followed by the building and construction of houses themselves, often out of makeshift materials such as bamboo, and later tin and finally bricks and mortar once land tenure had been legalized (Ray 2002; Sanyal 2009). Not only were houses built, but the refugee-squatters came to produce critical urban spaces such as markets, schools, roads, and so forth (Bose 2000; Ray 2002; Sanyal 2009). These kinds of upgrading and consolidation processes are common in informal settlements in many parts of the Global South but are generally analyzed through the lens of urban poverty rather than forced migration and refugee studies. The urban histories of refugee-squatters mark a fascinating blurred boundary between squatting and refuge and lay bare the politics of exclusion that lie at the heart of both state-making and urbanization.

The production of space on the fringes of cities such as Kolkata in the aftermath of Partition not only enabled a particular form of urbanization of the city, but also contributed to the production of certain kinds of urbanity and urban citizenship amongst the refugee-squatters. The occupation of land and the eventual legalization and regularization of land tenure and colonies also crafted particular relationships between citizens of Kolkata who saw refugees as encroachers on space, and refugees who saw these acts as part of their claims to citizenship. Nilanjana Chatterjee (1992, 207) deftly describes the fraught relationships between both groups in her beautifully crafted unpublished dissertation. Here, she notes how refugees felt "ashamed" to disclose their addresses and were deeply disturbed by the attitudes amongst locals that refugees had effectively trespassed on and stolen land by squatting and eventually acquiring land titles.

Kolkata is not the only city that has been recast through the activities of refugees and displaced persons. Indeed, as noted earlier, urban refugees are not new, and many cities including Delhi, Karachi, Beirut, among others, have been fundamentally reshaped through displacement and forced migration and through the labor and aspirations of these refugees. As we see more people continuing to be uprooted throughout the world for various exigencies, it is worthwhile considering these urban histories and how they may help us think about the possibilities of non-camp futures. This is not to engage in a problematic and celebratory account of displaced populations being "resilient" or "entrepreneurial" – terms that tend to gloss over the very real and quotidian forms of violence that continue to shape their lives – but to acknowledge displaced people as city-makers who have the right to the city and to consider ways in which we can stand in solidarity with them, rather than erasing their lives, histories, and presences.

Conclusion – rethinking "architectures of displacement"

Despite the emergence and expansion of non-camp spaces for displaced people, the analyses of refuge continue to be on camp-like spaces. We need to critically interrogate why that may be the case. Here I return to the discussion I had with the UN officer in Lebanon about supporting refugees and their insistence on focusing on informal settlements. Through this narrative, a picture emerges about the utility of the camp. As Richard Black (1998) among others have noted, the camp is discussed as a convenient technology of delivering aid and support effectively to populations that need them. Such a narrative hides the larger issues of controlling and sequestering the population. I would take that further and say that it also masks the bigger points about making the population visible, mappable, and knowable to different actors. It makes the spectatorship of displacement and suffering possible. Aid agencies, humanitarian NGOs, and donors can see, for example, a sociologically and geographically distinct, numerically specific population of people in need of distinct forms of help and support living in the camp. Here I draw on the work of Monika Krause (Krause 2014) on "the good project," which analyses how agencies sell projects to donors. Projects become manageable, and they and their beneficiaries become commodities. Using this lens, I argue that camps enable agencies to sell humanitarian projects to donors precisely because the aesthetic possibilities of the space make distinct projects within it persuasive and easy to capture visually. On the contrary, urban interventions that may support refugees *and* local populations are harder to sell because the superficial boundary between the displaced and the poor is far more blurred, making it harder to intervene or to encapsulate in an easy narrative and image. A recent report by ALNAP (Campbell 2018) noted that a few organizations are beginning to think about urban refugees and "developing toolkits" for addressing their needs. From the report it appears that the work is not only slow, but also piecemeal. A recently launched Global Alliance for Urban Crises (GAUC) is also attempting to refocus the work of NGOs to urban areas. But the purchase of this currently appears to be limited despite the fact that the needs of refugees in urban areas are considerable and complex.[5] Host governments and populations can see displaced people who they assume will cause problems and tensions safely penned into a designated space in which they are treated as humanitarian subjects. Academics, artists, reporters, and writers can enter into and view these distinct and unique spaces and discuss their specificities, their unique spatial forms, and political practices. Camps then become spaces where the spectatorship of suffering is possible.

Such essentialization of displaced people is less possible to do within urban environments, where they live cheek-by-jowl with the urban poor. Indeed, many refugees move into non-camp and urban environments precisely so that they can melt away into the local population (Malkki 1995b). The urbanization of refugees poses particular problems for constructing a narrative about a unique urban "architecture of displacement." Firstly, as refugees become dispersed through urban environments, it is difficult to find them and document where and how they live. Secondly, the unique suffering of refugees in urban environments tends to get blurred, particularly in informal settlements where large numbers of refugees often find shelter. Relations vary from those of solidarity and hospitality to racialization, exploitation, and harassment of displaced people (Coddington 2018; Landau 2006; Sanyal 2018). Refugees negotiate spaces with urban poor in these places, sharing with them the problems of poverty, lack of access to resources, and second-class citizenship. How do you talk about an architecture of displacement within a city when that is also the architecture of poverty and/or informality? How does this inability to capture the distinction between the displaced and the poor mark the awkward boundaries between citizenship, belonging, and rights? How does it also signal the failure of capturing the essence of displacement?

Camps have played an important role in defining the life and habitation of refugees. And while the focus on them is necessary, especially as they reincarnate into Europe, it is important to consider what we overlook when we construct an iconography of refuge through its camps. It is perhaps time that we rethink what architectures of refuge can be and how we can be part of a progressive conversation that pays attention to a wider range of spaces that refugees come to inhabit.

A shorter version of this article is published in Structures of Displacement (Birkhäuser 2021, 178–81) as the transcript of my talk at the symposium with the same name, held on October 18, 2019, at the University of Applied Arts Vienna, Institute of Architecture.

---

1 An interesting debate between Michel Agier and Liisa Malkki in *Ethnography* discussed why this may in fact be the case. See (Agier 2002; L. H. Malkki 2002). **2** Many refugee scholars, particularly those working on law, have argued that the mandate of UNHCR has been consistently watered down from an organization that advocates for the rights of refugees to one that has largely become a humanitarian organization, bending to the will of donor countries who want to keep refugees away from their shores. **3** ALNAP is a global network in the international humanitarian system. Per their organizational description, they facilitate learning, host events and conferences, maintain a large library of reports, and carry out their own research. **4** I make this point based on my own observations while working with various NGOs in different capacities. **5** The GAUC was launched during the World Humanitarian Summit, which took place in Istanbul in May 2016.

References

Agier, M. 2002. “Between War and City Towards an Urban Anthropology of Refugee Camps.” *Ethnography* 3, no. 3: 317–41. https://doi.org/10.1177/146613802401092779.

Bagelman, J. 2016. *Sanctuary City: A Suspended State*. New York: Palgrave McMillan.

Bakewell, O. 2014. “Encampment and Self-Settlement.” In *The Oxford Handbook of Refugee and Forced Migration Studies*, edited by E. Fiddian-Qasmiyeh, G. Loescher, K. Long, and N. Sigona, 127–38. Oxford: Oxford University Press. http://www.oxfordhandbooks.com/view/10.1093/oxfordhb/9780199652433.001.0001/oxfordhb-9780199652433-e-037.

Banerjee, S. 2003. “Displacement within Displacement: The Crisis of Old Age in the Refugee Colonies of Calcutta.” *Studies in History* 19, no. 2: 199-220. https://doi.org/10.1177/025764300301900203.

Bau, I. 1985. *This Ground Is Holy: Church Sanctuary and Central American Refugees*. First edition. New York: Paulist Press.

Black, R. 1998. “Putting Refugees in Camps.” *Forced Migration Review* 2: 4–7.

Bose, P. K., ed. 2000. *Refugees in West Bengal: Institutional Processes and Contested Identities*. Calcutta: Calcutta Research Group.

Brun, C. 2010. “Hospitality: Becoming ‘IDPs’ and ‘Hosts’ in Protracted Displacement.” *Journal of Refugee Studies* 23, no. 3 (September 2010): 337–55. https://doi.org/10.1093/jrs/feq024.

Brun, C., and R. O. Thorshaug. 2020. “Privatized Housing and Never-Ending Displacement: The Temporality of Dwelling for Displaced Georgians.” In *Displacement: Global Conversations on Refuge*, edited by S. Pasquetti and R. Sanyal, 116–30. Manchester: Manchester University Press.

Campbell, L. 2018. *What's Missing? Adding Context to the Urban Response Toolbox.* ALNAP, April 4, 2018. https://www.alnap.org/help-library/whats-missing-adding-context-to-the-urban-response-toolbox.

Chakrabarti, P. K. 1990. *The Marginal Men: The Refugees and the Left Political Syndrome in West Bengal.* Kalyani, India: Lumière Books.

Chatterjee, N. 1992. "Midnight's Unwanted Children: East Bengali Refugees and the Politics of Rehabilitation." PhD dissertation. Brown University.

Chatterji, J. 2011. *The Spoils of Partition: Bengal and India, 1947–1967.* Reissue edition. Cambridge: Cambridge University Press.

Chouliaraki, L. 2006. *The Spectatorship of Suffering.* First edition. London: SAGE Publications Ltd.

Coddington, K. 2018. "Landscapes of Refugee Protection." *Transactions of the Institute of British Geographers* 43, no. 3: 326–40. https://doi.org/10.1111/tran.12224.

Cuny, F. C. 1977. "Refugee Camps and Camp Planning: The State of the Art." *Disasters* 1, no. 2: 125–43. https://doi.org/10.1111/j.1467-7717.1977.tb00020.x.

Darling, J. 2009. "A City of Sanctuary: The Relational Re-imagining of Sheffield's Asylum Politics." *Transactions of the Institute of British Geographers* 35, no. 1: 125–40. https://doi.org/10.1111/j.1475-5661.2009.00371.x.

Darling, J. 2016. "Privatising Asylum: Neoliberalisation, Depoliticisation, and the Governance of Forced Migration." *Transactions of the Institute of British Geographers* 41, no. 3: 230–43. https://doi.org/10.1111/tran.12118.

Fábos, A. 2015. "Microbuses and Mobile Homemaking in Exile: Sudanese Visiting Strategies in Cairo." *Refuge: Canada's Journal on Refugees* 31, no. 1 (April 2015): 55–66. http://refuge.journals.yorku.ca/index.php/refuge/article/view/40149.

Feldman, I. 2015. "What Is a Camp? Legitimate Refugee Lives in Spaces of Long-Term Displacement." *Geoforum* 66: 244–52. https://doi.org/10.1016/j.geoforum.2014.11.014.

Fluck, W. 2010. "Poor Like Us: Poverty and Recognition in American Photography." *Amerikastudien / American Studies* 55, no. 1: 63–93.

Herscher, A. 2017. *Andrew Herscher – Displacements: Architecture and Refugee, Critical Spatial Practice* 9. London: Sternberg Press.

Jacobsen, K. 2006. "Refugees and Asylum Seekers in Urban Areas: A Livelihoods Perspective." *Journal of Refugee Studies* 19, no. 3: 273–86. https://doi.org/10.1093/jrs/fel017.

Katz, I. 2016. "A Network of Camps on the Way to Europe." *Forced Migration Review*, no. 51: 17–19.

Katz, I., D. Martin, and C. Minca (eds.). 2018. *Camps Revisited: Multifaceted Spatialities of a Modern Political Technology.* London: Rowman & Littlefield Publishers.

Kihato, C. W., and L. B. Landau. 2020. "Visibilising Suffering or Stealth Humanitarianism? The Perils of Promoting Durable Protection in Cities of the South." In *Displacement: Global Conversations on Refuge*, edited by S. Pasquetti and R. Sanyal, 193–209. Manchester: Manchester University Press.

Krause, M. 2014. *The Good Project: Humanitarian Relief NGOs and the Fragmentation of Reason.* Chicago: University of Chicago Press.

Kreichauf, R. 2018. "From Forced Migration to Forced Arrival: The Campization of Refugee Accommodation in European Cities." *Comparative Migration Studies* 6, article no. 7. https://doi.org/10.1186/s40878-017-0069-8.

Landau, L. B. 2006. "Protection and Dignity in Johannesburg: Shortcomings of South Africa's Urban Refugee Policy." *Journal of Refugee Studies* 19, no. 3: 308–27.

Lewis, J. 2008. "The Exigent City – Phenomenon – Refugee Camps – Architecture," *The New York Times Magazine*, June 8, 2008. http://www.nytimes.com/2008/06/08/magazine/08wwln-urbanism-t.html.

Malkki, L. H. 1995a. "Refugees and Exile: From 'Refugee Studies' to the National Order of Things." *Annual Review of Anthropology* 24: 495–523.

Malkki, L. H. 1995b. *Purity and Exile.* Chicago: University of Chicago Press. http://www.press.uchicago.edu/ucp/books/book/chicago/P/bo3624883.html.

Malkki, L. H. 2002. "News from Nowhere: Mass Displacement and Globalized 'Problems of Organization'." *Ethnography* 3, no. 3: 351–60. https://doi.org/10.1177/146613802401092797.

Martin, D. 2015. "From Spaces of Exception to 'Campscapes': Palestinian Refugee Camps and Informal Settlements in Beirut." *Political Geography* 44: 9–18. https://doi.org/10.1016/j.polgeo.2014.08.001.

Montclos, M.-A. P. D., and P. M. Kagwanja. 2000. "Refugee Camps or Cities? The Socio-Economic Dynamics of the Dadaab and Kakuma Camps in Northern Kenya." *Journal of Refugee Studies* 13, no. 2: 205–22. https://doi.org/10.1093/jrs/13.2.205.

Pasquetti, S. 2015. "Negotiating Control." *City* 19, no. 5: 702–13. https://doi.org/10.1080/13604813.2015.1071121.

Pasquetti, S., and G. Picker. 2017. "Confined Informality: Global Margins, Statecraft, and Urban Life." *International Sociology* 32, no. 4 (April 2017): 532–44.

Ramadan, A. 2013. "Spatialising the Refugee Camp." *Transactions of the Institute of British Geographers* 38, no. 1: 65–77. https://doi.org/10.1111/j.1475-5661.2012.00509.x.

Rao, V. 2006. "Slum as Theory: The South/Asian City and Globalization," *International Journal of Urban and Regional Research* 30, no. 1: 225–32. https://doi.org/10.1111/j.1468-2427.2006.00658.x.

Ray, M. 2002. "Growing Up Refugee." *History Workshop Journal* 53, no. 1: 149–79. https://doi.org/10.1093/hwj/53.1.149.

Roy, A. 2003. "Transnational Trespassings: The Geopolitics of Urban Informality." In *Urban Informality: Transnational Perspectives from the Middle East, Latin America, and South Asia*, edited by A. Roy and N. AlSayyad, 289–317. Lanham, MD: Lexington Press.

Roy, A. 2011. "Slumdog Cities: Rethinking Subaltern Urbanism." *International Journal of Urban and Regional Research* 35, no. 2: 223–38. https://doi.org/10.1111/j.1468-2427.2011.01051.x.

Sanyal, R. 2004. "Poverty as a 'Theme Park': Christian Norms and Philanthropic Forms of Habitat for Humanity." *Traditional Dwellings and Settlements Review* 15, no. 2: 19–31.

Sanyal, R. 2009. "Contesting Refugeehood: Squatting as Survival in Post-Partition Calcutta." *Social Identities* 15, no. 1: 67–84. https://doi.org/10.1080/13504630802692937.

Sanyal, R. 2011. "Squatting in Camps: Building and Insurgency in Spaces of Refuge." *Urban Studies* 48, no. 5: 877–90. https://doi.org/10.1177/0042098010363494.

Sanyal, R. 2014a. "Hindu Space: Urban Dislocations in Post-Partition Calcutta." *Transactions of the Institute of British Geographers* 39, no. 1: 38–49. https://doi.org/10.1111/tran.12000.

Sanyal, R. 2014b. "Urbanizing Refuge: Interrogating Spaces of Displacement." *International Journal of Urban and Regional Research* 38, no. 2: 558–72. https://doi.org/10.1111/1468-2427.12020.

Sanyal, R. 2018. "Managing Through Ad Hoc Measures: Syrian Refugees and Politics of Waiting in Lebanon." *Political Geography* 66: 67–75. https://doi.org/10.1016/j.polgeo.2018.08.015.

Siddiqi, A. I. 2018. "Writing With: Togethering, Difference, and Feminist Architectural Histories of Migration." In *Structural Instabilities*, edited by D. Barber, E. Rega, and *e-flux Architecture*. Special issue, *e-flux Architecture* (July 28). https://www.e-flux.com/architecture/structural-instability/208707/writing-with/.

Sphere Association. 2018. *The Sphere Handbook: Humanitarian Charter and Minimum Standards in Humanitarian Response*. Fourth edition. Sphere Association. www.spherestandards.org/handbook.

UNHCR. 2007. *Handbook for Emergencies.* Third edition. United Nations High Commissioner for Refugees.

Ventura, G. 2017. "Intention, Interpretation and Reception: The Aestheticization of Poverty in William Bouguereau's Indigent Family." *Visual Resources* 33, no. 3–4: 204–33. https://doi.org/10.1080/01973762.2017.1356662.

Yiftachel, O. 2009. "Critical Theory and 'Gray Space': Mobilization of the Colonized." *City* 13, no. 2–3: 246–63. https://doi.org/10.1080/13604810902982227.

Epilogue

Inhabitation: A Story of Return

Somayeh Chitchian

As I write these concluding pages of our volume, as this journey, a stage of it, is coming to an end, as these pages reach someone else's hands and hopefully will continue to grow from there, I can't help but wonder about the *where* and the *when* I am writing these pages – the *where* of the home, and the *when* of a pandemic. That *where* and *when* that was, not too long ago, out there for us to grab; that *where* and *when* that was accessible to us, our playgrounds of privilege; that *where* and *when* of academic unboundedness, suddenly coming to a halt. Still. Borders. Listen. Our homes.

A global pandemic of solitary existence has *displaced* us all. Or rather, we are finally witnessing our global displaced condition. The terrific boomerang effect, as Césaire put it (1955), of that which we have collectively afflicted, twisting and turning, displacing *us* as well. As if this displaced world is trying to finally "re-place" itself, as if it is trying to, painfully, recenter. And with it, it is re-placing us, a merciful act of re-placement, forcing us to return, to ourselves, to our centers, to our homes. That place of home that was once sacred, that place of one's complete belonging, that place of care and nurture, that place of unconditional love and rejuvenation, that place of family, community, togetherness, that place where wounds heal and hearts mend, that space of arrival, of homecoming, of the soul – a story of return.

Writing these pages at this particular point in time allows for a collective understanding of the scope of our different displacements. It allows us to finally see, plainly, the interconnections; that otherwise distant *there*, and that otherwise distant *then*; that which was *there*, not (of) here, that which was *then*, not (of) now; that, which was the camp, *there*, this which was the city, *here*; those who were migrants, *them*, we who were citizens, *us*; those who were refugees, *uprooted*, we who were architects, *sheltered* – the world, however, showed us otherwise. Our categories twisted, our visions blurred.

What I am trying to convey through these lines is our inherent interconnectedness in time and in space. It is a radical understanding of displacement not being *out there*, but actually *of here*. An understanding that confesses displacement being part and parcel of our modern condition. Colonial modernity not only displaces those who are on the move; it also distorts the vision of displacement altogether. Displacement is not necessarily an act of movement *in* space, it is a condition *in* time, on-the-move or not. Modernity is based on the displacement of time and the subsequent displacement and colonization of space, thus, putting us all in a displaced relationality to each other. Colonial modernity has displaced its colonies as much as its metropoles; by displacing *you*, I have displaced *myself*. The "imperialist, white supremacist, capitalist, patriarchal" interlocking systems of domination, as bell hooks always points out, displaces. Domination means displacement, domination is a displacing force. Domination is inherently the creation of a margin and a center (hooks 2014a), connected in a displaced time-space continuum. The center, however, is as much displaced as the margin. Made on the shaky and uneven grounds of domination, unsustainable, destructive of life and beings. However, it is to the margins we are forced to return, the margins of our spaces, the margins of our minds. It is in the margins that the language of "resistance" is spoken, the language of "struggle," the language of "arrival," of "renewal and self-recovery, where we can heal our wounds and become whole" again (hooks 2014b, 49).

Displacement and re-placing, therefore, go hand-in-hand; that which is displaced needs to be re-placed elsewhere and elsewhen. While acknowledging displacement forms a foundational component of the project of modernity – the ontoepistemic displacement of both time and space, as mentioned – it opens up the possibility for a critical (re)formulation of the notion of *return*.[1] The possibility of return, albeit incremental, incomplete, or as a claim alone, emerges from the site and the moment in which different politics and ethics of life arise, from the uncanny and the marginal, that marginal space and marginal time. It is in this domain of re-placing, outside and inside of forces of displacement, that this volume centralizes inhabitation as a terrain of theorization, seeing, making, and being – inhabitation of displacement as the architecture of (possible) returns. It is an understanding of the inhabitation of the margin, that is, marginal inhabitation, "as a site of resistance," "elevating the spirit" by "caring for one another" (hooks 2014b, 44), it is a story of return.

The aim of this concluding chapter is not so much to offer an answer, but to offer additional questions and frames of analysis for further exploration and expansion of these themes. The work of bell hooks has been an inspirational voice to discover, and an inspirational one to teach in an architectural school. Ringing at our doorstep each week, present in our classroom, she gave us a vocabulary that we deeply lacked, gifting us a frame that we had completely missed, offering us a different lens altogether. Her notions of *homeplace*, *black vernacular*, and *margin* are flowing through this piece, nurturing my thoughts while filling the classroom. An architectural theorist, to say the least, she portrays a different vision of what constitutes *architecture*. Her ideas resurge in every class discussion, as we rely on them to make sense of things, to have a vocabulary to explain. In her passionate work and beautiful writing, she takes us on a journey with her, a loving journey, showing us where and how to look, otherwise. Our gazes that have been distorted, *displaced*, she recenters; our homes which have been *displaced* in our minds, she recenters, showing us the marginality of our "centers" and the centrality of our "margins." She re-places our displaced selves. With her, we move "from margin to center" (hooks 1984, ix–x). This is a story of return.

It is through her notion of the *homeplace* that we revisit the "camp," we revisit the "city," through the eyes of their inhabitants. For a moment we leave their ascribed displaced identities aside to see them as makers and builders of their *homes*, their homeplaces, as temporary as they may be. That feeling of "safety and arrival," as bell hooks describes, even fleeting, that feeling of "arrival and homecoming," "the warmth, and comfort of shelter, the feeding of our [...] bodies, the nurturing of souls," these are the moments one inhabits. Moments of "dignity, integrity of being," learning "to have faith" (2014b, 41–42). This is an inhabited space, this is the space of "mutual care, repair, and imagining," as Maja Momić puts it, by way of Camillo Boano and Giovanna Astolfo (2020), in her contribution to this volume. Though these are hard lives lived, "creating and sustaining a home environment [...] the construction of a homeplace, however fragile and tenuous, ha[s] a radical political dimension," where "people could strive to be subjects, not objects [...] despite poverty, hardship, and deprivation," where one could "restore" the sense of "dignity denied on the outside" (hooks 2014b, 42). This is the inhabitation of displacement. Inhabiting a community, inhabiting a home, "midst of an oppressive and dominating social reality," "despite the contradiction of poverty," "working to create a homeplace that affirm[s] our beings" (hooks 2014b, 46). It is not a space of immobilization, a space of detention, it is rather the space of the mind, the space of the body, and the space of the community, inhabited, nurtured, liberated. It is a story of return.

The architectural language of the inhabited homeplace is vernacular, black vernacular for hooks. The black vernacular is a political space of "who controls and shapes the environment" (hooks 1995, 146). It is a critical and imaginative act of thinking about homes, incapable of being framed through the language of architecture and design, as we know them today, for those whom these terms exist only in the location of "impossibility," as hooks explains. Rather, the vernacular is the "concrete relationship to space" (1995, 147). Though oftentimes not articulated in terms of space and architecture, for hooks, her childhood vernacular met the needs of its inhabitants, extended and changed over time; there was a sense of possibility, even in conditions of "the absence [or lack] of material privilege." Space was thought of in a creative way, change was "nevertheless always possible," offering a wealth of information about the relationship of inhabitants to their space. These spaces of inhabitation can be seen as a "liminal space where they [...] stretch the limits of desire and the imagination" (1995, 149).

> Lack of material privilege need not to be synonymous with poverty of spirit or imagination. Significantly, in the past, even during the more dire circumstances of oppression and exploitation, African Americans could find ways to express their creativity – to display artistry. They dared to use their imagination in ways that were liberatory (hooks 1995, 150).

While hooks further acknowledges how construction of the "projects" and state-owned housing brought an end to the vernacular type of dwelling discussed so far, it "erase[d] all chances for unique perspectives to shape living spaces and replace[d] these with a blueprint of sameness," bringing about a sense "that one was powerless, unable to intervene in or transform [...] one's relationship to space" (hooks 1995, 150) To conclude, according to hooks:

> the vernacular is as relevant as any other form of architectural practice [...] Yet, to ignore this standpoint is to reproduce a body of work that is neocolonial insofar as it violently erases and destroys those subjugated knowledges that can only erupt, disrupt, and serve as acts of resistance if they are visible, remembered. Documentation of a cultural genealogy of resistance invites the making of theory that highlights the cultural practices which transform ways of looking and being in a manner that resists reinscription by prevailing structures of domination. Subversive historiography connects oppositional practices from the past with forms of resistance in the present, thus creating spaces of possibility where the future can be imagined differently – imagined in such a way that we can witness ourselves dreaming, moving forward and beyond the limits and confines of fixed locations (hooks 1995, 151).

This is the concept of inhabitation, the imagination and making of a different future, from the closest future to the farthest. Its architectural language is a vernacular one, a vernacular that lies outside of the studies of modern sciences, not to be interpreted or translated by them, not a postcolonial aesthetic regime to be imposed elsewhere. Rather, it is a position on the margin, transgressing *to* the margin. It is a story of return, another return.

1 "The notion of 'return' has defined the diasporic and extraterritorial nature of Palestinian politics and cultural life since the Nakba. Often articulated in the 'suspended politics' of political theology, it has gradually been blurred in the futile limbo of negotiations. Return is a political act that is practiced in the present as well as projecting an image into an uncertain future [...] these practices necessitate the adoption of a stereoscopic vision that navigates the complex terrain between two places – the space of refuge and the destroyed site of origins. Both are extraterritorial spaces [...] The former is defined as 'absentee property,' and the latter as a 'United Nations run area,' [...] Refugee life is suspended between these two sites, always double" (Hilal and Petti 2018, 29).

References

Césaire, A. (1955) 2000. *Discourse on Colonialism*, translated by J. Pinkham. New York: Monthly Review Press.

Boano, C., and G. Astolfo. 2020. "Inhabitation as More-Than-Dwelling: Notes for a Renewed Grammar." *International Journal of Housing Policy* 20, no. 4: 555–77.

Hilal, S. and A. Petti. 2018. "Returns." In *Permanent Temporariness*, edited by M. Nadotti and N. Axel, 29. Stockholm: Art and Theory Publishing.

hooks, b. 1984. "Changing Perspectives on Power." In *Feminist Theory from Margin to Center*, 83–93. Boston, MA: South End Press.

hooks, b. 1995. "Black Vernacular: Architecture as Cultural Practice." In *Art on My Mind: Visual Politics*, 145–51. New York: The New Press.

hooks, b. 2014a. "Choosing the Margin as a Space of Radical Openness." In *Yearning: Race, Gender, and Cultural Politics*, 145–53. New York: Routledge.

hooks, b. 2014b. "Homeplace: A Site of Resistance." In *Yearning: Race, Gender, and Cultural Politics*, 41–49. New York: Routledge.

List of Contributors

Samah Al Jundi-Pfaff is a refugee who was raised by a Palestinian refugee. She manages the *Let's Make It* project at the Museum Friedland. She studied English literature, which led her to education studies. She was a UNICEF Girls Education Officer when Syria was hosting Iraqi, Lebanese, and Somali refugees. Samah conducted accelerated learning training with the youth program of UNRWA during the recent war in and over Syria. Her project *Let's Talk* won the second place in the Hessen Family Prize 2016.

Gregor Brune studied architecture at Leibniz University in Hanover. His architecture firm RSE+ is based in Kassel, Stuttgart, and Göttingen, and has years of experience in housing projects. During the "refugee crisis" in 2015–16, he worked on two refugee-related projects in Göttingen and Hann. Münden, which also surveyed the local social infrastructure. Gregor received two first prizes for the design of administration buildings in Korbach and Göttingen in 2017 and 2019.

Somayeh Chitchian is an architect, doctoral candidate in urban studies, and instructor in architecture at the Harvard Graduate School of Design. She was a doctoral fellow at the Max Planck Institute for the Study of Religious and Ethnic Diversity from 2015 to 2019. Her research focuses on the extended corridors of migratory circulation and uses a logistical/infrastructural lens as both a material and theoretical tool for a respatialized approach to migration research beyond its inherent methodological nationalism.

Ayham Dalal is an adjunct assistant professor at Vassar College (USA), and a research associate at the Technische Universität Berlin (Germany). His research interests include architecture, migration, mobility, and displacement, with publications in various journals such as *Housing Studies*, *Urban Planning*, *Town Planning Review*, and *ARCH+*. Ayham is also the author of the book *From Shelters to Dwellings: The Zaatari Refugee Camp*, published by Transcript Verlag in 2021.

Petra Heber is a landscape architect and urban planner. She gained her master's in urban design at the Technische Universität Berlin and studied landscape architecture at the Technische Universität München. After research experiences in Nablus, Palestine, and Venice, Italy, she became interested in homemaking practices. In her master's thesis, she researched the appropriation of spaces in the Azraq and Zaatari camps in Jordan. Today, she works as an urban and landscape planner in Bamberg, Germany.

Irit Katz is an assistant professor in architecture and urban studies at the department of architecture, University of Cambridge, and a Bye-Fellow of Christ's College. She practiced as an architect in Tel Aviv and London and her academic work focuses on built environments shaped in extreme conditions, primarily in post-colonial settings. She co-edited *Camps Revisited: Multifaceted Spatialities of a Modern Political Technology* and is the author of the forthcoming book *The Common Camp: Architecture of Power and Resistance in Israel-Palestine*.

Nassim Mehran is an architect and holds a PhD in urban sociology. She had several years of professional experience in architectural design and project management in Iran. Since 2014 she has been working as a researcher and lecturer at Humboldt University. Applying interdisciplinary mixed-methods approaches, her focus is on the spatialities of urban inequalities, refuge, and migration; the ecology of housing and health; and participatory urban alternatives in a time of crisis and armed conflicts.

Maja Momić is an architect and urban researcher. She graduated in architecture from the University IUAV of Venice and is a doctoral candidate in urban design at HafenCity University Hamburg. In her doctoral thesis "Dwelling as a Fugitive Practice?" she explores refugees' dwelling practices in Hamburg through a mix of architectural and ethnographic methods. Her research interests concern the interrelation between dwelling practices and urban transformation processes.

Aya Musmar is an assistant professor of architecture, displacement, and feminism at the University of Petra, Amman. She applies a decolonialist feminist critique and explores how her transdisciplinary research can bear testimony to social injustice through architecture. Aya's PhD dissertation, "Witnessing the Refugee Camp: Feminist Positions, Practices and Pedagogies," was shortlisted for RIBA President's Awards in 2020. Aya is Co-I on multiple international research projects looking at the question of displacement and conflict.

Leticia Palomino is an architect and urban planner. She holds a master's degree in urban design from the TU Berlin, and a bachelor's degree in architecture from the Polytechnic University of Madrid. In her research and practice, Leticia focuses on sociopolitical aspects of architecture and urban planning, especially regarding migration and refugee housing. Her master's thesis investigates the relationship between urban planning, security, and social segregation in the Azraq camp, Jordan.

Lina Sánchez Steiner holds a degree in architecture from Javeriana University in Bogotá. Her PhD in urban studies at Bauhaus University Weimar was titled "The Refuge-City: Forced Displacement and Urban Spatial Transformations in Colombia." Her work was awarded the first prize of the Colombian Architecture Biennale 2014 in the Research category. She worked in urban planning and research centers in Colombia and Germany. Currently she is working at UP19 Stadtforschung + Beratung in Berlin.

Romola Sanyal is associate professor of urban geography at the London School of Economics. She studies forced migration, urbanization, and urban politics in the Global South through an interdisciplinary lens. She has worked in Lebanon and India with a focus on the urbanization and shelter politics of refugees. She is the co-editor of *Urbanizing Citizenship: Contested Spaces in Indian Cities* with Dr. Renu Desai, and *Displacement: Global Conversations on Refuge* with Dr. Silvia Pasquetti.

Shahd Seethaler-Wari studied urban planning and urban management at TU Berlin, and architecture at Birzeit University in Palestine. Her post-doctoral research at the Max Planck Institute for the Study of Religious and Ethnic Diversity (2016–19) focused on the spatial needs of asylum seekers and the role of architecture and infrastructure in refugee accommodations. Shahd recently joined the department of urban planning and housing development at the Berlin State Office for Refugee Affairs.

Anooradha Iyer Siddiqi is an assistant professor at Barnard College, Columbia University. She is writing two book manuscripts. *Architecture of Migration: The Dadaab Refugee Camps and Humanitarian Settlement* (Duke University Press) analyzes the history, visual rhetoric, and spatial politics of the Dadaab refugee camps in Kenya. *Minnette de Silva and a Modern Architecture of the Past* engages the intellectual and heritage work of one of the first women to establish an architectural practice in Ceylon/Sri Lanka.

Copy Editing: Christen Jamar
Project management: Alexander Felix, Nora Kempkens
Production: Amelie Solbrig
Cover design and dividing pages: Floyd E. Schulze
Cover motif: Shahd Seethaler-Wari
Layout and typesetting: Kathleen Bernsdorf

Paper: Magno Natural, 120 g/m²
Lithography: bildpunkt Druckvorstufen GmbH, Berlin
Printing: Beltz Grafische Betriebe, Bad Langensalza

Library of Congress Control Number: 2021942496

Bibliographic information published by the German National Library
The German National Library lists this publication in the Deutsche Nationalbibliografie; detailed bibliographic data are available on the Internet at http://dnb.dnb.de.

ISBN 978-3-0356-2370-3

e-ISBN (PDF) 978-3-0356-2371-0

P.O. Box 44, 4009 Basel, Switzerland
Part of Walter de Gruyter GmbH, Berlin/Boston

9 8 7 6 5 4 3 2 1

www.birkhauser.com